WHO WAS THE FIRST JEWISH SECRETARY OF STATE? (NOT HENRY KISSINGER)

WHO WAS KNOWN AS THE JEWISH MARK TWAIN?

WHO DONATED THE PERSONAL THE AM

WHO WAS THE JEWISH REVERE?

WHICH WEST POINT GRADUATE ORGANIZED THE ISRAELI ARMY?

WHO STRUCK IT RICH WITH A UNIQUE PAIR OF PANTS?

WHO WROTE THE ISRAELI NATIONAL ANTHEM 61 YEARS BEFORE THE COUNTRY WAS BORN?

WHO WAS THE JEWISH INDIAN TRADER WHO BOUGHT THE GRAND CANYON FROM AN INDIAN CHIEF?

WHO WAS THE FIRST JEW TO BE APPOINTED TO A PRESIDENTIAL CABINET?

WHICH JEWISH PIONEER REQUESTED THAT HE BE BURIED STANDING UP WITH HIS MUSKET AT HIS SIDE?

Here are the vivid, fascinating stories of over 100 Jewish men and women who for more than three hundred years have played vital roles in the making of our nation.
Some are still famed. Others are almost forgotten. All are part of a rich legacy not only for Jews but for all who are proud to be Americans.

L5
P857b

A Shapolsky Book
Published by Shapolsky Publishers, Inc.

Second Revised Edition © 1988, © 1986 by Bernard Postal and Lionel Koppman.
Copyright © 1978 by Bernard Postal and Lionel Koppman.

Historical material excerpted from *American Jewish Landmarks*, Vol. I, II, III, and IV by Bernard Postal and Lionel Koppman. Published by Fleet Press Corporation, NYC, © 1977, 1979, 1984, 1986, 1988.

For any additional information, contact:
Shapolsky Publishers, Inc.
56 East 11th Street, New York, NY 10003

10 9 8 7 6 5 4 3 2

2nd Edition, January 1988

Library of Congress Cataloging in Publication Data:
Postal, Bernard and Koppman, Lionel

Guess Who's Jewish in American History
Revised and illustrated edition
1. Jews — History; I Title
ISBN 0-933503-55-5

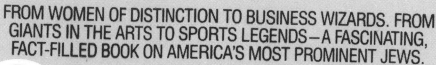

FROM WOMEN OF DISTINCTION TO BUSINESS WIZARDS. FROM GIANTS IN THE ARTS TO SPORTS LEGENDS—A FASCINATING, FACT-FILLED BOOK ON AMERICA'S MOST PROMINENT JEWS.

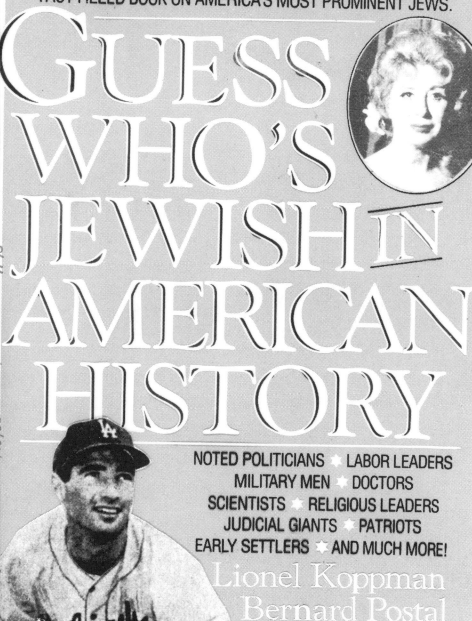

GUESS WHO'S JEWISH IN AMERICAN HISTORY

NOTED POLITICIANS ★ LABOR LEADERS
MILITARY MEN ★ DOCTORS
SCIENTISTS ★ RELIGIOUS LEADERS
JUDICIAL GIANTS ★ PATRIOTS
EARLY SETTLERS ★ AND MUCH MORE!

Lionel Koppman
Bernard Postal

More than 20 pages of rare photographs

"We could not subtract the Jewish contribution to American life without impoverishing our science, our literature, our art, our commerce, our law, indeed without vastly diminishing America. The Jewish contribution to the American experience is beyond calculation—and out of all proportion to the numbers of Jewish Americans involved."

NELSON A. ROCKEFELLER
Vice-President of the United States
(From a speech made on the occasion of the American Bicentennial)

PREFACE

At the heart of all history are innumerable biographies.

In assembling this collection of some of the well-remembered, as well as some long-forgotten names whose life stories are an integral part of American Jewish history, we have dug deep into the roots of American Jewry.

This gallery recreates the life and times of a unique aggregation of American Jewish personalities whose achievements and contributions brighten the pages of American and Jewish history from the earliest days of America to modern times—a chronicle spanning three centuries.

These portraits represent a cross-section of American Jewish men and women and comprise a miniature American Jewish *Who Was Who*. Collectively, they constitute an historical-biographical album that provides the source of the rich and colorful Jewish roots in America and their unbreakable but little-known links with the past.

BERNARD POSTAL AND LIONEL KOPPMAN
New York City, May, 1978

CONTENTS

INTRODUCTION

HOW IT ALL BEGAN

In the first week of September, 1654, 4 men, 2 women, and 17 children landed in the tiny Dutch outpost of New Amsterdam. These 23 were the first permanent Jewish settlers in North America, although not the first Jews in the American colonies. Perhaps a score of others are known to have been scattered in the English, Dutch, and French settlements before 1650, and even earlier in the Spanish domains of Florida and New Mexico, where they lived as secret Jews.

The journey for these 23 began in May, 1654, in Brazil. Marranos (secret Jews) had found a tenuous haven in Catholic Brazil for more than a century, after fleeing the Inquisition in Spain and Portugal when those lands expelled them at the end of the fifteenth century. When the Dutch conquered northern Brazil in 1624, the Marranos established the first open Jewish communities in the Americas at Bahia and Recife. After the Portuguese recaptured the area in 1654, the colonists were given the option of staying and pledging allegiance to Portugal or leaving. Preferring exile to Portuguese rule, the 600 Jews of Brazil disposed of their property, with the majority heading for Holland and a smaller group sailing for the British, French, and Dutch islands in the Caribbean.

One Netherlands-bound ship, carrying the 23 Jews and a party of Dutch Calvinists, was captured by Spanish pirates. En route to a Spanish port, the buccaneer vessel was seized by a French privateer and taken to the French West Indies. Stranded in a strange port, the pauperized refugees had only 933 guilders, and some clothing and house furnishings among them. When the French captain demanded 2,500 guilders for passage to New Amsterdam, the Jews agreed, pledging themselves to be collectively responsible for the debt, with all their belongings to be forfeited if the full amount was not paid.

Thus the "Jewish *Mayflower*," in September, 1654, reached New Amsterdam—a settlement of 800 inhabitants clustered at the tip of Manhattan Island.

During the bitter winter of 1654-1655, the indigent group was helped by the minister of New Amsterdam's Dutch Reformed Church. The governor, Peter Stuyvesant, used the

3

Jews' impoverishment as an excuse to demand that they "be not allowed further to infest and trouble this new colony," and declared that he intended to order the Jews out.

In January, 1655, the Jews appealed to the Dutch West India Company in Holland to revoke the ouster order, predicting, "the more of loyal people that go to live there, the better it is in regard to the payment of taxes and the increase of trade . . ." In the Company's reply to the Jewish plea, they reminded Stuyvesant that the Jews had suffered heavy losses in Brazil out of loyalty to Holland and that "these people may travel and trade to and in New Amsterdam and live and remain there, provided the poor among them shall not become a burden to the Company or to the community, but be supported by their own nation." One year later, the Company directed that the Jews be allowed to trade and buy land throughout the colony.

Tolerated but never really welcome, the Jews remained a tiny handful numbering not more than a dozen families in New Amsterdam until the 1680's. The records, however, indicate that there were isolated Jews in Delaware, Connecticut, Massachusetts, New Hampshire, and Rhode Island, between 1655-1677.

By the turn of the century, there were hardly more than 100 Jewish settlers in New York out of a population of 25,000, but they had already made an impact on the city's business and civic life, establishing the framework of a community organization and a tradition of public service on which succeeding generations were to build.

GENERATIONS OF IMMIGRATION

One of the most remarkable aspects of the Jew in America is the gathering together of more Jews in this country than anywhere else in the world.

Massive immigration from the Russian and Austro-Hungarian regions of Europe was the salient factor in the creation of this unprecedented concentration of Jews. Between 1880 and 1924, more than two million Jews reached the United States in flight from pogroms, revolution, war and postwar upheavals, economic discrimination, and social degradation. They came as whole families and often as entire communities. Landing primarily in New York, most of them settled there. In the great metropolis they found other Jews who shared their religious traditions and social mores, and helped them in getting a foothold in their new world.

As early as 1820, the trickle of Jews who came from the Polish province of Posen, following the Napoleonic Wars, swelled into a stream of Yiddish and German-speaking immigrants, reaching major proportions in the 1840's. Extremely poor, most of them arrived with only clothing and household goods. A second wave of immigrants, including a good many of culture and means, arrived after the collapse of the 1848 revolutions in Germany, Austria, Bohemia, and Hungary. The Jewish population in the country in 1825 was 6,000, and by 1848 had more than doubled to 13,000.

The older Sephardic families (Spanish and Portuguese Jews), which constituted the upper crust of Jewish society until the 1850's, had little contact with the newly arrived German and Polish Jews. Because many of the newcomers had no trade or money to set up a small business, they turned to peddling. To divert these newcomers from peddling, unsuccessful attempts were made to settle them around the country in agricultural colonies.

By 1880, 25,000 East European Jews had reached the United States, escaping from the harshness of their life in Russia and Poland. The older communities were ill-prepared to cope with the beginning of this folk exodus that was to transplant one-third of East European Jewry to the United States in a generation and a half. This tidal wave from

5

Eastern Europe was to swell the Jewish population in New York alone to 600,000 by the end of the century. The Lower East Side had become "a seething human sea, fed by streams, rivulets, and rills of immigration, fleeing all the Yiddish-speaking centers of Europe."

The Industrial Removal Office was set up to offer free transportation to families willing to leave New York. A Jewish Immigrants Information Bureau was organized in Europe to encourage immigrants to take passage for Galveston, Texas, which helped facilitate the settlement of Jews in the South and Middle West.

The last great wave of Jewish immigration occurred between 1933 and 1945, from Germany and Hitler-occupied Europe.

Each layer of Jewish immigration either created its own institutions or modified existing ones to meet special needs of time and place. Out of their diverse origins, traditions, and experiences, each generation of newcomers poured its own quality, variety, color, and unique contribution into the mainstream of American life. Enriched and influenced by each other, all the waves of immigration fused to create the present Jewish community and its enduring contributions to American life.

THE STRUGGLE FOR EQUALITY

The 23 unwanted refugees in New Amsterdam found no freedom. They fought the first of many battles to achieve equality for themselves and others. The first victory over Peter Stuyvesant's bigotry was more than an entering wedge for the achievement of further civil and religious rights for other disenfranchised and oppressed minorities.

They fought Connecticut's charter of 1662 (which remained in force until 1818) and which proclaimed that "the Christian faith is the only and principal end of this plantation." Delaware, the first state to ratify the Federal Constitution, did not remove religious tests for officeholders until 1792. Prior to the American Revolution, full citizenship rights in Maryland were given only to those who professed a belief in Christianity. In Louisiana, the Black Code of 1724 excluded Jews from the entire territory and banned the practice of Judaism there.

In 1797, Solomon Etting and Barnard Gratz began the long struggle, lasting nearly 30 years, to achieve full civil equality for the Jews of Maryland. The fight for these rights, led by Thomas Kennedy, a non-Jewish member of the State Assembly, began when a committee met "to consider the justice and expediency of placing the Jewish inhabitants on equal footing with the Christians." Thirty years later, the bill, which became known as "Kennedy's Jew Baby," passed on February 26, 1825. Kennedy, who had spearheaded the long fight for enactment of this bill, had never met a Jew until he became involved in this early civil rights struggle.

New Hampshire, the first of the 13 colonies to declare its independence from Great Britain, was also the last of the original states to grant complete political equality to Jews. Until 1877, Jews and Catholics were excluded by state law from some political offices. And although Jews enjoyed religious freedom in New Jersey as a result of Queen Anne's declaration to Governor Hamilton in 1702 that "you are to permit a liberty of conscience to all persons (except Papists) . . . ," curbs on holding office remained in effect until 1844, when the new state constitution established religious and civil equality for all.

With the adoption of New York State's first constitution in

7

1777, the Jews were granted full citizenship and complete equality. This final emancipation set a precedent for the other states and paved the way for the achievement of similar rights by Catholics.

The right of rabbis to serve as Army chaplains, the last battle for Jewish religious equality in the United States, was first established during the Civil War. Through negotiations with members of Congress and the War Department by representatives of the Jewish community, President Abraham Lincoln recommended that the law be amended to permit the appointment of rabbis as chaplains. Three were commissioned to serve with the Union forces at the front.

Anti-Semitism and discrimination, however, persisted both before the Civil War and after, fanned by the leading role played in the Confederacy by Judah P. Benjamin, Secretary of State of the Confederate States, and Senator David Yulee, of Florida. It was further aggravated by the notorious Order No. 11 issued by General Ulysses Grant on December 11, 1862, which expelled all Jews "as a class" from the Department of Tennessee. It was the most sweeping anti-Jewish regulation in all American history, remaining in effect until January 7, 1863, when President Lincoln rescinded it. Issued as part of the Union Army's attempt to halt trading with the Confederacy, the Order created indignation among native-born Jews and alarm among the new immigrants. Grant, who always regretted the ruling, sought to make amends when he became President by appointing Benjamin F. Peixotto, a prominent Jewish attorney and president of the B'nai B'rith, as United States Consul General to Rumania in 1870, in the hope that he would be able to halt the anti-Jewish policies of that country.

Grant's Order No. 11 contributed greatly to the post-Civil War stereotype of the Jew as peddler and profiteer, and, coupled with the rising anti-alien sentiment of 1870-1890, these prejudices became the seedbed of American anti-Semitism.

The Reverend Henry Ward Beecher's stirring sermon "Jew and Gentile," preached in 1877, was a classic repudiation of anti-Semitism. His denunciation was aimed at a growing "no Jews allowed" pattern developing in hotels and resorts, as well as other, more severe restrictions.

Jews were excluded from joining bar associations and college fraternities, and insurance companies would even refuse to issue policies to Jewish businessmen. Biased, sensation-seeking journalists contributed to the rise of anti-Semitism by drawing a distorted picture of the Lower East Side in New York City. Henry James spoke of the East Side as "a vast aquarium in which innumerable fish, of overdeveloped proboscises, were to bump together, forever, amid heaped spoils of the sea." Only a few perceptive non-Jewish observers—Jacob Riis, Hutchins Hapgood, and Lincoln Steffens, among others—sensed the enormous ferment of progress these newly arrived immigrants were creating. At the very time when Czarist persecution resulted in bringing shiploads of Jews to America, American racists began assailing the "Hebrew Conquest."

Before World War I, Adolph S. Ochs, publisher of *The New York Times*, wrote to all the daily newspapers reminding them that the word "Jew" is a noun and should not be used as an adjective or adverb, as in "Jew-boy" or "Jew-down."

One of the major victories against Jew-baiting came in 1927, when Henry Ford addressed a public apology to Louis Marshall, a prominent Jewish leader, for seven years of vilification of the Jews in *The Dearborn Independent*.

In 1964, the black civil rights struggle in Mississippi drew support from many rabbis, as well as from Jewish social workers. Two Jewish youths from New York, Andrew Goodman and Michael Schwerner, who had gone to Mississippi to help blacks register to vote, were found murdered, together with black civil rights worker James E. Chaney, their bodies buried in the muddy bank of a country water dam.

BUSINESSMAN AND WORKINGMAN

Jewish enterprise, innovation, and a sense of social justice were potent factors in the rise of American Jews to commercial and financial eminence, and in the emancipation of the workingman.

Handicapped by restrictions under the Dutch and later, to some extent, by the British, the early Jewish settlers earned their livelihood chiefly as Indian traders or butchers. By 1700, however, some Jewish merchants had made their influence felt in trade and commerce. Nevertheless, most Jewish businessmen were still itinerant traders or retailers of such modest means that few were listed as taxpayers.

Hayman Levy, an early Colonial merchant, is reputed to have given the fabulous John Jacob Astor, a non-Jewish immigrant, his first job beating peltries at one dollar a day. Jacob Franks was chief purveyor of goods to the British during the French and Indian Wars. Isaac Moses, a shipowner, plied the American coast from Montreal to Savannah. He was a partner of Robert Morris, the Revolutionary patriot, and with Samson Simson, another shipowner, among the founders of New York's Chamber of Commerce. A number of Jewish merchants were engaged in the slave trade with the West Indies. One of the wealthiest Jews following the Revolutionary War was Ephraim Hart, a partner of John Jacob Astor, who in 1792 helped found the New York Stock Exchange.

Before the wave of immigration from Germany in the early nineteenth century, Jews were primarily engaged in stock brokerage, manufacturing, the professions, and public service. Bernard Hart, grandfather of author Bret Harte, furnished arms and clothing to the citizens' army during the War of 1812; Harmon Hendricks owned a copper smelter which supplied Paul Revere's foundry and provided metal used in building Robert Fulton's steamboat, the *Clermont,* and the historic warship *USS Constitution.*

The immigrants who were not artisans or professionals turned overwhelmingly to petty trade, particularly peddling and the used clothes business. Of the 6,000 peddlers in the United States in 1860, most were said to have been Jews. The renovated used apparel sold by Jewish immigrants found a

10

ready market in the South and West as the discarded fashions of the style-setting East. Moving around the country with hard-to-get merchandise, the omnipresent peddlers became the nuclei of new Jewish communities in the South and West, and the founders of great mercantile and industrial enterprises. One secondhand dealer, Levi Strauss, who failed in the California gold rush, manufactured a special kind of pants for the miners and added the word "Levi's" to the English language. The German Jews, who gave communities along the East Coast strength of numbers, were quickly absorbed into the middle class because the rags-to-riches saga was far more common among those who arrived between 1830 and 1850 than among any other previous immigrant groups. Out of these generations came the Lehmans, Guggenheims, and Lewisohns, the Strauses, Schiffs, Speyers, and Seligmans.

The Seligmans, Joseph and Jessie, two former pack peddlers, went into banking after supplying clothing to the Union Army. Horatio Alger probably conceived the idea for his "rags-to-riches" books while serving as a tutor in the household of Joseph Seligman. The Seligmans, who sold nearly $200 million dollars in American bonds during the critical days of the Civil War to European bankers, also underwrote some of the first railroads in the West and Southwest. Joseph, who was instrumental in getting a pension for President Abraham Lincoln's widow, was offered the post of Secretary of the Treasury during the administration of President Ulysses S. Grant, but declined.

Lazarus Straus, who came to New York from Georgia in 1865 to pay off long-forgiven ante-bellum debts, was the father of the remarkable Straus brothers—Isidor, Oscar, and Nathan. Lazarus built R.H. Macy, one of the largest department stores in the United States, from a small crockery shop; Isidor became a member of Congress; Nathan was beloved as one of the country's best-known philanthropists; and Oscar was the first Jewish Cabinet member, Secretary of Commerce and Labor in President Theodore Roosevelt's administration.

Mayer Lehman (father of Herbert H. Lehman, senator and governor of New York State) and his brother, Emanuel, of Montgomery, Alabama, were Confederate patriots before they established the international banking firm of Lehman Brothers. The Guggenheims, celebrated for their art and literary fellowships, art museum, and support of aeronautical research, were the heirs of a nineteenth-century immigrant

who struck it rich when he invested profits from lace manufacturing in silver and copper mines.

When the wave of East European immigration commenced
in the 1880's, efforts were made by the Industrial Removal
Office and the Jewish Agricultural Society, with the assistance
of the Baron de Hirsch Fund, to relocate many of these
newly arrived away from the teeming Lower East Side of
New York City. Farm colonies were established as far west
as Ferry County in Washington; Cremieux County, South
Dakota; Douglas County, Oregon; and Gunnison, Utah.
Hardship and hard luck dogged most of these colonies. While
the land was provided free of charge, almost everything else
connected with tilling it was expensive, and chances of crop
failure were high. Drought, blizzards, and crop-destroying
plagues, as well as remoteness from markets and their own
inexperience, plunged most of these would-be farmers into
debt. Without ready cash to maintain themselves, they became hopelessly tangled in permanent indebtedness. When
most of these farm colonies failed, the immigrants gradually
drifted to nearby towns and cities, engaging in small trades.
They were, however, to become the core of a vital western
Jewish community.

There were, however, several very successful Jewish farm
colonies in South Jersey. Although these Jewish pioneers did
not know how potatoes grew, their lack of experience was
compensated for by proximity to nearby factories for supple-
mentary income and nearness to the wealthy Jewish communities of New York and Philadelphia. These established
communities kept them in the Jewish public eye and heart,
thus enabling them to get the broad support needed to tide
them over the difficult years.

In the late 1880's, the German Jews dominated the
clothing and tobacco industries. The need for cheap, docile
labor, and the religious beliefs of the newly arrived East Europeans, combined to lead many of them to the garment
trades, where they could more easily observe the Sabbath and
Kashruth (kosher eating code). They preferred employment
with Jews who might be more sympathetic to their special
needs for time off for afternoon and evening prayers or ab-
sences on the Sabbath. Although some Jewish employers did
not scruple to force Jewish workers to accept lower wages for

such privileges, there were many active on philanthropic immigrant aid committees.

Many of these immigrants eked out a living by setting up shops in their tenement hovels—sunless rooms which doubled as living quarters and factory—giving rise to the term "sweatshop." Parents and children worked side by side under appallingly unsanitary conditions. The word sweatshop became synonymous with disease-breeding ghettos occupied by exploited workers.

Most of the first generation East Europeans never climbed beyond the wage worker level. On the whole, they needed two generations to achieve what the German Jews had accomplished in one.

The most dynamic force to emerge from the sordid conditions under which the East European immigrant lived and worked was the Jewish labor movement, which began with an outburst "of righteous discontent on the tenement-sweatshop frontier," in the early 1880's. From "the corner of pain and anguish," as Morris Rosenfeld, the ghetto's Yiddish poet laureate, called it, came the first laments, then protests, and, finally, unions. Out of this ferment emerged one of America's foremost union leaders, Samuel Gompers, an English Jew. However, despite the formation of small union groups, some short-lived strikes, and the beginnings of the Socialist Labor Party, many of these gains melted away during the depression of 1893. Although the plight of the exploited workers had aroused wide public sympathy, it was the victims themselves who broke the sweatshop system by going on to form stable and powerful unions "born of despair, with poverty as the midwife."

The tragic Triangle Shirtwaist factory fire, which took the lives of 143 girls and women, was one of the great turning points in the history of the Jewish worker. *Heaven Will Protect the Working Girl,* Charlie Harris' 1909 tune, became a national and international hit. The International Ladies Garment Workers Union, the Fur Workers Union, and the Amalgamated Clothing Workers Union were founded during the turbulent period between 1900 and 1914.

The great outcry of sympathy and protest following the Triangle fire brought state legislation that provided for factory fire prevention, building inspection, sanitary working conditions, workmen's compensation, and shortened hours of labor for women and children. Strike gains and legislative reforms solidified the Jewish unions behind leaders who modified the militant radicalism of their predecessors into an industrial democracy and moved the Jewish workers into the mainstream of the American labor movement.

Today, however, the Jewish trade union movement is nearing its end. Once constituting an overwhelming majority of wage workers, the Jewish population is now predominantly middle and upper-middle class, despite pockets in some of the larger cities of poor or near-poor. The children and grandchildren of those factory workers are now professionals, civil service workers, executives, scientists, teachers, etcetera.

The East European Jews were "one generation proletarians, in most cases neither sons nor fathers of workers," who looked to self-employment or education as the escape route from the wage worker class. They came from communities where tailors, shoemakers, bakers, and other artisans were on the lowest rung of the social and communal ladder. Because they considered such occupations a humiliation, they slaved and saved to achieve a better life.

IN THE PEOPLE'S SERVICE

Inextricably woven into the tapestry of American history, Jews have had a large hand in shaping the country's civic, cultural, and professional life, and in coloring its liberal social and political outlook. In every generation, Jews were distinguished for community responsibility, a passion for social and political reform, a zest for culture, and a gift for expressing their vitality in word, song, and art.

The liberal political bent of Jewish voters goes back to the days when Thomas Jefferson coalesced the opponents of the domestic and foreign policies of the Federalist party into a new political alignment. Samson Simson, first Jewish member of the New York Bar, was among the founders and vice-president of the Jeffersonian Democratic party in 1795. The Reverend Gershom Mendes Seixas, patriot of the American Revolution, preached a sermon sharply at variance with the views of the other clergy, who supported the Federalists in their denunciations of the new republican regime in France following the French Revolution.

The German immigrants on the East Coast were leading organizers of the new Republican party, with a number of them Lincoln presidential electors in the 1860 and 1864 elections. The Seligman brothers were sponsors of the pro-Lincoln rally at Cooper Union in New York City, which paved the way for Lincoln's nomination in 1860.

As the newer waves of immigrants acquired political sophistication, they generally joined in supporting political reform movements, regardless of party. They supported the candidacy of Theodore Roosevelt, and as President he fought immigration curbs, intervened with Rumania against its anti-Semitic policies, and protested the pogroms in Russia. He appointed Oscar S. Straus as Secretary of Labor, an event of great import to American Jews because no Jew had previously served at the Cabinet level. In 1912, William Howard Taft said that Jews "make the best Republicans," and forty years later, Adlai Stevenson said they make the best Democrats. Each was right in his own day.

Despite their changing economic status, Jewish voters were a source of great strength to the Democratic party. They were later to help raise large sums of money for Franklin D. Roosevelt's first presidential campaign. Samuel L. Rosenman became his leading speechwriter and counsel, and later head of the White House "brain trust." Jews continued to give their almost complete support to Harry S. Truman, one of the first heads of government to recognize the State of Israel.

One of the first signs of a more conservative Jewish vote occurred during the 1972 presidential election, in which there was a swing to the right in support of President Richard M. Nixon. This was in reaction to an assault on Jewish interests and Israel by the New Left and by some black militants.

National polls generally indicate that Jews usually register and actually vote more consistently than other ethnic blocs of the citizenry. However, in recent elections a large proportion of voters reported themselves "undecided" and no longer aligned to one party. The Jewish vote has become "a ballgame," as one candidate noted.

IN PURSUIT OF LEARNING

The impact of Jews on education and the cultural arts has been compared to "a sort of cosmopolitan galvanic battery" which is always charging up an intellectual ferment.

The fruitful association of Jews with learning dates back to early Colonial times, when the Reverend Gershom Mendes Seixas, a leading Jewish leader during the American Revolution, was elected a trustee of King's College (Columbia College). As early as 1723, Judah Monis received a Master of Arts degree from Harvard, the first ever granted a Jew in America. Appointed an instructor in Hebrew at Harvard, he wrote and published the first Hebrew grammar in North America in 1735.

Although the struggle for an economic foothold and their sometime conflicts with rebellious children tarnished the dream of "the goldene medina" (the golden land) for many first-generation immigrants, they eventually took full advantage of every opportunity for educational advancement in the second generation. As soon as they learned English, immigrant Jews crowded public schools, public libraries, and free lectures wherever they were available. Such free tuition schools as City College of New York, which was long known as the "Jewish college of America," had an alumni roster which read like a roll call of the country's leading figures in law, business, art, science, literature, and philosophy. From Bernard M. Baruch and Jonas Salk, to Arthur Kornberg, Nobel Prize winner, the achievements of City College's Jewish graduates are written large in the history of the twentieth century. Perhaps the two most distinguished immigrant alumni were Supreme Court Justice Felix Frankfurter and Morris Raphael Cohen, one of the few original philosophers America has produced.

Usually working by day, the second-generation children began attending professional schools at night, turning in great numbers to medicine, science, law, and teaching. Out of the immigrants' ambition for professional careers for their children came the now-familiar boast "my son the doctor."

After centuries of oppression in the ghettos of Europe, with little hope of education or advancement, the flowering of Jewish culture and learning burst forth in America in the second generation of immigrants.

THE CULTURAL FERMENT

Eagerness to use talents pent up during hundreds of years of oppression also galvanized and stimulated American culture. The role of Jews in the worlds of theater, music, literature, art, and mass entertainment has been described as "sometimes strident, generally exciting, and often original and profound."

In 1859, a newspaper said that "if any segment of the population makes extensive sacrifices on behalf of newspapers, the theater, and scholarly and artistic efforts, it is first and foremost, among all immigrants, the New York Jews." Older families, however, had set the precedent.

One of the prominent artists of the eighteenth century was Myer Myers, a leading silversmith, whose work is still preserved in museums, and who is considered to be a peer of Paul Revere. Mordecai M. Noah and Samuel B. H. Judah were successful playwrights in the 1830's and 1840's, and Henry B. Phillips was a widely known popular actor. The first permanent Italian opera company was established in 1843 by Max Maritzek. The New Orleans-born pianist, Louis Gottschalk, was a musical sensation between 1853 and 1863.

Leopold Damrosch and Oscar Hammerstein were pioneers in the American musical world. Damrosch, friend of Wagner and Liszt, had come to America in 1871 as Temple Emanu-El's musical director. He later founded the Philharmonic Society of New York and became conductor of the newly opened Metropolitan Opera House. His son, Walter, persuaded Andrew Carnegie to build one of America's great concert halls, Carnegie Hall.

In the world of the theater, the names of David Belasco and the Frohman brothers, Charles, Daniel, and Gustav, were known throughout the country. The Frohmans produced over 700 plays and introduced some of the stage's greatest stars.

In 1882, Boris Thomashefsky, a choir singer, organized one of the great cultural outlets for the East European Jew—the Yiddish theater. By the turn of the century, he was the most popular actor, playwright, director, and producer in the Yiddish theater and a matinee idol beloved by many a Jewish girl. Jacob P. Adler, who brought over the first

company of experienced Yiddish actors in 1890, ushered in
the most exciting epoch of Yiddish drama. At the height of
its popularity, the Yiddish theater filled four houses Monday
through Thursday via a benefit system through which Jewish
clubs and associations bought blocks of tickets. The claim has
been made that the modern theater party, backbone of
Broadway hits, was invented by East Side Jews who seldom
said they were going to the theater, but always to a benefit.
The early years produced such stars as Ludwig Satz, Bertha
Kalish, Jennie Goldstein, Rudolph Schildkraut, and David
Kessler. In the later years, stars such as Molly Picon, Luther
Adler, Paul Muni, Edward G. Robinson, Menashe Skulnik,
Maurice Schwartz, and Herschel Bernardi were to emerge
from their Yiddish theater experience to achieve international
fame.

The movies, to which immigrants flocked, dealt the first
body blow to the Yiddish stage, from which it never recov-
ered.

The founding fathers of the motion picture industry were
almost all Jews, many of them East European immigrants.
These celluloid empires were built by such names as Adolph
Zukor, Jesse Lasky, Carl Laemmle, William Fox, Lewis
Selznick, Samuel Goldwyn, the Cohn brothers, and Louis B.
Mayer. It was the Warner brothers who dared to gamble on
the first all-sound picture, *The Jazz Singer,* starring Al Jolson.

From the earliest days of radio and television, those media
counted the Sarnoffs, Paleys, Flamms, and Strauses among
their most enterprising leaders. In the early days of vaudeville, radio, and television, the most popular headliners were
Jewish comedians and singers. Eddie Cantor, George Burns,
the Marx Brothers, the Ritz Brothers, Phil Silvers, Sid
Caesar, Milton Berle, Joey Bishop, Fannie Brice, Al Jolson,
Ed Wynn, George Jessel, and Jack Benny all rose to the top
without reliance on Jewish gags. The ethnic Jew of vaudeville
had been replaced by *Abie's Irish Rose.* The daily life of the
Goldbergs, as recounted by Gertrude Berg, occupied the regular radio attention of all America for 25 years. Later, however, such comedians as Sam Levenson, Jerry Lewis, Shelly
Berman, Alan King, Myron Cohen, and Lenny Bruce found
their humorous foils in the environment out of which they
came.

America's musical life has been enriched in special abun-
dance by such towering figures as Irving Berlin, son of a

synagogue cantor, and George Gershwin, a self-taught pianist. Berlin's earliest songs, such as "Alexander's Ragtime Band," became musical landmarks, while millions of Americans marched off in World War II to "God Bless America." His more than 1,000 tunes have been called "a continuous obbligato to American history." Gershwin combined popular and classical music in his immortal folk opera, *Porgy and Bess* and in his symphonic jazz composition, *Rhapsody in Blue.*

Jewish musicians, singers, and conductors, who began arriving in the late 1890's from East Europe, paved the way for a flock of virtuosi and later native-born artists of worldwide renown. The names of Vladimir Horowitz, Artur Rubinstein, Mischa Elman, Efrem Zimbalist, Jascha Heifetz, Nathan Milstein, Rosalyn Tureck, Gregor Piatigorsky, Fritz Reiner, Bruno Walter, Serge Koussevitzky, Yehudi Menuhin, Alma Gluck, Regina Reznik, Rosa Ponselle, Leonard Warren, Richard Tucker, Jan Peerce, Robert Merrill, and Beverly Sills are but a few of the Jewish greats of the twentieth-century musical world.

The Guggenheim Foundation fellowships, which have been granted for nearly 40 years, have become an intellectual knighthood to musicians, artists, writers, scholars, and scientists of promise, as the Guggenheim and Hirshhorn Museums are meccas for art lovers.

The new American art form called musical comedy was dominated by Marc Blitzstein, Harold Rome, Jerome Kern, Lorenz Hart, Oscar Hammerstein II, Richard Rodgers, Frederick Loewe, and Alan Jay Lerner. These "grassroot operas" displaced the musical extravaganzas of Florenz Ziegfeld.

The theater has been enriched by a long line of Jewish luminaries: Elmer Rice, George S. Kaufman, Moss Hart, Lillian Hellman, Sidney Kingsley, Arthur Miller, Clifford Odets, Dore Schary, S. N. Behrman, Lee Strasberg, David Merrick, Kermit Bloomgarden, and Neil Simon.

One of the great photographic artists of the twentieth century was Alfred Stieglitz. Other artists who achieved international fame were Jo Davidson, Sir Jacob Epstein, William Zorach, Ben Shahn, Abraham Walkowitz, Moses and Raphael Soyer, and Maurice Becker.

Jews have long been influential in the American literary field. Alfred A. Knopf, Benjamin Huebsch, Charles Boni, the Guinzbergs, Horace Liveright, Bennett Cerf, Max Schuster, and Richard Simon dynamically changed the book publishing industry after World War I. They introduced new European authors, encouraged American writers, and dramatically enlarged the American reading audience. Literary critics such as Waldo Frank, James Oppenheim, Louis Untermeyer, Leslie Fiedler, Babette Deutsch, Alfred Kazin, John Simon, Norman Podhoretz, Nat Hentoff, and Paul Rosenfeld have helped to shape American literary taste and thought. Horace Kallen, Sidney Hook, Irving Kristol, Irving Howe, Irwin Edman, David Riesman, Daniel Bell, and Nathan Glazer became important social and cultural influences.

Mordecai M. Noah, founder, editor, or publisher of seven different daily newspapers between 1820 and 1840, was one of the first eminent Jewish figures in American journalism. On his *Enquirer* he employed James Gordon Bennett, who, according to legend, started the *Herald* with $100 borrowed from Noah.

Noah's uncle by marriage, Solomon H. Jackson, in 1823 launched *The Jew*, the earliest known English-language Jewish publication in the United States, started specifically to counteract the widespread efforts to convert Jews at that time. When *The Jew* suspended publication, there were few Jewish journals until 1849. *Israels Herold* had a brief existence as the first German-Jewish weekly, and *The Asmonean*, an English-language weekly, was published from 1849 to 1858. *The American Israelite,* founded by Rabbi Isaac M. Wise and Edward Bloch in Cincinnati in 1854, was a vehicle used to proclaim the tenets of Reform Judaism. Today there are approximately 500 Jewish newspapers throughout the United States, of which the largest is *The Jewish Week and American Examiner,* the most widely read and probably the most influential American Jewish weekly in the country.

Joseph Pulitzer, with his innovations and unorthodox methods on *The New York World,* was to emerge as one of the fourth estate's most controversial newspapermen. Son of a Jewish father, Pulitzer was assailed as a renegade Jew whose "face is repulsive not because the physiognomy is Hebraic but because it is Pulitzeresque." Pulitzer's relentless battle against political corruption and his struggle with Hearst's jingoistic efforts which led to the Spanish-American War are all but forgotten. He is remembered, however, for the Pulitzer Prize. These annual awards for outstanding achievement in the fields of journalism, letters, and music were established by Pulitzer and have been awarded since 1917.

Adolph S. Ochs built an enduring memorial in *The New York Times.* A one-time Tennessee printer's devil, Ochs acquired the bankrupt *Times* in 1896 and built it into one of the world's most influential newspapers. His high standards and capacity for choosing brilliant associates made the newspaper a symbol of honest and socially responsible journalism.

Herbert Bayard Swope, Franklin P. Adams, Meyer Berger, Walter Winchell, Mark Hellinger, Louis Sobol, Leonard Lyons, Al Capp, Rube Goldberg, and Milton Gross were legendary Jewish names in American journalism. Columnists Walter Lippmann and Walter Weyl were once described by President Theodore Roosevelt in a moment of annoyance as "two uncircumcised Jews." Norman Cousins was the prime factor in the success of *The Saturday Review,* and Sime Silverman founded the bible of show business, *Variety.* Samuel Newhouse, once a clerk on the *Bayonne Times,* rose to become the owner of twenty newspapers and a number of magazines, as well as radio and television stations.

One of the most colorful episodes in Jewish journalistic history was the rise of the Yiddish press. Created by and for immigrants, the Yiddish press flourished as long as mass immigration continued. It taught the immigrants about the ideals and traditions of the bewildering new world, kept them in touch with happenings in the old world, and was influential in molding their political, cultural, and social integration. It began in 1871 when a Jewish politician published *The Jewish News* in English, German, Yiddish, and Hebrew in order to win votes. There were many other Jewish newspapers between that date and 1897 when *The Forward* was launched. *The Forward* rose to great influence on the tidal waves of immigration under the extraordinary editorship of Abraham Cahan. It became the largest and most important newspaper in the Jewish world and a major weapon in the emergence of the Jewish labor movement and in the Americanization of two generations of immigrants. As a mediator between Yiddish and American cultures, Cahan "helped infuse the one with the other and thus had a share in creating a Jewish American culture." His letter column, "A Bintel Brief" (bunches of letters), created one of the most popular open forums for immigrants.

There emerged during this fruitful period the poetry and prose of Morris Rosenfeld, Abraham Reisen, Solomon Bloomgarden, and H. Leivick. The works of I. Peretz, Mendele Mocher Seforim, Sholom Aleichem, Sholem Asch, Zalman Schneur, Israel Singer, Isaac B. Singer, and Elie Wiesel all first appeared in Yiddish papers.

Every reader the Yiddish dailies helped Americanize became a lost reader, and by the late 1920's, circulation started to drop in spite of efforts to halt this irreversible trend.

THEIR BROTHER'S KEEPER

From the days when they were still only a tolerated minority with a precarious foothold in New Amsterdam, Jews have given leadership and support to almost every liberal, humane, and forward-looking movement.

It began with Asser Levy, who gave 100 florins to the fund raised to defend New Amsterdam against the British invasion in 1664; seven years later, he also advanced money to the Lutherans to help them build their first church. Minister Gershom Mendes Seixas' lectures at St. Paul's Church in 1800 set an enduring example of interfaith amity, which much later resulted in the National Conference of Christians and Jews. The records of the Manumission Society from 1799 to 1809 contain the names of many Jews who emancipated their slaves and helped maintain the underground railway for runaway slaves. Ernestine Rose was involved in the early struggle for women's rights in the 1830's, and during the Irish famine of the 1840's, Jews conducted a number of fund-raising relief appeals.

At the time of the Civil War, most of the Jewish immigrants from Germany, Bohemia, and Austria sided with the abolitionists. When Rabbi Morris Raphall preached a sermon early in 1861 attempting to justify slavery on biblical grounds, he was bitterly assailed in Jewish circles.

Nathan Straus set up over 300 pasteurized milk stations throughout the country; Lillian Wald, a social worker, organized settlement houses and started the Visiting Nurse Corps; Dr. Stephen S. Wise, Joel and Arthur Spingarn, and Dr. Henry Moskowitz were all founders of the National Association for the Advancement of Colored People; Professor Edwin R. A. Seligman was the first chairman of the Urban League; and Arthur Garfield Hays was instrumental in establishing the American Civil Liberties Union. All these are but a few examples of the deep commitment to social justice and philanthropy exhibited by the descendants of peddlers and sweatshop workers. The great philanthropists Lucius N. Littauer and Julius Rosenwald contributed millions to American educational institutions. The latter was responsible for the construction of over 5,357 schools, homes, libraries, health clinics, and YMCAs for blacks in 15 southern states. Rosenwald especially braved bitter prejudices in his far-reaching efforts to improve the conditions of blacks.

MANNERS AND MORES

Since the handful of Jewish refugees found a grudging haven in New Amsterdam over three centuries ago, they have risen from an immigrant, low-income, embattled group to a largely native-born, well-educated, mostly middle-class citizenry accepted as an inseparable element of America.

Though more widely dispersed than ever before throughout the country, Jews never became dissolved in the melting pot but rather became imbedded in two cultures, Americanism and Judaism. At times they have adopted the manners of their non-Jewish friends, colleagues, and neighbors, but they have also held on to many of the mores of their parents and grandparents. Despite wretched living conditions, the Jewish working class of the immigrant generations was middle class in moral and health standards, in its worshipful adoration of education, and in its eagerness to escape from poverty.

At the turn of the century, contemporary descriptions of life on the Lower East Side of New York City, where there was the highest concentration of Jews in the nation, painted a generally accurate picture of the dismal conditions there, but seldom mentioned the lack of crime or the absence of drunkenness, venereal disease, and illiteracy. Jewish paupers were strangers to the New York Almshouse, nor were they ever buried in Potter's Field, the pauper's graveyard.

There were some Jewish toughs who warred with Irish and Italian gangs, and some Jewish gangs did become breeding grounds for criminal rings which fostered their share of poolroom operators, brothel-keepers, and petty grafters. Louis "Lepke" Buchalter of Murder, Inc. notoriety, was a descendant of the immigrant waves which commenced in the 1880's.

The first Jewish athletes were prizefighters who learned boxing to defend themselves and later became title contenders and champions, as the crowds yelled "kill the kike" or "hit the Hebe." Andy Cohen of Texas became a baseball player on the Giants team; Hank Greenberg achieved big league stardom; Sandy Koufax became a national baseball hero as a pitcher for the Dodgers, while Ronnie Blomberg, an Atlantan, was cheered as "the kosher boomer" by Yankee fans.

Lon Myers and Abel Kiviat represented the United States in Olympic track and field events, Sid Luckman became one of the greats of collegiate and pro football, and Nat Holman was known as "Mr. Basketball."

No matter where the Jews moved, their dietary predilections have influenced the eating habits of their surrounding areas. The kosher food industry, though concentrated in New York, has become a multimillion-dollar national enterprise. There are more than 2,000 different kosher products made by some 400 companies. The Heinz Company promoted its kosher ketchup in full-page ads headlined "MY BROTHER IS A SCHLEMIHL!" These foods are generally available throughout the country at hotels, on planes, and in hospitals in frozen or precooked forms. National radio, television, and newspaper ads now feature Jewish and kosher products—"You don't have to be Jewish to like Levy's rye bread," or "Be a herring maven."

Non-Jewish epicures who relish the gastronomic pleasures of what has been called "belly Judaism" also know and use many Yiddish words and expresssions. While Yiddish is declining as a spoken and printed language, it has won a place as a piquant element in American "slanguage." The linguistic amalgam has spilled into American English through many expressive words and phrases which have been spread by Broadway, radio, television, and columnists.

Little surprise is evoked when non-Jews refer to a legal arrangement as "kosher," identify a fool as a "schlemihl" or a well-rounded female as "zaftig." "Gelt," "mazuma," "kibitzer," and "meshuggah" became lingua franca of many comedians' routines. Al Capp's "shmoo" is related to the Yiddish "schmaltz" and "shmo"—the latter being an abbreviation for a Yiddish obscenity. A cosmetics firm named its new soap "Fancy Schmancy."

Politicians and reporters talk about a political mishmash; shlock and shmattas have become synonyms for junk and rags; and chutzpa is widely used to describe brazenness or extreme nerve. A leading manufacturer of heating units advertised that his product worked best when treated with "a Jewish mother's love."

The amazing success of Allan Sherman's record My Son the Folksinger and the show Fiddler on the Roof, indicated that the nation could still be intrigued by the flavor and sentiment of old world and immigrant idiosyncracies.

The story of the Jewish immigrants and their descendants became bestsellers through the novels and short stories of Herman Wouk, Bernard Malamud, Saul Bellow, Philip Roth, Bruce Jay Friedman, Herbert Gold, Chaim Potok, and Isaac Bashevis Singer. Their prose provides a continuing insight into the changing patterns of Jewish life and Jewish American history.

A final observation about the Jews of America: it is not Henry James' remark about his fears of "the Hebrew conquest," but the statement by Ford Madox Ford, the eminent English literary critic, who remarked when he came to the United States in 1926:

> . . . the intellectual vividness, partly due to the immense Jewish population . . . the only people who really loved books with a passionate yearning that transcended their attention to all terrestrial manifestations."

PATRIOTS

Although the United States dates its independence from July 4, 1776, the War of the Revolution had still to be won before the new government could function on a peacetime basis. America had to be made a fact through struggle and privation by the patriots of those days. It was not until 14 years after the first July 4th that George Washington took the oath of office as President.

When the struggle began, despite the meagerness of their numbers, and despite the fact that many of them had migrated only a short time before, the Jews were not found wanting in their participation in the war, even though America at that time was far from recognizing absolute political and religious liberty, either in statute or in practice.

The Revolution, however, was an important factor in bringing men of different persuasions together for the first time. The unity of revolutionary action ultimately stimulated the latent American sentiment for religious liberty and equality.

In 1788, with the ratification of the new Federal Constitution, for the first time since the Roman Imperial edict of 212 C.E., *there existed a nation in which Jews were full citizens.*

The ideals of the Revolution appealed to the liberal tendencies of the Jew, who had known suffering and was eager to achieve freedom. Such families as the Franks of Philadelphia, the Sheftalls and Minises of Georgia, the Ettings of Maryland, the Pintos of Connecticut, and the Gomez, Seixas, Simon, Hendricks, and Phillips families of New York, committed their lives and their fortunes to the undertaking of their time—the winning of the war.

When George Washington was inaugurated as President in 1789 in New York City, Rabbi Gershom Mendes Seixas, spiritual leader of the Spanish and Portuguese Synagogue, was among the invited guests. Despising bigotry, the tall, dignified figure of Washington was the embodiment of America to all those present.

ASSER LEVY
c. 1628—6182

In the history of the struggle to attain equal rights in America, Asser Levy emerges as one of the first and foremost figures. His campaign for these rights was to affect the millions of immigrants who were to come in the following 300 years.

Levy, together with 22 other impoverished Jewish passengers, arrived from Brazil in the Dutch colony of New Amsterdam in 1654, aboard the *Saint Charles*. This destitute group, fleeing the Portuguese Inquisition in Brazil, constituted America's first Jewish refugees. While they were not the first Jews in the Americas or the Caribbean Islands, they were the first to create an issue over citizenship and human rights.

When the governor of the Colony, Peter Stuyvesant, sought to expel them on the grounds that their poverty would make them wards of the state, Levy sent a petition directly to Holland, urgently requesting permission to remain.

On February 15, 1655, Stuyvesant announced harshly that the group could remain as probationers, but under severely imposed restrictions. Although they would be allowed to exercise their religion "in all quietness . . . within their houses for which end they must without doubt endeavor to build their houses close together in a convenient place. . .," they would not be permitted to build a house of worship. In addition, they were forbidden to seek any assistance from the citizenry or the government, or to engage in the retail trade or fur trade—the most profitable activities of the Colony.

Having established their right to this uneasy permanence, albeit under severe circumstances, Levy then slowly sought to have the impositions removed. In another appeal to Holland, he stated that the Jews were subject to all of the taxes of legalized citizens but possessed none of the community rights. He was successful in having most of the restrictions removed, with the exception of the right to bear arms and to become a burgher (citizen).

With the freedom to trade, Levy and the small group prospered, gaining commercial importance and the respect of the governor. By 1656, even Stuyvesant relented, recommending to his superiors that Jews of the Colony be permitted to build a house of worship.

When the need to maintain a militia arose, in order to guard the city from possible Indian attack, the question of whether Jews should be required to serve was debated. The decision of the City Council was that they not be permitted and that a tax be levied against all Jewish males from 16 to 65 in lieu of military service.

Levy, with the aid of one Jacob Barsimson, petitioned the Council to reconsider this burdensome tax. The authorities, incensed at the audacity of these Jews, who had only recently had other restrictions removed, rejected their plea. Continuing their agitation, Levy and Barsimson were reluctantly permitted to bear arms, and with the passage of a new law in 1657, under which the Jewish settlers were able to become burghers, the last impediment to equal rights was lifted.

When Levy died in 1682, he left a large estate of two thousand pounds and a very respectable name. By all standards he had become one of the leading citizens and merchants of the city.

When he began this first struggle for full citizenship for immigrants, he unknowingly set a constitutional precedent, the foundation of the "open door policy" of American immigration law.

FRANCIS SALVADOR
1747—1776

Francis Salvador, nephew of a prominent English financier, was the first Jew to give his life for the American Revolution.

He came to America from England in 1773 to manage his family's plantations in South Carolina. He was a friend of the most prominent men of his day—Pinckney, Rutledge, Drayton, and others—and soon gained fame for his impassioned efforts in the cause of liberty and justice.

Salvador sat in the two Provincial Congresses and was elected to the First General Assembly of the new state of South Carolina—the first time in 1,900 years that a Jew had served in an elective office.

Soon after part of the British fleet landed in Charleston, they were successful in arousing the Cherokee Indians to attack the outlying settlements. Mounted on his horse, Salvador sped through the countryside rousing the men on the plantations to action. On the evening of July 31, 1776, Major Andrew Williamson, with Salvador as his aide and a detachment of 330 men, set out on an expedition against the Indians and Tories. Suddenly, the enemy opened fire and Salvador was ambushed and scalped. He died at the age of 29.

In City Hall Park in Charleston, South Carolina, mounted on a granite shaft, is a bronze marker memorializing Francis Salvador with these words:

> Born an aristocrat, he became a democrat—An Englishman, he cast his lot with America; True to his ancient faith, he gave his life For new hopes of human liberty and understanding.

Salvador has also been called "the Jewish Paul Revere."

DAVID SALISBURY FRANKS
c. 1749—c. 1812

David Salisbury Franks and Benedict Arnold were the major figures in a *cause célèbre* during the American Revolution, known as "L'Affaire Franks."

Franks, a member of a distinguished Jewish family in Philadelphia, was engaged in business in Montreal on the eve of the American Revolution. The American forces occupied that city for a short time, and when they retreated, Franks enlisted as a volunteer and saw active service in a Massachusetts regiment. In Philadelphia he became an aide-de-camp to General Benedict Arnold and fell under suspicion of abetting Arnold's plans for the betrayal of West Point.

Arnold's treachery had aroused tremendous bitterness, and everyone even remotely associated with him was suspected of treason. Franks was arrested and was tried before a court-martial in 1780. Hints were made that he had been in contact with his kinsman and namesake, David Franks, a known Tory who had been imprisoned as an enemy. Arnold himself wrote a letter from behind British lines seeking to vindicate Franks of any complicity.

Although Franks was acquitted and subsequently assigned to Washington's army, there were grumblings and dark whisperings in the regiment against him. When Franks learned of this, he took the matter up with Washington, asking that another investigation be made, on the grounds that "Arnold's baseness gave the tongue of Calumny ground sufficient."

Washington knew of Franks' services to the American

cause and unhesitatingly granted Frank's plea for justice. One month later a special board of inquiry was convened at West Point by order of Washington. After examining all the facts, the board issued a lengthy report which completely exonerated Franks. He was immediately promoted in rank and sent on several missions abroad as a confidential courier to Benjamin Franklin in Paris and John Jay in Madrid. Later he accompanied Thomas Jefferson to Paris to draft the peace treaty.

Enemies continued to hound him and efforts were made to dismiss him from the diplomatic service. In 1786 he was recalled, returning to the United States financially embarrassed and jobless. His fatal association with Benedict Arnold was a millstone.

He spent years hoping for another assignment and applied for positions making "disinterested tenders of his services."

In January, 1789, Congress granted him 400 acres of land in recognition of his services during the war.

HAYM SALOMON
1740—1785

Haym Salomon, one of the most notable patriots of the American Revolutionary period, was born in Lissa, Poland, in 1740. As a young man he acquired a working knowledge of eight languages and an unusual understanding of finance, which enabled him to move in banking circles of the major European commercial centers. He came to America in 1775 and began peddling among the troops at Lake George.

Salomon soon became known for his warm attachment to the American cause and was actually arrested for a short time by the British. He joined the Sons of Liberty, a secret group dedicated to the cause of freedom. He was instrumental in persuading many Hessian mercenary troops to join the American cause, and he assisted in the escape of French and American prisoners of war. He was forced to flee to Philadelphia in 1778.

In May, 1781, Robert Morris, a Superintendent of Finance, seeking an able, honest broker to help sell bills of exchange, engaged Salomon as his chief agent. In August, Morris asked Salomon to assist in raising the necessary funds for a drive to stop General Cornwallis. Following the surrender of Cornwallis at Yorktown, Salomon continued to serve

Morris, who allowed him to advertise himself as "Broker to the Office of Finance."

The multilingual, knowledgeable financier also loaned money to delegates of the Continental Congress who were in desperate need, among them James Madison.

Salomon was a member of the historic Mikveh Israel Congregation in Philadelphia, and when he died in 1785, the Sons of the American Revolution erected a plaque honoring him. Annual memorial services are held here in his honor. In 1975, the United States Post Office issued a commemmorative stamp in tribute to Haym Salomon.

BARNARD GRATZ
1738—1801

Pennsylvanian Barnard Gratz, a patriot of the American Revolution, was one of the key figures in the opening of the West to trade and settlement.

Born in Upper Silesia in 1738, Gratz, the grandson of a rabbi, came to Philadelphia in 1754. Within a few years, Barnard and his brother Michael established a firm which engaged in trapping and trading in the territory west of Pittsburgh.

Foreseeing that the American frontier would inevitably be pushed beyond the Mississippi River, they acquired large tracts of land in what is now Ohio, Kentucky, Indiana, and Illinois for economic development and colonization.

When the British embarked on a mercantile policy the colonists considered unjust, American merchants engaged in a boycott through the Nonimportation Resolutions. The Gratz brothers were among the first signers in 1765 of this early act of rebellion against the English.

During the American Revolution, Gratz gave invaluable aid to the patriots' cause by running supplies through the British blockade.

For more than two decades after the American Revolution, Gratz continued to supply and support outposts in the Northwest Territory. He was an important factor in winning the goodwill of the Indian tribes of the area.

Gratz was one of the leaders in the long fight which began in 1797 to amend the constitution of Maryland to enable Jews to hold public office. Victory in this civil rights issue, how-

ever, was not achieved until 1826, when State Assemblyman
Thomas Kennedy's "Jew Baby" bill was passed.

BENJAMIN NONES
c. 1755—c. 1821

Known as the "Jewish Lafayette," Benjamin Nones left his
native city of Bordeaux, France, and came to the American
colonies sometime between 1775 and 1776 to offer his
services to the fledgling Continental Army. He entered the
ranks as a volunteer private and rose rapidly to captain and
then major. A citation from his commanding officer read:

> I take advantage of the occasion and with such pleasure
> in my quality of Captain of the Volunteers attached to
> the suite of Pulaski's Legion to certify that Mr. Ben-
> jamin Nones has served as volunteer during the sieges of
> Charleston and Savannah. His behavior in all actions has
> been marked with all the bravery and courage which the
> military must show for the defense of the liberty of his
> country.

As the officer in charge of four hundred men, he was attached to the command of Baron De Kalb. When De Kalb
was mortally wounded, it was Nones who risked his life to
carry him from the field.

Following the end of the war, he settled in Philadelphia,
where he became an active member in communal affairs.
When a number of anti-Semitic remarks were made by the
publisher of the *Gazette,* as a result of Nones' support of
Thomas Jefferson for the Presidency, Nones published a
masterful rejoinder in the *Aurora,* another Philadelphia newspaper:

> I am a Jew. I glory in belonging to that persuasion
> which even in its opponents, whether Christian or
> Mohammedan, allow to be of divine origin of that
> persuasion on which Christianity itself was originally
> founded, and must ultimately rest—which has preserved
> its faith secure and undefiled, for nearly three thousand
> years, whose votaries have never murdered each other in
> religious ways, or cherished the theological hatred so
> general, so unextinguishable among those who revile
> them.

I am a Republican. Thank God I have not been so headless and so ignorant of what has passed, and is now passing in the political world. I have not been so proud or so prejudiced as to renounce the cause for which I have fought.

But I am poor. I am so, my family also is large, but soberly and decently brought up. They have not been taught to revile a Christian because his religion is not so old as theirs.

Nones was a member of the Masonic Order and president of Mikveh Israel Congregation in Philadelphia.

PIONEERS

When Jews first emigrated to America in the seventeenth century, they were impelled by the same reasons as Christians—to escape religious and political oppression. The vast new land, which dwarfed many countries of Europe, had a powerful appeal for ghetto-enclosed Jews in offering a life based on personal merit and tolerance. They saw a promise of equality and worked for the fulfillment of that promise. Alive to the unlimited potential, they were to dare the challenge of the wilderness to help build a new country. Most of the fifty states had Jewish settlers long before the frontier areas became territories or achieved statehood.

It is difficult to overestimate the parts played by the Franks and Gratz families, fur traders and sutlers of the early eighteenth century, in opening up the lands that were someday to become Ohio, West Virginia, Kentucky, Indiana, Illinois, and Missouri. These traders were among the first pioneers and colonizers, who held the country until the land-hungry settlers could follow the trails they had blazed. They brought supplies and mail to the outpost trappers and to the soldiers who moved in later to protect the land. Jews launched the first line of passenger boats which connected the small settlements along the Ohio River. As town-builders, there is an unbroken line of villages and municipalities from Pennsylvania to Oregon named for hardy Jewish pioneers—a line that extends from Aaronsburg, Pennsylvania, to Heppner, Oregon.

While the names and accomplishments of some of the early Jewish pioneers have been lost or forgotten, many are known through archival material, tombstones, and monuments.

Abraham Mordecai, veteran of the Revolutionary War, founded the city of Montgomery, Alabama, Solomon Barth, an Indian trader, once bought the Grand Canyon from an Indian Chief. Emanuel Lazarus, in 1826, was one of the first white men to enter California from the East. In 1859, Fred Z Salomon was one of the signers of a charter which created the city of Den-

43

ver. *Moses Elias Levy was the largest landowner in Florida, having acquired 60,000 acres in 1819. In 1734, Philip Minis was the first white child born in Georgia.*

When George Rogers Clark captured lands in Illinois in 1778, Dr. Isaac Levy was practicing medicine in the area. John Hays was a postmaster and sheriff in Illinois from 1790 to 1818. Isaiah Isaacs and Jacob I. Cohen, two Virginians, once hired Daniel Boone to survey lands they owned on the Kentucky frontier. Dr. Jacob Lumbrozo came to Maryland in 1656 and was the first Jewish doctor to practice in the United States.

Elias Stulheis, director of a colonization effort, helped settle the city of Natchez, Mississippi, between 1718 and 1733. The magic cry of "gold" brought Jews to Montana in 1862. Isaac Moses served in the military force of General William Loring in 1846 in his overland march to Oregon. The earliest Jewish settlers in Oklahoma arrived following the Civil War as towns grew up along the Chisholm and Shawnee Trails when Texas cattlemen began their great herd drives to the railheads.

David Eisenberg operated a trading post in Bismarck in 1869, and Leopold May opened a wagon-outfitting depot in Omaha in 1855. With the discovery of the Comstock silver lode in 1862 in Nevada, hundreds of Jews settled in such towns as Virginia City and Silver City. It was Simon Marks who was attached to a geological party of General George A. Custer's 7th Cavalry Division, which first found gold in the Black Hills of the Dakotas.

Though there are thousands of examples of the pioneering spirit of the Jews, some steeped in legend, the American Jewish community is an old one—older than the original thirteen colonies.

ABRAHAM MORDECAI
c. 1775—1850

"Old Mordecai," as he was called in his later years, was not the first Jewish settler in Alabama, but he was one of the most colorful.

Much of his life was spent among the Indians, whom he believed to be descended from the Ten Lost Tribes of Israel. He was bolstered in this belief by the Indians' chanting in grateful tones, "Yavohoya, Yavohoya," during their corn festival dances. It reminded him of "Jehovah," especially so since the Indians told him it meant the Great Spirit.

Born in Pennsylvania, Mordecai settled in Montgomery County, Alabama, in 1785, thus becoming the first native-born American citizen to settle in that county. Before coming to Montgomery County he was engaged in trading. Using pack ponies, he penetrated beyond the Pensacola Trading Trail, bartering with the Indians. Legend has it that he never despaired of one day hearing the familiar sound of a Hebrew answer from some Indian to his Hebrew questions, in order to prove his favorite theory.

Mordecai performed a number of missions for the Indian agent, James Seagrove, including a visit to the Creek tribal chiefs to arrange for the ransom of captive settlers.

For twenty years Mordecai carried on extensive trade in skins, hickory-nut oil, and other items with the Indians, which he would convey to such centers as New Orleans and Mobile in canoes. Through the years he acquired a thorough knowledge of Spanish, while the Indian language had almost become his mother tongue.

Although there are two versions to the story about how Mordecai lost his ear, both tales agree he definitely did lose it. The most plausible version recounts how when Chief Towerculla of the Coosawda Tribe learned of Mordecai's intrigue with a married Indian squaw, he approached his house with twelve warriors, pinned Mordecai down, and thrashed him with poles until he was unconscious, then cut off his ear and left him to the care of his wife.

Mordecai had married an Indian woman following the Revolutionary War, but was separated from her in 1836, when the Government ordered the Creek Indians westward.

In 1802, Mordecai, with the aid of two other Jews, built

45

the first cotton-gin in Alabama. But this was burned down by
the Indians. Then in 1813 he went to Georgia, where he
joined General Floyd's Militia.

He died in 1850, in his late nineties, in a lonely hut at
Dudleyville, beside a coffin of his own design which had
served as his eating table most of his life. A memorial marker
erected by the Daughters of the American Revolution near
his grave reads:

To the Memory of Abraham Mordecai
Soldier of the Pennsylvania Line,
American Revolution.
Indian Trader and Early Settler
in Montgomery County.
Scout in Floyd's Georgia Militia, 1814.

HENRY CASTRO
1786—1862

Castroville, a town west of San Antonio, Texas,
memorializes Henry Castro, an early pioneer in Texas, and
friend and adviser of Sam Houston.

Castro, a descendant of a distinguished Marrano family
(one of his ancestors, Jose de Castro, was the fourth
Portuguese Viceroy of the Indies), was born in France in
1786. Though little is known of his early years, records indicate that he was a member of a guard of honor which accompanied Napoleon in the invasion of Spain.

When he emigrated to the United States (c. 1820), he
settled for a short time in Providence, Rhode Island. Castro
received a diplomatic appointment to the Kingdom of Naples
and, on completion of this mission, organized a banking firm
with a French partner. When Texas became a republic in
1836 after seceding from Mexico, the new government under
President Sam Houston appealed to Castro for desperately
needed financial aid. After the loan was arranged, Houston
again asked Castro's help in attracting settlers for the survival
and growth of the new Republic of Texas. In 1842, Houston
entered into an agreement with Castro which conveyed a
large tract of land west of the Medina River for colonization.

Two years later, when Castro was appointed Consul-General to France from Texas, he devoted much of his time to
publicizing the new colony to prospective settlers from

France, Alsace, and the German provinces. When he returned, the colony was formerly inaugurated and a town plan laid out. In a unanimous vote by the settlers, the town was named Castroville. By 1846, Castro had settled over 5,000 immigrants in his colony. Transporting them in 27 ships, he spent more than $150,000 of his own money during the first year in furnishing the newly arrived with food, cattle, farming implements, and seed.

When the Civil War broke out, Castro's financial position became precarious. Determined to reach France to raise capital, he was unable to leave through any of the blockaded ports of Texas. He attempted the trip through Mexico, but died at Monterey and was buried at the foot of the Sierra Madre mountains.

In 1876, the State of Texas paid tribute to the memory of Henry Castro, pioneer of the West, by naming one of its new counties in the Panhandle in his name. In the plaza of his town of Castroville, a granite slab commemorates its founding father.

MICHAEL GOLDWATER (GOLDWASSER)
c. 1823—1903

From 1860 through present times, the name of Goldwater has figured prominently in Arizona's colorful and exciting history.

One of the early pioneers in the Territory of Arizona, Polish-born Michael Goldwater, turned up at La Paz, scene of a major gold strike, in 1860. His grandson, Barry, was destined to be nominated for the office of President of the United States in 1964 on the Republican party ticket, and to be reelected to the Senate after losing his bid for the Presidency.

Goldwater set up a freighting business, hauling provisions and supplies to army posts, meanwhile guarding against attacks by the Apache Indians. He opened his first store in 1864, and the town of Ehrenberg that grew up around it was named for Goldwater's friend Herman Ehrenberg. The store served as the town hall, post office, and general meeting place. His brother Joe was the first postmaster of the town.

In 1872, the Goldwaters decided that the new village of Phoenix held promise, and they opened a store there, with Michael in charge, while Joe remained in Ehrenberg. Joe later established stores in Tombstone, when a rich silver strike was made there, and in other frontier towns of Bisbee, Yuma, and Benson.

Michael had eight children—five sons and three daughters. One son was a professional gambler, one a tobacco salesman, and one a wanderer. Two sons, Morris and Baron, followed in their father's work. Morris moved to Prescott, which was the capital of Arizona until 1889. He was a pioneer telegraph operator who was instrumental in getting a telegraph line in Arizona, and served as mayor of the city for 20 years.

Baron Goldwater, who remained in Phoenix, developing a wide-ranging mercantile and industrial empire, was the father of Barry Goldwater. Although Barry's mother was not Jewish and he was raised as an Episcopalian, he has never denied his Jewish origin. At the Presidential nominating convention of 1964, Senator Everett Dirksen presented him as "the grandson of a Polish-born Jewish peddler."

In 1964, when Prescott marked its centennial, Morris Goldwater, the Senator's uncle, was named "Man of the Century." For 63 years, he had been a leader in countless civic and business affairs. He was the father of the city's water system, founder of its volunteer fire department, secretary of the Prescott Rifles, member of both houses of the Territorial Legislature, a prominent banker, and a booster of roads and railroads. A leader of the Territory's Democratic party, Goldwater was elected vice-president of the 1910 constitutional convention, where he was one of the framers of Arizona's first constitution, a preliminary to statehood.

<h1 style="text-align:center">HENRY ALTMAN</h1>
c. 1835—1905

As the Union Pacific construction crews and surveyors pressed their track-laying across southern Wyoming, merchants, peddlers, and freighters moved into Cheyenne. Four months before the tracks reached Cheyenne in November, 1867, two Jews were among the early merchants to arrive. One was Simon Bamberger, who went on to Salt Lake City and fame to become the first non-Mormon governor of Utah; the other was Henry Altman, who became one of the builders of Wyoming.

Both men had earned their livelihood by renting tents, cashing pay vouchers, peddling, and driving wagons. Altman had come from North Platte, Nebraska, where he had been a peddler for some years. On the way to Cheyenne, he had acquired a reputation as a courageous driver when he outwitted a band of Indians attacking his wagon. At Cheyenne, Altman opened a store and branched out into cattle raising.

In 1880, the Altman cattle ranch was one of the largest in Wyoming and its owner was one of the founders of the Wyoming Stock Growers Association. A member of the Territorial Legislature, Altman was instrumental in succeeding in having Wyoming admitted to the Union in 1889, even though its population of 62,500 did not qualify for statehood.

Altman also served in the State Legislature. By 1900, he was called "the grand old man of Wyoming."

OTTO MEARS
1840—1931

One of the most colorful and influential figures in Colorado in the 1860's was the Lithuanian-born Jew, Otto Mears. Indian fighter and conciliator, trail blazer, farmer, road builder, colonizer, and railroad magnate, Mears was largely responsible for opening vast stretches of previously impassable mountain areas to trade, agriculture, mining, and settlement.

A 12-year-old orphan in 1852 when his relatives in Lithuania sent him to an uncle who lived in California during the Gold Rush, Mears found no uncle when he arrived in San Francisco. After working at odd jobs, he joined the First California Volunteers during the Civil War, fighting through the campaigns in New Mexico and Arizona, and serving under Kit Carson.

After he was mustered out in 1864, Mears settled in Colorado's San Luis Valley, where he became friendly with the Indians, including the Ute chief, Ouray. To provide transportation for the lumber and grain of the mountain valleys, he hacked out one of the State's first toll roads at Poncha Pass. This became part of a 300-mile network of urgently needed highways which Mears built to open southwest Colorado to settlement. He also built a large section of the Rio Grande Southern Railroad.

A plug-hatted, bewhiskered character who spoke the Ute Indian language with a Yiddish accent, Mears became a Presidential elector when Colorado was admitted to the

Union in 1876. In 1883 he was elected Lieutenant-Governor.

When he died in California at the age of 91, he requested that his ashes be scattered over the mountains of his beloved Colorado.

SOLOMON BARTH
c. 1853—1928

An early prospector in Arizona, Solomon Barth claimed ownership of the Grand Canyon, one of the world's most famous natural sites. A Jewish Indian trader, Barth had entered into an agreement with an Indian chief for the transfer of ownership of the Canyon.

Pony express rider, miner, and gambler, Barth had worked in La Paz in 1862 for Michael Goldwater. In 1864, he won a contract to carry mail between Prescott and Albuquerque, New Mexico. In 1868, he was captured by the Apaches, stripped, and threatened with torture. When he was set free, he walked barefoot to a nearby friendly Zuni village. Two years later, he obtained the mail contract between other towns and forts.

The town of St. Johns on the Coronado Trail was founded by Barth in 1874, when he won several thousand head of sheep and a large sum of money in a card game. Barth named the town for the first woman resident, Señora Maria San Juan de Padilla de Baca.

He served in two state legislatures and was a county treasurer. When he died in 1928, the flags were at half-mast throughout the state. His brother Nathan was the first sheriff of Apache County.

RELIGIONS

During the American Colonial period, the spirit of the Hebrew prophets was one of the most potent forces in the land. The Puritans, in particular, were profoundly influenced by the teachings of the Old Testament. They borrowed broadly from its codes and respected the Hebrew language. Many of them, such as Ezra Stiles, president of Yale University, studied rabbinics with his friend Rabbi Isaac Touro of Newport, Rhode Island, and sought instruction from itinerant rabbis who came to the Colonies. When Stiles was inducted at Yale, he delivered an oration in Hebrew and later made the language compulsory for freshmen. The Yale coat of arms bears the Hebrew words Urim *and* Thummim *(Light and Truth). Dozens of prominent figures in Massachusetts and Rhode Island were Hebraists, and every man who graduated from Harvard College in those early days was expected to have sufficient fluency in Hebrew to read the* Pentateuch *in the original.*

The Old Testament gave vigor to Colonial preachers, who hammered away at the analogy between their mistreatment by the British and the enslavement of the Jews in Egypt. In 1776, Benjamin Franklin, Thomas Jefferson, and John Adams, members of a committee to recommend an official seal for the new Republic, originally endorsed a design whose theme was the escape of the Israelites from the despotic Pharaoh, with the legend "Rebellion to Tyrants is Obedience to God."

Those Jews living in the shadow of Independence Hall in Philadelphia realized that this struggle against tyranny was their millennial struggle against oppression and injustice. The Liberty Bell's inscription from Leviticus (25:10), "Proclaim liberty throughout the land unto all the inhabitants thereof," *was to remind them and succeeding generations of this Old Testament command.*

Thus Jewish religious aspirations were linked with those of the early patriots and the Founding Fathers, as the country drew profound inspiration from the Hebrew scriptures. There is historic justice in the fact that the United States became a haven for millions of Jews who found here the religious freedom denied them abroad. It is, therefore, no surprise that the first successful Reform movement in Judaism developed in the United States. Freedom of speech and worship offered an incentive toward changes in custom and ritual, with the practices and philosophy of Judaism subjected to considerable modernization in America. Changes in Jewish ceremony and the introduction of English into the services were accompanied by intense interest in the synagogue. By the latter half of the nineteenth century, Reform rabbis were in service in almost every important community in the country. Wherever they went, they were exponents of a broad, universal, liberal religious spirit.

Paralleling the development of Reform congregations, there has also been a Conservative and Orthodox movement among American Jews, which has similarly grown in strength and importance. While most of the early congregations had rabbis drawn from men who had received their education in Europe, seminaries now exist all over the United States for rabbinical training. The oldest of these is the Hebrew Union College in Cincinnati, Ohio, which prepares men for the Reform rabbinate.

Content in the fact that the country permitted full religious expression, Jews have strongly resisted threats to establish a state-supported church, generally seeking to keep religious institutions out of affairs of state. They joined the struggle against the introduction of any religious dogma in public school systems, which they considered the great nurseries for the cultivation of American democracy.

Although the Jewish community has always been a minority one in the United States, they had a flourishing congregation in the early settlement of New Amsterdam when it numbered only a few thousand white inhabitants.

GERSHOM MENDES SEIXAS
1745—1816

Gershom Mendes Seixas, born in New York in 1745, the fourth of seven children of Isaac M. and Rachel Seixas, was the first native-born Jewish preacher, and a leading patriot of the American Revolution.

At the age of five, Seixas read portions of prayers at the Spanish and Portuguese Synagogue, the first congregation in North America, founded shortly after the settlement of the first Jewish pilgrims in 1654. At 23, he was unanimously elected to the office of *hazzan* (minister) of this congregation.

At the outbreak of the American Revolution, he sided fervently with the American patriots. Rather than continue worship under the British occupation of New York, Seixas closed the doors of the synagogue and left with the Torah Scrolls for Stratford, Connecticut, later going to Philadelphia. Following the end of the war, he returned to New York to continue his duties at his synagogue.

At the inauguration of George Washington as first President of the United States, Seixas was one of the clergymen to be invited.

In 1784, he was elected by the New York State Legislature as a member of the first Board of Regents of the University of the State of New York. He was one of the incorporators of Columbia College and served for almost thirty years as a trustee. The inscription under his portrait hanging in Earle Hall of Columbia University reads:

Gershom Mendes Seixas
1745
Regent, University of the State of New York
1784-1815
Minister of Congregation Shearith Israel
and
American Patriot

He is buried at the Chatham Square Cemetery in New York City, the second oldest Jewish burial ground in the United States, having been consecrated in 1656.

Supreme Court Justice Benjamin N. Cardozo and the poet Emma Lazarus were among the notable descendants of Ger-

55

shom Mendes Seixas. In 1836, his son Joshua Seixas taught Hebrew to Joseph Smith, the founder of Mormonism. This event is memorialized on the third floor of the Mormon Temple at Kirtland, Ohio, where Smith recorded these lessons in his diary.

ISAAC LEESER
1806—1868

Isaac Leeser, one of the most notable Jewish personalities of the nineteenth century, was born in Prussia and came to the United States in 1824. He settled in Richmond, Virginia, and first gained fame through the publication of six essays, which appeared in the *Richmond Whig* in answer to an anti-Semitic article. These essays were later published as a book, *Jews and the Mosaic Laws,* in 1833.

Elected reader of Mikveh Israel, the oldest congregation in Philadelphia, Leeser was an outspoken opponent of innovations and reforms in the ritual, advocating unity among the varying Jewish leaders of his time. He revised the King James translation of the Bible, and published *The Occident and Jewish Advocate,* one of the first important Jewish periodicals in America. He organized Maimonides College, and was one of the founders of the Jewish Publication Society. Two of his congregants created major Jewish institutions—Hyman Gratz (Gratz College) and Moses Aaron Dropsie (Dropsie University).

One of his most enduring contributions was the establishment of the army's Jewish chaplaincy corps. In his capacity as Secretary of the Board of Ministers of the Hebrew Congregations in Philadelphia, he wrote to President Lincoln requesting the appointment of a Jewish army chaplain for Jewish soldiers serving with the Union army. In 1862, Congress changed the law to permit the appointment of rabbis as chaplains.

Following the assassination of Lincoln, Leeser officiated at the Jewish community's memorial services for the slain President in Washington, D. C.

ISAAC MAYER WISE
1819—1900

When an Albany, New York, synagogue engaged Rabbi Isaac Mayer Wise in 1846, little did they realize that they had acquired a stormy petrel, one destined to change American Judaism.

Wise, born in Bohemia in 1819, studied for the rabbinate in Prague. He came to America in 1846, filled with the progressive ideas which were prevalent in Europe at that time.

Unable to find work in New York City, he accepted a job at the Orthodox Beth El Synagogue in Albany, New York, as rabbi. From the beginning, he shocked the congregation when he introduced his first reforms in the ritual. Denunciations from the members and the Jewish press led to a congregational split.

While still rabbi of the progressive group, Wise received an offer for a post in Cincinnati, the gateway city to the Middle West and the South. He accepted the offer, convinced that with the influx of immigrants arriving daily, the new arrivals would be more accepting of his reforms than the entrenched East Coast orthodoxy. This decision was the start of his amazing career as teacher, orator, editor, author, reformer, organizer, and administrator.

Determined to dedicate his life to the creation of an informed and progressive laity and an American-trained rabbinate, Wise joined with Isaac Leeser, leader of the traditional movement in Judaism, in a call for unity in religious life. Although many conferences were convened to achieve this unification, ultimately they failed, due in part to the extreme positions taken by the radical reform leaders.

Undaunted, Wise continued his efforts by founding *The American Israelite*, the first continuous American Jewish periodical. It was through this medium that he promoted his ideas for Reform Judaism, and it was to become his most effective instrument.

In 1855, he opened the short-lived Zion College in Cincinnati, the earliest attempt at creating a Jewish university in the United States. In 1873, at a meeting in Cincinnati,

Wise and the leaders of 34 national synagogues founded the Union of American Hebrew Congregations. The Union adopted a broad program aimed at preserving Judaism in America and adapting it to the needs and desires of American Jews.

Not content with this major accomplishment, he energetically pursued his other goal—the establishment of a Jewish college. In 1875, the Hebrew Union College was founded—the first permanent American seminary to train youths for the rabbinate. The first group was ordained in 1883. By 1889, when a sufficient number of rabbis had been graduated, Wise brought into being the Central Conference of American Rabbis—the first permanent body of Jewish religious leaders.

When the waves of Orthodox East European Jews began arriving in the United States in the 1880's from the isolation of the *shtetl,* they were confronted with a Judaism which they did not recognize or understand. While they considered the English-speaking members of the Reform movement as having abandoned their faith, the American Jews considered their bearded co-religionists as alien in character and out of touch with the pertinent issues confronting world Jewry in general, and American Jewry in particular. However, the spirit of freedom in the United States was infectious for the young Jewish immigrant, who slowly rebelled against the rigidity of old-world Orthodoxy, with many joining the new Conservative or Reform movements.

The reformation Isaac Mayer Wise brought to American Judaism not only changed Orthodoxy but opened the way for other movements, such as Conservative Judaism, founded by the great scholar Solomon Schechter, and the Society for Ethical Culture, founded by Felix Adler.

When Isaac Mayer Wise died in 1900, the great national institutions he helped create had already brought order out of chaos in Jewish life in America and set the organizational pattern for all other segments of American Jewry.

SABATO MORAIS
1823—1897

There is a touch of irony in the fact that Sabato Morais, a Sephardic rabbi, was a founder and first president of one of the great seats of religious learning, the Jewish Theological

Seminary of America—an institution of Conservative Judaism.

In 1845, the 22-year-old Italian-born Jew, Sabato Morais, applied for the post of assistant rabbi of London's Spanish and Portuguese Congregation, but was turned down because of his limited knowledge of English. He was, however, accepted for a lesser post as Hebrew master of their school for orphans. When Isaac Lesser, spiritual leader of the historic Congregation Mikveh Israel in Philadelphia, resigned, Morais applied and was elected to the post in 1851.

An ardent abolitionist, Morais used his office on many occasions to deliver anti-slavery sermons. His deep commitment to this burning issue led to his being prohibited from preaching. The prohibition lasted a full year, and when he returned to his pulpit, he was requested to abstain from discussing all political subjects. The request had come from a congregant who was a close friend of a fellow Pennsylvanian, President James Buchanan, who despised abolitionists as impractical troublemakers.

The only letter President Lincoln ever wrote to a Jewish congregation was in response to a copy of a sermon delivered by Rabbi Morais on the occasion of the issuance of the Emancipation Proclamation. In his brief reply, Lincoln acknowledged receipt of the sermon and extended his thanks to the congregation for their expressions of kindness and confidence.

In 1867, Morais joined forces with Dr. Isaac Leeser in establishing the first Jewish college in America, Maimonides College, and during the six years of its existence was Professor of Bible and Biblical Literature. He welcomed the establishment of Hebrew Union College in Cincinnati and served as official examiner there. He was, however, a traditionalist, and in 1886 issued a call, signed by himself and several other rabbis, declaring that, "It is imperative to make a strong effort for the perpetuation of Judaism in America," and that, "It is proposed to form an institution in which Bible and Talmud shall be studied to a religious purpose."

On January 2, 1887, the Jewish Theological Seminary was established to disseminate the tenets of Traditional Judaism—the original name of Conservative Judaism. Located on Morningside Heights in New York City, the Seminary today is considered one of the world's foremost institutions of Jewish scholarship.

Its original library consisted of 1,000 volumes. Today, the Seminary's library is second only to the Anglo-Judaica collection in the British Museum.

On the occasion of his 64th birthday, Dr. Morais was awarded an honorary degree of Doctor of Laws from the University of Pennsylvania—the first Jew to be so honored by this institution.

SOLOMON SCHECHTER
1847—1915

Solomon Schechter, one of the great Hebrew scholars of the late nineteenth and early twentieth centuries, was the leading spokesman in the United States for Conservative Judaism.

Born in Rumania in 1847, he left his native town of Focsani as a young man to continue his Talmudic studies in Vienna and Berlin, where, under the guidance of outstanding Jewish teachers, he mastered the scholarly method of interpreting ancient texts.

In 1882, at the invitation of Claude Montefiore, Schechter went to England. It was here that his scholarly achievements were so remarkable and his mastery of English so rapid that he was appointed a lecturer in Rabbinics at Cambridge University. While at the University, Schechter journeyed to Cairo, Egypt, to investigate a *genizah* from which mutilated fragments had come to him from time to time. (A *genizah* is a special hiding place where incomplete or damaged Hebrew-written documents which may not be destroyed were kept.) While in Cairo, Schechter discovered the hiding place of some 100,000 manuscripts and fragments which had been buried for centuries. The documents included handwritten letters from Maimonides, love songs from the period of the Crusades, Hebrew religious and secular texts, and Greek translations of the Old Testament.

It was in this treasure trove that Schechter also found part of the Hebrew original of the Book of Ecclesiastes. Schechter gave the bulk of these discoveries to Cambridge.

In 1901, he left England to become President of the Jewish Theological Seminary in New York. Under his zealous guidance, the Seminary soon acquired a reputation for scholarship and leadership throughout the world. He was also the

founder of the United Synagogue of America, an association
of Conservative congregations.

FELIX ADLER
1815—1933

When Dr. Andrew D. White, one of the founders of
Cornell University, and minister to Russia in 1894, had an
exchange of conversations with Count Leo Tolstoy, the eminent Russian writer was asked his impressions of the American literary scene. His reply was very negative, with the
exception of his pleasure in the writings of Felix Adler.

Born in Germany in 1851, Adler, the son of a rabbi, came
to the United States at the age of six. His father Samuel was
to become the spiritual leader of one of the most influential
rabbinical posts in America, Temple Emanu-El in New York
City. When young Felix was graduated from Columbia University in 1870, he went to Germany to continue his studies,
and at the age of 23, he received his doctorate.

Expecting to succeed his father, Adler's first sermons ex-
pounded the more radical theories of the Reform movement.
However, this repelled the congregants, and he was not offered the post. His father, deeply disappointed, feared that his
son's extreme attitudes would erode not only the strength of
Talmudic teachings but also, eventually, the very foundations
of Judaism. His deepest fears about his son's views were realized when Felix Adler abandoned Judaism.

Later, when a professorship in Hebrew and Oriental literature at Cornell University was offered to him, Adler accepted. It was at Ithaca where he struggled to formulate and
clarify his philosophy of life and conduct based on ethics and
morality. He resigned from Cornell after three years and returned to New York City.

In May, 1876, he delivered an address in which he announced the formation of the New York Society for Ethical
Culture. The Society invited people of all faiths to join in a
commitment to a moral excellence as the highest duty of
man. It imposed no sanctions for lapses nor did it offer re-
wards. Its guiding principle was an interpretation of the
Golden Rule: "So act as to elicit the best in others, and by so
doing elicit the best in thyself." It was to have no prayers,
ceremonies, or rituals, and its meetings were to be discourses
on moral and ethical living.

The movement spread quickly, with branches formed in major cities of the United States and Europe. Such outstanding British leaders as Prime Minister J. Ramsay MacDonald, J. Maynard Keynes, and Graham Wallas, supported the ideas and ideals of the Society.

The Society became widely known for its advanced educational methods for children, and its classes were studied by educators from all parts of the world. Adler established the first free kindergarten for poor children, which later grew into a vocational school—the first to include both manual training and ethical instruction in its curriculum. Recognition for the school's teaching methods came when John D. Rockefeller, Jr., contributed $400,000 to the Society's educational program.

Always active in civic affairs, Adler participated in a number of commissions investigating conditions of child labor, tenements, and city corruption. Honors came to him in the form of invitations to teach at the Universities of Berlin and Oxford. He was the author of many books, of which the best known are *Creed and Deed, An Ethical Philosophy of Life,* and *The Reconstruction of the Spiritual Idea.*

When Adler died in 1933, a friend wrote that he "was a personality of spiritual majesty and light, one is awed in his presence; one does him unconscious reverence. A reverence all the more remarkable because his are none of the external attributes of authority."

CYRUS ADLER
1863—1940

Cyrus Adler—scholar, diplomat, religious leader, and Secretary of the Smithsonian Institution—was born in Van Buren, Arkansas, in 1863. The family moved East following the death of Adler's father.

Adler, who showed a marked interest in Bible studies from early childhood, was graduated from the University of Pennsylvania. While attending college, he studied privately with the biblical scholar Rabbi Sabato Morais, who was also one of the most ardent abolitionists of the antebellum period.

Adler received his Ph.D. from Johns Hopkins University in Semitics, the first American to be granted a degree in this field of study. His specialty was Assyriology, but his studies embraced the entire field of Semitics, including Arabic, Syriac, and Ethiopic.

He taught Semitics for a number of years at Johns Hopkins University while serving as a curator of the National Museum in Washington, D.C.

Adler was commissioned by President Benjamin Harrison as a government representative to seven countries in the Middle East. Upon his return to Washington in 1892, he was appointed librarian of the Smithsonian Institution, and later secretary.

His discovery of the so-called Jefferson Bible created a literary sensation. It was published with an introduction by Adler in 1904, at the express authorization of Congress. When asked why he left out his own name from the title page, Adler replied, "Jesus and Jefferson are sufficient for one title page."

While serving at the Smithsonian, Adler helped organize the Jewish Theological Seminary and the Jewish Publication Society in Philadelphia. He was a founder of the American Jewish Historical Society and an editor of the *Jewish Encyclopedia*. In 1908, he left the Smithsonian to become president of Dropsie College for Hebrew and Cognate Learning in Philadelphia.

He was a founder of the American Jewish Committee and the National Jewish Welfare Board, and president of the Jewish Theological Seminary.

In 1939, President Franklin D. Roosevelt summoned Adler to confer with him and dignitaries of the Catholic and Protestant denominations on religious matters.

On Adler's death in 1940, President Roosevelt eulogized him:

Scholar, patriot, humanitarian and religious leader who held fast to the ancient verities, an earnest worker in the cause of peace and advocate of goodwill among men.

STEPHEN SAMUEL WISE
1874—1949

Stephen Wise, the outspoken rabbi and gifted orator whom many referred to as "God's angry man," was also a potent force for political reform, his activities leading to the resignation of New York's Mayor Jimmy Walker.

Born in Budapest, Hungary, in 1874, the son of a rabbi,

Wise was brought to the United States at the age of one. He received his doctorate from Columbia University and began his rabbinical career at New York's B'nai Jeshurun, a congregation founded in 1825.

In 1905, when Temple Emanu-El, the largest Reform house of worship in the United States, invited Wise to become its rabbi, he rejected the post when the board of trustees made it clear that, "The pulpit would always be subject to and under the control of the trustees." In declining the post, Wise stated:

> A free pulpit, worthily filled, must command respect and influence; a pulpit that is not free howsoever filled, is sure to be without potency or honor. In the pursuit of the duties of his office, the minister may from time to time be under the necessity of giving expression to views at variance with the views of some or even many members of the congregation.

In reaction to what he saw as a lack of vitality and influence on the part of the Reform movement, he founded the Free Synagogue in 1909. In a lecture to explain his goals, he stated:

> We mean to be vitally, intensely, unequivocally Jewish. Jews who would not be Jews will find no place in the Free Synagogue, for we, its founders, wish to be not less but more Jewish in the highest and noblest sense of the term.

The response to the Free Synagogue was gratifying. Some attended out of curiosity, while others sought a kind of affiliation they could not satisfy in existing institutions. More than a hundred "religious pioneers," among them some of the leading figures in American Jewry—Jacob H. Schiff, Adolph Lewisohn, Henry Morgenthau—announced their intention of joining. Beginning in 1910, services were held at Carnegie Hall, giving the new congregation the largest seating capacity of any religious group in the country.

Wise's oratory excoriated the evils in the world of business, industry, and politics. Preaching a liberal Judaism that rejected the kind of reform that was the "center of wealth and fashion," he created a social service division which was to practice Jewish teachings as part of congregational life.

When Zionism had only a marginal following in New York, Wise was its most passionate spokesman. In 1925. his sermon "Jesus the Jew" created such a furor that the Orthodox rabbinate excommunicated him as a heretic. To prepare rabbis for congregations of all denominations, he organized the Jewish Institute of Religion, which became the focus of significant Jewish scholarship and religious experimentation.

As a champion of social justice. Wise was constantly involved in wide communal efforts. Following the race riots of 1909, he joined with Lillian Wald and others in issuing the "Lincoln's Birthday Call," which led to the formation of the National Association for the Advancement of Colored People.

At the outbreak of World War I, Wise took a strong pacifist stance in opposing the increase in armaments and the rise of militarism. However, in 1917, he endorsed President Woodrow Wilson's declaration of war. Always in the forefront of immediate issues of the day, Wise supported the women's suffrage movement and labor's right to organize.

A long-time foe of Tammany Hall, he joined the political reform movement in 1930, becoming a prime mover in the action that led to the resignation of Mayor Jimmy Walker. In his support of the fusion candidate in the election of 1933, Wise helped elect the Yiddish-speaking Fiorello La Guardia as mayor. When the growing menace of the Nazi movement loomed, he led a protest march through the streets of New York, calling for an economic boycott of Germany. As one of the country's leading Zionists, Wise helped secure President Wilson's endorsement of the Balfour Declaration in 1917.

The Stephen S. Wise Congress House in New York City, named for this eminent American, is the headquarters of the American Jewish Congress, a national organization which continues Wise's work in the fight against racial and religious bigotry.

ALEXANDER DAVID GOODE
1911—1943

One of the most inspiring stories of heroism and devotion during World War II was that of four chaplains, Lieutenants Clark V. Poling, Alexander D. Goode, John P. Washington, and George L. Fox, who perished aboard the troop transport

SS Dorchester. Of the four, two were Protestants, one Jewish, and one Catholic.

The ship was torpedoed while passing the coast of Greenland early on the morning of February 3, 1943. With complete disregard for their own safety, the chaplains made their way on deck among the confused, fear-stricken men, encouraging them, praying with them, and assisting them into lifejackets and lifeboats. The chaplains calmed their fears, throughout the whole disaster, setting a supreme example of courage and calmness.

From eyewitness reports of the survivors, the chaplains stood together on the forward deck, removing their own priceless lifejackets, and gave them to the troops when the general supply ran out. As the ship sank, the men in the lifeboats saw the chaplains, linked arm in arm on the deck, praying aloud, each in his own way. The manner of their dying has been cited as one of the most noble deeds of the war.

Rabbi Alexander D. Goode was born in 1911 in Brooklyn, New York. He studied at Hebrew Union College, and the University of Cincinnati, and was ordained in 1937. He received his Ph.D. at Johns Hopkins in Semitics in 1939.

When the war was declared, Goode offered himself for service as a chaplain in the United States Army in sincere patriotism and with a sense of consecration. He was the first Jewish chaplain to die during the war.

The Distinguished Service Cross was awarded posthumously on December 3, 1944, to the families of the chaplains.

There are numerous memorials around the country honoring their sacrifice, and in 1948 a Four Chaplains Commemorative stamp was issued.

ABOLITIONISTS
AND PRO-SLAVERS

The Jewish population of the United States before and during the Civil War period numbered about 180,000. In the great debate on the issue of slavery, Jews were found on both sides of the issue, generally sharing the views of those they lived among. There were many who favored compulsory emancipation and others who merely opposed the further extension of slavery (the free soilers).

Although anti-slavery sentiment had existed during the American Revolution, the abolitionist movement did not reach crusading proportions until the 1830's. One of its mainsprings was the strong support it received from religious groups, including many of the prominent rabbis of the time. Isaac Leeser, Sabato Morais, Benjamin Szold, and David Einhorn were prominent rabbis who were outspoken advocates of abolition, using their pulpits to denounce slavery as a moral evil. Morris Raphall, however, attacked the abolitionists for their misrepresentation of the biblical view of slavery and for their agitation against the legitimate right of slaveholding. Rabbi Isaac Mayer Wise probably reflected the mixed sympathies of his border city of Cincinnati by remaining silent on the issue.

Many Northern Jews were convinced that the Union had to be preserved, even if this meant the immediate destruction of the slave system. The agitation for this argument usually came from recent Jewish arrivals who had fled revolutions in Germany, Austria, and Hungary. Imbued with a sense of liberty and hatred of slavery, they naturally gravitated to the social and political outlook of the Republican party and its views on abolition.

In the South, most Jews had adapted themselves to the idea of owning slaves, and they joined their fellow Southerners in the belief that their "way of life" could not survive without fighting.

Solomon Haydenfeldt, a County Court judge in Alabama, wrote to the governor in 1849 to protest the fur-

ther importation of blacks into the state. Opposed to slavery on economic grounds, Haydenfeldt was nevertheless an ardent "states' righter," convinced that the South would eventually solve the slavery problem without the interference of the Federal Government.

August Bondi marched and fought with John Brown in his raids in Kansas, and the Bondi family was forced to flee their home as a result of his abolitionist views.

Moritz Pinner was militant on the issues of slavery and secession which convulsed Missouri. Pinner launched the anti-slavery newspaper Kansas Post, *in Kansas City, Missouri, with the encouragement of the famed abolitionist leader, William Lloyd Garrison, to marshal the sentiments and support of German-Americans for an abolition bloc.*

Isidor Bush was one of the 15 elected by the Union Party to the Missouri State Convention in 1861 to decide whether Missouri would secede. It was Bush's vote which helped keep the state in the Union.

Judah P. Benjamin, Senator from Louisiana until secession, defended slavery in numerous debates against Daniel Webster, and was referred to as "an Israelite with an Egyptian heart."

Jews were not immune to the bitterness of the storm and stress engendered by secession and war. No previous conflict had seen so many Jews in uniform and, in some instances, brother fighting brother. Eight thousand Jews served during the war—6,000 with the Union army and 2,000 in the Confederate forces.

JUDAH PHILIP BENJAMIN
1811—1884

Judah P. Benjamin, illustrious patriot of the Southern Confederacy, had a reward of $50,000 posted for his capture following Lee's surrender at Appomattox. He has the distinction of being the first Jewish Secretary of State in American history.

Born in the Virgin Islands, Benjamin came to New Orleans in 1828. Gifted with rare oratorical talent, he was so successful as a lawyer that at the age of 31, he was already recognized as one of the state's leading attorneys. In 1851, he was elected to the State Senate, where he pushed for the passage of a law abolishing imprisonment for debt. Benjamin had served in the State's upper chamber for less than a year when it selected him to represent Louisiana in the United States Senate.

When Louisiana seceded from the Union in 1861, Benjamin spoke his farewell to the Senate, and ten days later was named Attorney General of the Confederacy by Jefferson Davis. In November, 1861, he was transferred to the more active post of Secretary of War, and later was appointed by Davis as Secretary of State. As a result of the positions he held, his brilliance, and his close association with Davis, Benjamin was called "the brains of the Confederacy."

After the Confederacy surrendered, a reward of $50,000 was offered for his capture. He escaped to Florida and then went to England. He became one of Britain's most distinguished lawyers, and in 1872, he was appointed Queen's Counsel. He died in Paris in 1884.

His large estate, Bellechase, and other properties were seized by the government following the end of the war. Bellechase, the pillared mansion on the west bank of the Mississippi, was one of the city's shrines for many years.

DAVID LEVY YULEE
1810—1886

David Levy (Yulee), born in the West Indies in 1810, was destined to become the first Jew to serve in the United States Senate.

His wealthy father, Moses Elias Levy, had made a fortune

in lumber and was one of the largest land owners in Florida. David attended school in Norfolk, Virginia, where his father had placed him with Moses Myer, one of Virginia's leading citizens. After managing one of his father's plantations in St. Johns County, he studied law and was admitted to the bar in St. Augustine in 1832. Five years later, he was elected to the Territorial Legislature, where he championed statehood for Florida. He helped draft Florida's first constitution in 1838, and three years later was chosen Congressman-at-large from the Florida Territory. When Florida was admitted to the Union in 1845, Levy was named to the United States Senate.

Soon after he became a Senator, David Levy changed his name to David Levy Yulee. While Yulee's political enemies, including ex-President John Quincy Adams, attacked him as "the alien Jew delegate," he cut himself off from any connection with Jews, quietly encouraging the growth of a legend that his father was not Jewish but a Moroccan prince named Yulee, who had assumed the name of Levy for business purposes.

Because of his pro-slavery views, Yulee was known as the "Florida fire eater." As early as 1840, he urged secession from the Union. Two months before the South seceded, Yulee was one of a number of Southern senators who helped plan the Confederate States of America. He was the first member of the Senate to announce the secession of one of the Southern states.

Following the end of the Civil War, he was arrested and confined in a Federal prison for five years. Yulee and Jefferson Davis were the last two Confederate leaders to be pardoned. After his release, he returned to Florida to help rebuild the East-West railroad, which he had organized in the 1850's, and to assist in the reconstruction of the state.

When he died in 1886, the *Washington Post* described David Levy Yulee as the Senator from Florida "who was better known than the state he represented."

MORRIS JACOB RAPHALL
1798—1868

Morris Jacob Raphall, the first rabbi to open a session of the House of Representatives with prayer, was well-known for his attacks on the abolitionist movement and his controversial sermon in defense of slavery.

Born in Stockholm, Sweden, in 1798, Raphall, the son of a banker, completed his studies at the German University at Erlangen. After settling in England, he became one of British Jewry's chief spokesmen to the Christian world. Publisher of the first Jewish periodical in England, the *Hebrew Review and Magazine of Rabbinical Literature*, he gained a wide reputation as a scholar, orator, and exponent in the fight for political rights for Jews.

When he came to the United States in 1849 to serve as rabbi of Congregation B'nai Jeshurun, in New York City, which had been established in 1825, his lectures and sermons attracted large crowds, including many church dignitaries. In 1860, Raphall, known for his magnificent diction, delivered the benediction in the House of Representatives.

On January 4, 1861, just prior to the inauguration of Abraham Lincoln, President James Buchanan proclaimed a National Fast Day in a futile effort to unite the country before the outbreak of the Civil War. It was on this day that Raphall delivered his sermon, "Bible and Slavery." Placing Judaism squarely in opposition to abolition, he denied that the Bible prohibited slavery and insisted that biblical law sanctioned this right. Although Raphall made a clear distinction between biblical slavery and the system in the South, his sermon was a major attack against the abolitionists and their agitation against the legitimate right of slaveholding.

The sermon provoked both wide praise and criticism. It was reprinted in Southern newspapers and was acclaimed there as a scholarly defense of the South's position. In the North, he was bitterly assailed by Jewish and non-Jewish abolitionists and liberals. His chief critic, Rabbi David Einhorn of Baltimore, a militant foe of slavery, had to flee to Philadelphia to escape mob violence after his fiery denunciation of the sermon. The noted encyclopedist, Michael Helprin, led a scathing attack against Raphall in articles in the *New York Tribune*.

Although an ardent spokesmen in the cause of slavery, Raphall sought a Union army commission during the Civil War for his son. He approached Adolphus S. Solomons, a founder of the American Red Cross and a leading Jew in Washington, for an introduction to President Lincoln. Lincoln, aware of the fact that Raphall had not led the prayer for the preservation of the Union in his synagogue on the day set for this occasion, rebuked him for it. Raphall told the President that the service had been conducted by his assistant. Lincoln, understanding that Raphall could not have conducted the service because of his pro-slavery attitudes, did obtain the commission for his son.

When the long war was over, so too was Raphall's influence and reputation. He died in 1868, three years after Lee's surrender at Appomattox.

DAVID EINHORN
1809—1879

When David Einhorn unsparingly denounced slavery as the cancer of the country from his pulpit in Baltimore, Maryland, he placed his life in danger from a mob, and had to flee to Philadelphia. This was but one in a long series of controversies for the radical Reform rabbi and theologian.

Born in Bavaria in 1809, Einhorn received his studies at rabbinical training in Furth, and continued his studies at universities in Erlangen, Wurzburg, and Munich. In 1838, he was named rabbi of the community of Wellhausen, but because of his liberal views, the Bavarian government refused to approve the appointment. He was later named to a post in Birkenfeld, in the Grand Duchy of Oldenberg.

Though he had already rejected the divine authority of the Talmud and upheld the right to diverge from ceremonial laws, he now favored the introduction of the vernacular in services, endorsing the elimination of prayers for the restoration of sacrifices and for a Jewish state. His radical religious ideas constantly jeopardized his position, as he went from Chief Rabbi of Mecklenburg-Schwerin to a post at the Reform Congregation of Budapest, which the government closed two months after his arrival.

Denied any opportunity in Europe, he accepted the rabbinate at Har Sinai Congregation in Baltimore in 1855. His arrival in the United States coincided with the Cleveland Rabbinical Conference, which, under the leadership of Isaac Mayer Wise, adopted a platform designed to permit a broadly based union among the various factions in American Judaism. Einhorn regarded this platform as treachery to the Reform cause and condemned it bitterly. This was the beginning of a rancorous feud between Isaac Mayer Wise and Einhorn on the practice of Judaism and in the introduction of ritual modifications in the religious services.

Einhorn, in his new post at Har Sinai Congregation, encountered further difficulties. Unable to justify human bondage in a free country, he carried on a fanatical anti-slavery campaign in Baltimore—a city of strong pro-Southern sympathies. Warned by the police and the military of an impending riot which might endanger his life, he fled to Philadelphia, where he became rabbi at Kenesseth Israel and later at Congregation Adath Israel in New York.

Never far from contention, Einhorn's radicalism had brought about a schism in the American Reform movement. Under the leadership of Isaac M. Wise and Kaufmann Kohler, Einhorn's son-in-law and disciple, basic Jewish customs were reestablished in Reform Judaism.

ISIDOR BUSH
1822—1898

In the burning issue of slavery which divided the country, Isidor Bush, a staunch abolitionist, emerged as an active leader in the stormy political events surrounding the question of whether Missouri would remain in the Union or secede.

Born in Prague in 1822, Bush was a descendant of the first Jew ever to be raised to the nobility in Austria. His father was a partner in a prominent Hebrew publishing house in Vienna, where Bush worked. At age 20, he began publishing *Kalendar und Jahrbuch für Israeliten*, Austria's first popular German-language annual of scholarly Jewish articles. An active leader in Vienna of a committee to further Jewish emigration, Bush left Austria after the failure of the Revolution of 1848.

Within a few months after reaching New York in 1849, he began publishing *Israels Herold*, a German-Jewish weekly—the first of its kind in the United States. Although the paper lasted only three months, it did further Jewish unity, undertaking the first effort to write a history of the Jews of New York. Shortly after his publication folded, Bush settled in St. Louis, Missouri, where he became successively a storekeeper, vintner, bank president, railroad freight agent, and publisher of *The Bushberg Manual*, an internationally known grape handbook. His vineyards in Jefferson County were known for many years as Bushberg, and he was credited with many improvements in grape-growing.

Although he was engaged in this variety of occupations

and enterprises, Bush's deeper interests were of a literary and political nature. Elected to the City Council and the Board of Education, he joined in organizing the Union party, which was dedicated to fighting the efforts of the slave holders to secede. Despite a physical handicap which prevented him from active service during the Civil War, he served as a civilian secretary to General John C. Fremont.

Widely known for his abolitionist views, and a firm believer in the preservation of the Union, Bush was elected by the Union party to the 1861 state convention, casting his vote to keep the state in the Union. In 1863, he was appointed to the most important committee of that year's state convention—the committee on emancipation. Bush fought for immediate freedom of the slaves. Dissenting from the majority vote, which recommended that emancipation be postponed until 1870, he pleaded eloquently but vainly for immediate abolition. "I pray you have pity for yourselves, not for Negroes," he urged the convention. "Slavery demoralizes, slavery fanaticism blinds you. It has destroyed God's noblest work—a free and happy people."

As a delegate to the constitutional convention of 1865, Bush joined the majority in mandating the immediate and unconditional abolition of slavery, thus making Missouri the first of the slave states to achieve this goal. On the adoption of the constitution, however, Bush was one of thirteen delegates who refused to vote for the new charter. He opposed its enactment because it disenfranchised all citizens known to have been Confederate sympathizers. Ten years later, Bush's position was vindicated when Missouri ratified a new constitution which repudiated the disenfranchising action.

When he died in 1898, at the age of 76, Bush was one of the most distinguished figures in American Jewish life, with a unique career in public affairs.

AUGUST BONDI
1833—c.1897

August Bondi, an immigrant who at the age of 15 was one of the youngest participants in the Austrian revolution of 1848, responded to Horace Greeley's plea in the *New York*

Tribune "to the freedom-loving men of the states to rush to Kansas and save it from the curse of slavery."

Bondi had seen slavery at firsthand in New Orleans, where his family landed on their way to St. Louis. By 1851, after participating in many anti-slavery rallies, he became an ardent abolitionist. He broke off his plans to marry a woman who owned slaves because "my father's son was not meant to be a slave-driver.' Always searching for excitement, he went to Texas to join a guerrilla expedition seeking to free Cuba, but he never left Galveston. He missed by one day getting a berth with Commodore Perry's mission, which opened Japan to the West in 1854.

For a time, Bondi tried typesetting, bookkeeping, and teaching; he was even a roustabout on the Mississippi levees and a bartender on a river steamer. None of these pursuits satisfied Bondi, and as he said years later in his autobiography, ". . . any struggle, any hard work would be welcome to me." This was the hot-headed liberal who found himself in Kansas at the side of John Brown, "God's angry man."

By May, 1855, the smoldering animosity between the free soilers and the pro-slavers was almost at the point of civil strife. Threatened by the pro-slavers, Bondi and a friend, Jacob Benjamin, secured the aid of John Brown's sons and joined Frederick Brown's military company. Anxious to take part in the free state election in December, 1855, Bondi, although ill with fever, had himself put in a cart and was carried to the polls. There he met John Brown. A few months later, when Lawrence, Kansas, had been sacked by border raiders, Brown sent Bondi back to the Pottawatomi with most of his riflemen to protect the remaining free soil families. Bondi also saw action in the Battle of Black Jack.

In 1861, he answered Lincoln's call for volunteers, enlisting in the 5th Kansas Volunteer Cavalry. He became a first sergeant and served for three years. He was badly wounded in the fighting in Arkansas in 1864 and received a discharge on grounds of disability. Following the war, Bondi lived briefly in Leavenworth, and then settled in Salina.

Bondi always credited his mother for his zeal against slavery. "My mother said that as a *Jehudi* I had a duty to perform, to defend the institutions that give equal rights to all beliefs."

LABOR

Although labor unions are now one of the strongest economic and political forces in America, guiding working conditions from apprenticeship through retirement, this status emerged only after long struggles during the country's transition from an agrarian society to the world's leading industrial nation.

Associations of journeymen under a guild system existed in the Colonial era, but trade unionism had its real beginnings in the period of the expansion of industry following the Civil War. This rapid growth was concurrent with the massive waves of unskilled immigrants who provided cheap, docile labor for factories, railroads, and mines.

The Jewish immigrants to America from 1880 to 1912 knew well the curse of economic exploitation. In East Europe, a generation before, their parents had earned the equivalent of two dollars a month. Determined to escape the appalling conditions of the Polish and Russian ghettos, they came to the United States where many found employment at slave wages with destructive working conditions in the developing clothing industry, where the sweatshop system had already taken root.

The growing discontent of other workers in the American labor force, who were also hostages to the cycles of business depressions, combined to force early confrontations with the leaders of industry. As early as 1877, Samuel Gompers called on the workers in the cigar industry to strike against the pitiful labor conditions imposed on them. Blacklisting, lockouts, scabs, and Pinkerton guards were the employers' response to force workers back to their grim, precarious livelihoods.

Out of the tragic conflicts and the chaos of the fight for union recognition, a number of Jewish leaders emerged—Samuel Gompers, Sidney Hillman, David Dubinsky, among others. The efforts of these men resulted in achieving a decent standard of living for the masses. Their pioneering leadership was responsible for the creation of a successful, continuous arbitration machine which pointed the way to industrial peace. Such innovations as unemployment insurance, labor banking, union housing, adult education programs, and medical care, were developed by these men.

In forging an industrial democracy, the liberal Jewish forces had the moral support of rabbinical associations. These bodies, deeply convinced that there could be no social freedom without economic security, helped to formulate the social justice programs which were incorporated into union negotiations.

The early unionizing efforts of these men were the seed of liberation for all American workers.

SAMUEL GOMPERS
1850—1924

Over the tomb of President Woodrow Wilson in Washington National Cathedral, there is a huge stained-glass window dedicated to Samuel Gompers, one of America's labor giants, the founder and first president of the American Federation of Labor.

Born in London in 1850, Gompers came to America with his parents when he was 13 and worked at his father's trade of making cigars.

Joining the Cigarmakers Union and the National Trade Union in 1870, he won his trade union spurs in these early labor organizations. He was among the early exponents of craft unionism and helped organize a number of unions. When the AFL was formed in 1886, he was chosen to be its first president. When he died in 1924, the AFL had grown to a membership of 5,000,000. A commemorative 3¢ stamp was issued in 1950 by the United States Post Office honoring this great labor leader on the centennial of his birth.

It was Gompers who led and helped win the battle against sweatshops and starvation wages. He succeeded in outlawing the company union and labor injunctions, and defeated the first Communist attempt to control the American labor movement. In 1894, he succeeded in getting Congress to declare the first Monday in September as Labor Day, a national holiday.

He kept the union free from political entanglements in its early years and refused to entertain various cooperative business plans, socialistic ideas, and radical programs, maintaining that increased wages and shorter hours were the just aims of labor.

During World War I, he served on the Council of National Defense, winning status for the unions by his patriotic mobilization of labor behind the war effort.

SIDNEY HILLMAN
1887—1946

The explosive phrase "clear it with Sidney" became a central issue in the 1944 Presidential campaign in the Republican party effort to defeat Franklin D. Roosevelt.

Sidney Hillman, born in Lithuania in 1887, was to have studied for the rabbinate. At the age of 18, however, caught up in the struggle against the despotism of the Czar, he took part in the abortive Russian Revolution of 1905. He was imprisoned and faced execution or exile to Siberia just before a general amnesty brought him freedom.

He came to the United States in August, 1907. In 1910, an unknown clothing worker at the Chicago men's clothing factory of Hart, Schaffner and Marx, earning $6 a week, Hillman took the lead in organizing a strike against deplorable working conditions and low wages. By 1914, he was elected president of the newly founded Amalgamated Clothing Workers Union.

Under his leadership, the union grew rapidly to become one of the largest and most respected labor organizations in the nation. He played a key role in reducing the work hours from a 48-hour week in 1916 to a 44-hour week in 1919. His union pioneered in the organization of the first Amalgamated Bank, in cooperative housing projects for its members, and in unemployment insurance funds.

It was during the 1930's that Hillman's fame spread far beyond the labor movement, when he played a major role in the drafting of the National Industrial Recovery Act in the earliest days of the New Deal. In 1933, at the height of the Depression, President Franklin D. Roosevelt appointed him to the Labor Advisory Board of the NRA. He also played a leading role in the passage of the Social Security Act and the National Labor Relations Act in 1935. In 1938, President Roosevelt said that the American public owed Hillman a debt of gratitude for the enactment of the first federal wage and hour law.

When the CIO Political Action Committee was formed in 1943, Hillman was named its first chairman, and in this capacity he played a decisive role in the 1944 Democratic convention and in the Presidential campaign.

His death on July 10, 1946, was front-page news and an occasion for mourning throughout the nation. His body lay in state for 24 hours at Carnegie Hall, and thousands witnessed the funeral procession through the streets of New York.

Two months after his death Sidney Hillman was posthumously awarded the Medal of Merit by President Harry S. Truman.

DAVID DUBINSKY
1892—

David Dubinsky, president of the International Ladies' Garment Workers Union from 1934-1966, served the union in one of the most tumultuous, dramatic, and productive periods of the trade union movement in America.

"D.D.," as he is affectionately known, was born in Brest-Litovsk in Russian Poland in 1892. At the age of 16, Dubinsky was arrested for his part in a baker's strike. He spent over a year in political prisons and was banished to Siberia. Escaping enroute to Siberia, he returned for a short time to Russian Poland before arriving in New York City in 1911.

Dubinsky learned the women's coat and suit cutting trade and became a member of the Cutters' Local 10. He joined the Socialist Party in 1911 and remained a member until 1936, when he supported Franklin D. Roosevelt for reelection.

By 1916, Dubinsky was deeply involved in union activities, establishing himself as a rank-and-file leader, and in 1920 he was elected president of the local. In the next few years he gave vital support to the leaders of the union in their fight to repulse anti-union efforts and an attempt by Communists to take over the union. In 1929 he was the unanimous choice for secretary-treasurer of the ILGWU at their convention in Cleveland.

In this capacity, Dubinsky instituted a tight fiscal policy aimed at lifting the union out of the precarious financial position it found itself in after years of struggle with the Communists. Just as the union was beginning to make progress, Wall Street collapsed, bringing the country's economy to ruin. It was in this atmosphere of despair three years later that Dubinsky became president of the union following the death of its president, Benjamin Schlesinger.

At the outset of his presidency during the Great Depression, the union had 25,000 members and was heavily in debt. By 1934, Dubinsky was able to report an increase in membership to 200,000 and assets of $1 million.

One of the first labor leaders to realize the importance of political action, Dubinsky helped found the American Labor Party in 1936. When the Communist faction gained control, Dubinsky resigned and helped organize the Liberal Party. His efforts at ousting racketeers from union leadership culminated in the anti-racket codes adopted by the AFL and CIO in 1957.

The United States' highest civilian honor, the Medal of Freedom, was presented to David Dubinsky in 1969 by President Lyndon B. Johnson. The citation reads:

> David Dubinsky is a national leader of foresight and compassion. He has advanced the cause of the working-man in America—and the broader cause of social justice in the world—with unfailing skill and uncommon distinction. The American people are richer for the service he has given them.

POLITICS AND
PUBLIC LIFE

When Nathan Simson was elected to the humble post of Constable of the South Ward of New York City in 1718, the first chapter was written in the long history of Jewish participation in elective and appointive public office in America—a record that has included the highest posts, with the exception of the Presidency and Vice-Presidency.

To encourage immigration to the colonies, the British Naturalization Act of 1740 gave Jews the right to become citizens after seven years of residence, but not the right to hold public office. Fewer than 200 Jews were naturalized under this law, because many of the individual colonies ignored the Act. A new law in 1773 gave immigrants the right to hold office, but this too was ignored in many areas.

In practice, Jews and Catholics had few political and civil rights in any of the thirteen colonies before 1776. In Connecticut, until 1965 [sic] the state's constitution contained an obscure and long-ignored article that gave rights of residence only to members of "every society or denomination of Christianity." A number of the colonies required that all officeholders avow a belief in the divine inspiration of the New Testament.

It was not until 1806 that Judah Hays, a cousin of the famed philanthropist Judah Touro, was elected fire warden in Boston.

Rhode Island's early religious tolerance did not extend to political equality for Jews until 1842. Although Maryland did not pass its "Jew Baby" bill until 1825, Reuben Etting was appointed United States Marshal for that state in 1801 by President Jefferson.

Pennsylvania removed all disabilities to holding elective office in 1790. The Virginia Bill of Rights, adopted in 1776, implied that religious difference did not disqualify any man for public office, but that state, as well as Geor-

89

gia and South Carolina, denied political liberty to Jews for at least a decade after the Revolution. Francis Salvador did, however, become a member of the provincial legislature in 1774 in South Carolina. He was the first Jew to die fighting the British during the Revolutionary War.

Mordecai Sheftall, one of the great Jewish figures in the early history of Georgia, was elected to the legislature in 1796, probably the first Jew to become a member of a state legislature in the United States.

North Carolina barred from public office anyone who did not accept "the truth of the Protestant religion," until 1868. When Joseph Henry, a practicing Jew, was elected to the lower house of the North Carolina legislaure in 1809, it provoked a great debate. Demands for his expulsion led to prolonged oratory. His impassioned speech in defense of full religious liberty won him the right to his seat. The legislature interpreted the religious test against Catholics and Jews to mean that they could hold legislative office but not executive office.

Although none of the states admitted to the Union after the adoption of the Constitution denied either the vote or the right to hold office, there were only a small number of Jews in political office until 1887.

Jews were among the founders of Thomas Jefferson's Democratic-Republican party in New York, Philadelphia, and Charleston, and later of Tammany Hall. Mordecai M. Noah, grand sachem of Tammany in 1820, was Sheriff of New York County in 1822. German-Jewish immigrants helped found the Republican party in a number of states, and were delegates to the 1860 and 1864 Republican National Conventions that nominated Abraham Lincoln for President.

At the beginning of the nineteenth century, as the Jewish immigrants pushed south and west in newly opened territories and states, they quickly became an integral part of frontier politics. John Hays was Sheriff in the Indiana Territory and later collector of Internal Revenue. Joseph Phillips was elected secretary of the Illinois Territory, and Samuel Judah was Speaker of the lower house of the Indiana legislature from 1830-1833. Abraham Jonas, a friend and political ally of Lincoln, served in the Illinois legislature in 1842.

During the California Gold Rush, Washington Bart-lett, a member of a distinguished Charleston family, was Mayor of San Francisco in 1849 and later Governor of the state. Henry Lyons and Solomon Heydenfeldt were Justices of the California State Supreme Court in the 1850's.

In other western communities where gold and other precious metals were discovered, Jews were early figures in public life. Fred Solomon was the first treasurer of the Colorado Territory in 1860. Frances Jacoby, elected to the Colorado legislature in the 1870's, was not only the first Jewish woman to hold this office, but the first female member of any state legislature. Wolfe Landauer was Mayor of Denver in 1889, and Otto Mears was Lieu-tenant-Governor of Colorado in 1883.

Morris Goldwater, son of the pioneer Michael ("Big Mike") Goldwater, was one of the early leaders of the Democratic party in the Arizona Territory, and served as chairman of the first constitutional convention. His son, Senator Barry Goldwater, was the Republican candidate for President in 1964.

Columbus Moises, Henry Jaffa, and Nathan Jaffa were all prominent men in public life in the New Mexico Territory. Nome and Anchorage, Alaska, had Jewish mayors in territorial days, and Ernest Gruening, governor for many years, was one of the first two senators elected when Alaska gained statehood.

The first Jewish member of the United States Senate was David Levy Yulee, elected in 1845 from Florida. There have been 13 other Jewish senators.

From 1841 to the present, there were 92 Jews elected to the House of Representatives; 7 members of Presi-dential cabinets; 19 state governors; over 200 mayors of leading cities; and 3 chairmen of the major political parties.

Only one Jew, Abraham Ribicoff, has held four of the seven highest offices to which an American can aspire. He has served in both houses of Congress, as Governor of Connecticut, and as a member of President Kennedy's cabinet.

Jews have served as ambassadors and ministers since 1853. They have been appointed Solicitor-General; Gover-nor of the Federal Reserve Board; heads of the TVA and the Atomic Energy Commissions; Secretaries of Defense; chairmen of the Council of Economic Advisors, Federal Communications Commission, and Federal Tariff Commission; directors of the Census Bureau, Bureau of Labor Statistics, and United States Mint; Surgeon General; Controller of the Currency; counsels to the President; and Chairman of the Civil Aeronautics Board.

MORDECAI MANUEL NOAH
1785—1851

At Grand Island, New York, near Buffalo, a slab of Ohio sandstone with the following inscription in Hebrew stands as the only visible reminder of Mordecai Manuel Noah's quixotic colonization scheme which created a tremendous stir among American and European Jews in 1825:

> Shema Yisroel Adonai Elohenu Adonai Echod
> Ararat, A City of Refuge for the Jews
> Founded by Mordecai Manuel Noah
> in the month of Tizri (September) 1825
> & in the Fiftieth Year of American Independence

Noah, born in Philadelphia in 1785, was raised by his grandfather, Jonas Phillips, a Revolutionary patriot. Noah was a descendant of Dr. Samuel Nunez, a Marrano who settled in Savannah, Georgia, in 1733. His father served in the American Revolution, and there is a legend that George Washington attended the wedding of his parents.

After working as an apprentice builder and carver, a clerk in the United States Treasury, and as a reporter, Noah moved to Charleston, South Carolina, where he became editor of the *City Gazette*. Author of a series of anonymous letters on political issues, he fought several duels as a result of political disputes. He received and declined an appointment as United States Consul at Riga. In 1813, President James Madison named Noah Consul to Tunis, with instructions to ransom a group of Americans held captive by the Barbary pirates. He succeeded in his mission, but in the process found that the State Department had rejected his expenditures as unauthorized. In addition, Noah was dismissed from his post by Secretary of State James Monroe on the grounds that at the time of his appointment they did not know he was a Jew. Ultimately, Noah was vindicated.

In 1820, Noah tried to buy Grand Island, New York, as the future site of a Jewish colony. Earlier he had organized a syndicate which bought 2,500 acres on this island. There is no evidence that he ever saw this land before he envisaged it as the site of Ararat in his "Proclamation to the Jews," dated 1825. The manifesto reaffirmed Noah's faith in the restoration of Zion, but in the meantime, he invited all the Jews of

93

the world to come to Ararat as a way station in preparation for a new life in Palestine. Indeed, he even invited the American Indians, in the strange belief that they were descendants of the Ten Lost Tribes.

Dubbing himself "Governor and Judge of Israel," he commanded that a census be taken of the Jews throughout the world; he forbade polygamy and levied taxes on all Jews to finance Ararat. This fantastic document concluded with a plan for organizing the mass migration of Jews to Grand Island.

Noah scheduled September 15, 1825, as the date of the proclamation (just one month before the opening of the Erie Canal) and for a ceremony to dedicate Ararat's cornerstone. At the celebration, a cannon boomed and a magnificent procession of city officials, army officers, Masonic dignitaries, clergymen, and Knights Templar led the way. Noah, garbed in his conception of the robes of a judge of Israel, repeated his bizarre proclamation. This service was both the beginning and end of Ararat. Though Noah's scheme earned him ridicule and condemnation, some writers have described him as the first political Zionist.

After the abortive settlement scheme, Noah returned to New York City, where he became a well-known politician, playwright, and journalist. He was even appointed the head of Tammany Hall and once served as Sheriff of New York. When his opponents protested that a Jewish sheriff might have to hang Christians, Noah countered, "Pretty Christians they are to require hanging."

He died in 1851 and his funeral is said to have been one of the most elaborate in the history of the city. One of the last Jews to be buried within the limits of the old City of New York, his last resting place is in the Shearith Israel Cemetery on West 21st Street in New York City.

ABRAHAM JONAS
1801—1864

A close friend and political ally of Abraham Lincoln, Jonas, a leading lawyer of Quincy, Illinois, played a pivotal role in the election of Lincoln to the Presidency.

Born in Exeter, England in 1801, Jonas settled in Cincinnati in 1819. For the next nine years, he lived in Kentucky, where he was elected to the state legislature and also served as Grand Master of the Masons. Following his move to Quincy, Illinois, he was admitted to the bar and served in the legislature at the same time as Lincoln. Considered one of the Whig party's leading debaters and political organizers, Jonas was appointed postmaster of Quincy by Presidents Zachary Taylor and Millard Fillmore as a sign of their esteem for his party loyalty.

Jonas and Lincoln served as Frémont Presidential electors in 1856 when the new Republican party made its first bid for the Presidency. They corresponded regularly, and it was Jonas, as a party chairman, who arranged for the Lincoln-Douglas debate in Quincy during Lincoln's unsuccessful try for the Senate. When the venerable Horace Greeley of the *New York Tribune* passed through Quincy to discuss national politics and Presidential candidates with party leaders, Jonas conferred privately with him on the possibility of naming Lincoln.

During the national campaign of 1860, Democratic opponents charged Lincoln with affiliation with the fanatical anti-alien Know Nothing party—a predecessor of the Ku Klux Klan. It was Jonas that Lincoln turned to for assistance in dispelling this myth. In denying the charge, he wrote his friend, "I am not a Know-Nothing . . . how could I be? How can anyone who abhors the oppression of Negroes be in favor of degrading classes of white people?"

Their friendship continued during the Civil War, despite the fact that Jonas' four sons were serving in the Confederate army. When Jonas lay dying in 1864, his family sought Lincoln's help on behalf of Charles Jonas. Lincoln's deep feelings for his old friend moved him to issue an order to the War Department to "allow Charles Jonas, now a prisoner of war at Johnson's Island, a parole for three weeks to visit his dying father."

ADOLPH SUTRO
1830—1898

Adolph Sutro, immigrant from Prussia, rose to become Mayor of San Francisco and one of its greatest benefactors.

Born in 1830, the son of a prosperous cloth manufacturer, Sutro came to America in 1850 with his family and settled in Baltimore. Restless and adventuresome, he was persuaded by the excitement of the California Gold Rush to go West, where he spent nine years selling tobacco. When the Comstock Lode in Nevada was discovered, he moved there in the hope of an opportunity to apply the engineering knowledge he had patiently acquired by study. Though he failed in his search for gold, he did develop a new process for extracting and reducing quartz. The results were successful, and his financial prospects brightened.

Appalled by the dangers and disasters encountered by the miners in extracting ore, Sutro conceived the idea of a ventilating and draining tunnel that could clear hot water and gaseous vapors from the mines and speed production. Obsessed with the vision of the tunnel, it was to take 13 years to complete.

Though Sutro was able to obtain a charter for the right of way and the aid of a number of European mining engineers and bankers, plans for the enterprise were halted by the mining companies, who turned against him in an effort to capture control of the tunnel company and the large profits it was expected to earn. The victim of slanderous propaganda, "Sutro's coyote hole," as it was called, was rejected by Congress as an impractical scheme. Untiringly, he went about seeking other endorsements and backing for his project, and it was finally the miners of Nevada—the people most vitally concerned—who responded with aid.

In 1879, 13 years later, Sutro, stripped to the waist, fired the blast breaking the tunnel through into the first mining shaft. Hailed as an engineering miracle, Sutro sold his interest in the tunnel for $5 million.

Settling in San Francisco, Sutro invested part of his fortune in real estate which skeptics considered worthless. With his engineering knowledge, however, he converted the barren soil into a fertile forest which bears his name and also paved roads leading to Mount Sutro, which he gave to the city. Owning one-tenth of the entire real estate of the city, Sutro became one of the richest men in the state.

Sutro Heights, overlooking the Golden Gate, was the area he chose for his imposing home, which was known as "Sutro's Gingerbread Palace." Before its demolition in 1939, the house had played host to five Presidents and was the rendezvous of such notables as Sarah Bernhardt, Mark Twain, and Bret Harte. (After the house was torn down, the land was donated by his daughter, Dr. Emma Sutro Merritt, for a public garden.)

After Sutro was elected Mayor of San Francisco in 1895 on a reform-populist ticket, he made further land donations for the beautification of the city. Sutro died in 1898, never to witness the massive earthquake which was to destroy most of his beloved city eight years later.

In 1940, a plaque at the entrance of Sutro Heights was erected by the Native Sons of the Golden West. It bears the following inscription:

In memory of Adolph Sutro, mining engineer, philanthropist, pioneer builder of San Francisco. Born April 29, 1830—Prussia. Came to the United States 1850. Settled in San Francisco 1851. Built Sutro Heights which he presented to San Francisco as a public park. Also gave to San Francisco the site of the University of California Hospital. As an engineer, designed Sutro drainage and ventilating tunnel for Comstock Lode, Virginia City, Nevada. Mayor of San Francisco 1895-1896. Died San Francisco July 8, 1898.

ADOLPHUS SIMEON SOLOMONS
1826—1910

Born in New York City in 1826, the son of an English journalist, Solomons was the epitome of the cultivated nineteenth-century American Jew. Civic leader, philanthropist, and personal friend of Abraham Lincoln, Solomons was one of the founders of the American Red Cross.

A graduate of City College of New York, he went to work for a printing firm and was later appointed a special dispatch bearer to Berlin for Secretary of State Daniel Webster. Solomons and his bride, Rachel Seixas Philips, a descendant of Reverend Gershom Mendes Seixas, settled in Washington, D.C., where he started his own printing company. For many years he was the official government printer, until the Government Printing Office was established.

A member of the Board of Delegates of American Israelites, Solomons was the most prominent Jew in the capital during the Civil War period. He was one of a group which appealed to Lincoln to rescind General Grant's Order No. 11.

It was in Solomons' office that the last-known photograph of Lincoln was taken. In his book *Reminiscences of Abraham*

Lincoln, Solomons recalls asking Lincoln to sit for a new photo. The President posed for the picture, but it did not turn out well because "Lincoln wore a troubled expression." Sensing Solomons' disappointment, he agreed to pose again, saying, "Tell me a funny story and we will see if I can't do better." This incident took place five days before the assassination of the President.

When the District of Columbia was granted self-government, Solomons was elected to their House of Representatives and served as chairman of the important Ways and Means Committee. In 1873, President Grant proposed Solomons for Governor of the District, but he declined the office. Through his years in Washington, his name was identified with the establishment of every important social and welfare agency. As a leader of the Jewish community, he took part in all the inaugural ceremonies from the time of Abraham Lincoln to that of William H. Taft.

The most significant of his humanitarian tasks was as a member of the first meeting, which took place in his home, to consider the formation of an American Red Cross in May, 1881. When President Chester Arthur signed the Red Cross Treaty in 1882, Solomons, together with Clara Barton, was appointed to represent the United States at Geneva.

In his later years, Solomons became general agent in the United States of the Baron de Hirsch Fund, an influential international organization set up to help ameliorate the conditions of Jews and to assist in Jewish colonization projects.

On his death in 1910, Louis Marshall, the noted constitutional lawyer, paid tribute to Solomons: "He believed in the sacred duty of personal service and he performed that duty as a religious act, with cheerful heart, serious mind, and willing hand."

ISIDOR RAYNER
1850—1912

Born in Baltimore, Maryland, in 1850, Isidor Rayner has the distinction of having been the first Jew to be suggested for the candidacy of the President of the United States.

Son of a wealthy Maryland industrialist, Rayner was educated at the Universities of Maryland and Virginia, and was admitted to the bar at the age of 21. His long career in politics began in 1878 with his election to the Maryland General Assembly. He was later elected to Congress, where he served three terms. A staunch supporter of President Cleveland, he was an advocate of the direct election of Senators by voters rather than by state legislatures. He resigned his seat to become Attorney General of Maryland.

Rayner gained national prominence as counsel to Rear Admiral Winfield S. Schley during a Court of Inquiry investigating a controversy over the naval victory at Santiago Harbor during the Spanish-American War. Exhausted after delivering a five-hour speech before the presiding officer, Admiral George Dewey, hero of the Battle of Manila, Rayner declared, "I will be willing to give my health if I can clear the Admiral."

Already a nationally known figure, he was elected to the United States Senate in 1904, where his prestige grew as he led the successful fight against the attempt to disenfranchise the blacks.

Strongly opposed to the colonial policies of Theodore Roosevelt following the Spanish-American War, he charged in his maiden speech that "it was never intended that we should assume a protectorate, political or financial, over the islands of the Caribbean." During this speech, he made a plea for aid for the persecuted Jews of Russia, urging "a demand upon the barbarous Prince to grant these people their rights or no longer be allowed to maintain contact or intercourse with civilized governments."

As a Senator for seven years, he was a strong defender of the states rights and opposed the centralization of the Federal government. A leading figure in the Democratic party, he refused on two occasions to let his name be placed in nomination for the Vice-Presidency. During the Democratic convention of 1912, when a deadlock developed on the nomination for the Presidency, William Jennings Bryan, thrice standard-bearer for the Democratic party, proposed that Isidor Rayner be named as candidate for President.

Just before his death in November, 1912, President-elect Woodrow Wilson was considering him for a cabinet post.

MOSES ALEXANDER
1853—1932

Alexander, born in Bavaria in 1853, is celebrated in American Jewish history as the first professing Jew to be elected Governor of a state. He became the eleventh Governor of Idaho in 1914.

When he arrived in Idaho in 1890 from Chillicothe, Missouri, where he had been a successful merchant and had served as Mayor, the area, which had been part of the Oregon Territory, had just achieved statehood. Five years after settling in Boise, he was a well-established merchant, with branch stores in Lewiston and Pocatello.

Traveling widely through the state on business, he became well known and highly respected. One of the surest ways of getting a hearing in a Boise gathering in the 1890's was to start by saying, "Mose was telling me today . . ."

When a reform party invited him to be its mayoral candidate, he accepted and was elected in 1897. He declined to succeed himself, but his reelection on a coalition ticket made him a leader of the Democratic party. Defeated in his first try for Governor in 1908, he ran again in 1914 in a campaign that made political history and produced legends which old-timers related for years.

Alexander's lively wit made him the kind of hard-hitting campaigner who appealed to miners, lumberjacks, ranchers, and farmers. Crossing the state on horse and in a wagon, he stopped wherever voters could be gathered. At one hamlet, Alexander spotted a shed and made ready to speak from atop it to a cluster of farmers. One of his entourage protested, "But Mose, they store manure under that shed." Ignoring the caution, Alexander wryly remarked, "This is the first time in my life I've ever spoken from a Republican platform."

He was bitterly attacked as "just a clothing merchant," assailed as a "foreigner," and smeared as an "uneducated carpetbagger." He turned all this to advantage and was elected Governor.

Although he had to contend with a hostile legislature, he gave the state a businesslike administration that won him many friends. At the end of his first legislative session, he was faced with a pile of bills to sign. Asked what he was going to do with them, he riffled through the pile and said, "I'll sign the thin ones and veto the thick ones."

He was reelected in 1916 and pushed through legislation that gave the state its first workmen's compensation law, paved the way for a highway system, created irrigation and reclamation projects, and established prohibition. He retired in 1918, but ran again in 1922, when he was defeated.

Alexander's first election created a sensation among the Jews of America. The Yiddish and American Jewish press were ecstatic in amazement and gratification. One paper, advising young Jews to go West, said, "If you go West, be proud and frank, and above all be a good Jew like the Governor of the state of Idaho."

On his first trip East as Governor, Alexander was guest at a memorable reception in Boston's Faneuil Hall.

As late as the 1940's, when old-timers in Idaho spoke of "the Governor," they meant Moses Alexander.

The town of Alexander in Caribou County is named for him, and Alexander House in the state capitol of Boise was deeded to the state in 1977 by the Governor's grandson, Nathan N.; it is listed in the National Historic Register of the United States National Park Service.

OSCAR SOLOMON STRAUS
1850—1926

Oscar S. Straus, lawyer by profession, merchant by family tradition, and civic leader and historian by inclination, was the first Jew to be appointed to a Presidential cabinet.

Straus, born in 1850, was the son of Lazarus Straus of Talbotton, Georgia. Impoverished by the Civil War, the family moved to New York, where the elder Straus was eventually to become the head of R. H. Macy & Company.

Oscar was graduated from Columbia University and practiced law until 1881, then joined the family business. In 1887, he was appointed Minister to Turkey by President Grover Cleveland and held the same post under Presidents McKinley and Taft. He was also a member of the Permanent Court of Arbitration at The Hague.

At the height of the anti-Jewish persecutions in Russia at the turn of the century, New Hampshire became the scene of a dramatic event in Jewish American history in which Straus took part.

Theodore Roosevelt had initiated a meeting at Portsmouth in an attempt to mediate a peace settlement of the Russo-Japanese War. It was here that the emissaries of the Czar sat down with leaders of American Jewry in their attempt to secure promises from Russia to halt the barbarous pogroms.

In 1906, President Theodore Roosevelt appointed Straus Secretary of Commerce and Labor. When Roosevelt ran unsuccessfully for President in 1912 on the Bull Moose ticket, Straus was the party's candidate for Governor of New York.

A memorial to him at the Department of Commerce building in Washington, D.C., was dedicated October 26, 1947, by President Harry S. Truman. The following words are inscribed on the memorial:

Our liberty of worship is not a concession nor a privilege but an inherent right.

HERBERT HENRY LEHMAN
1878—1963

Although he started his career as an investment banker, Herbert H. Lehman gained fame as a governor, senator, statesman, and director-general of the first United Nations relief organization.

Lehman was born in New York City in 1878. His father, Mayer, had originally settled in Alabama in 1848, but moved to New York following the end of the Civil War. Mayer, together with his brother Emanuel, established the Lehman Brothers' banking house; they were also among the founders of the New York Cotton Exchange.

In 1908, following his graduation from Williams College, Lehman became a partner in the family banking business. It was during this period that his lifelong interest in public welfare began when he became a volunteer worker at the Henry Street Settlement House on New York's Lower East Side, and at the start of World War I, he was one of the founders of the Joint Distribution Committee.

When the United States entered the war in 1917, Lehman, ten years beyond draft age, volunteered for duty. He first served as an aide to Franklin D. Roosevelt, then an Assistant Secretary of the Navy, and later as a captain on the General Staff. His services in procuring, shipping, and distributing supplies for the American Expeditionary Forces won him the Distinguished Service Medal and a colonelcy. Following the end of the war, Lehman, as chairman of the Joint Distribution Committee, helped in the rebuilding of Jewish life in the devastated areas of Eastern Europe.

He made his political debut in 1926 as manager of Alfred E. Smith's campaign for Governor of New York. Two years later, when Franklin D. Roosevelt accepted the nomination for Governor to strengthen Smith's bid for the Presidency, Lehman was prevailed upon to run for Lieutenant-Governor. Although Smith was defeated, Roosevelt and Lehman were elected by a slim margin. This marked the beginning of a close political and personal friendship between the two men that endured until Roosevelt's death.

As Lieutenant-Governor for four years, Lehman was given more responsibility than any previous occupant of this office. On the many occasions he was Acting Governor in Roosevelt's absence, and he became known as an able administrator and leader. In 1932, when Roosevelt was elected President, Lehman succeeded him as Governor, and was reelected in 1934 and in 1936. At the end of his term, when he yearned for retirement, Roosevelt prevailed upon Lehman to run again, calling him "my good right arm."

In his ten years as Governor, Lehman had fought successfully for liberal legislation which made New York the bellwether for progressive state government. Several weeks before the expiration of his term in 1942, Lehman resigned to accept President Roosevelt's appointment as Director of the Office of Foreign Relief and Rehabilitation. In this post, he brought relief supplies to the peoples of North Africa, Sicily, and the liberated areas of Italy, until the establishment of UNRRA. The 44 nations participating in this relief organization unanimously elected Lehman the first Director-General, and he served in this capacity from 1943 to 1946.

In a special senatorial election in New York in 1949, Lehman defeated John Foster Dulles for this office. Reelected in 1950, he was an uncompromising champion of liberal legislation and an outspoken critic of Senator Joseph R. McCarthy.

In or out of public office, Herbert Lehman remained identified with the Jewish community. As Governor and Senator, he never hesitated to speak out on behalf of Jewish causes or to take an active role in Jewish life.

When Lehman died, President Lyndon B. Johnson came to New York on December 8, 1963, for the funeral at Temple Emanu-El—just 16 days after he succeeded President John F. Kennedy.

BERNARD MANNES BARUCH
1870—1965

Bernard Baruch, a millionaire before the age of 32, was called everything from a Robin Hood who took from the rich but did not give to the poor, to a great living legend.

Son of Dr. Simon Baruch, a Confederate surgeon during the Civil War, Bernard Baruch was born in Camden, South Carolina, in 1870. When the family moverd to New York, Baruch attended City College and, following his graduation, went to work as a clerk on Wall Street for $3 a week. Within five years he was worth $3.5 million through stock market speculation. He retained his fortune by selling out in 1928, one year before the crash of 1929, saying, "I liked hard cash around, especially in times of trouble."

During World War I, his career as an "adviser to Presidents" was launched when President Woodrow Wilson appointed him to the Council of National Defense, and chairman of the powerful War Industries Board. In 1919, he served as a member of the American Commission to Negotiate Peace, and an economic adviser to the American Peace Commission. For his public service, he was awarded the Distinguished Service Medal by President Wilson.

Presidents Franklin D. Roosevelt and Harry Truman also turned to him during and after World War II. Baruch prepared the report on postwar industrial conversion, and was the United States' Representative to the United Nations Atomic Energy Commission for the formulation of plans for international control of atomic energy.

He was a great admirer of Presidents Roosevelt, Hoover, and Eisenhower, but less so of Harding. In commenting on Harding, he quoted the axiom that the office of the Presidency makes the man, but that in Harding's case it was a notable exception.

His biographer noted that "he was great and he was small. He could find pleasure in Churchill as well as Billy Rose. He was naïve and sophisticated, vain on little things and humble on great ones."

He said of himself, "An elder statesman is somebody old enough to know his own mind and keep quiet about it."

THE MILITARY

The Jewish role as fighting men remains one of the largely unwritten chapters of Jewish history the world over, and nowhere more so than in the United States.

The beginnings of Jewish soldiering in this country go back to the Colonial era, when Asser Levy demanded the right to bear arms and compelled the Dutch colony of New Amsterdam to allow him to stand guard against possible Indian attacks. Jews accompanied Colonel George Washington during the French and Indian Wars and fought with the British against French Canada and in frontier battles in Pennsylvania and Virginia.

When the Revolutionary War began, nearly 200 Jews served with the American forces out of a total Jewish population of 3,000. They were at Valley Forge, the Battle of Camden, the Battle of Bunker Hill, and with Washington's troops when they crossed the Delaware. They engaged in privateering expeditions against British shipping, accounting for the sinking of over 30 British merchantmen. They served in the Mexican War of 1845-1848, as well as in the earlier struggle of the Texans to win their independence from Mexico. There were seven Jews at the Battle of San Jacinto, which gave birth to the Republic of Texas.

When the Civil War started in 1861, some 6,000 Jews served in the Union army and 2,000 in the Confederate army. Five Jewish soldiers were awarded the Congressional Medal of Honor. The highest ranking Jewish officer in the Union Army was Major-General Frederick Knefler, commander of the 79th Indiana Regiment, who distinguished himself at the Battle of Chickamauga. Captain Ullman of the 5th Pennsylvania Cavalry survived the war, but died with General George A. Custer in the Sioux massacre at Little Big Horn June 25, 1876.

There were equally heroic Jewish achievements in the Confederate army. Moses Ezekiel, later to become one of America's great sculptors, fought bravely in the cadet battalion of the Virginia Military Institute. Max Frauen-

*thal distinguished himself by his bravery at the Battle of
Spottsylvania Court House in 1864. Dr. Simon Baruch,
father of the statesman-financier Bernard M. Baruch,
was General Robert E. Lee's Surgeon General. Eugenia
Phillips was a beautiful Confederate spy who narrowly
escaped hanging.*

*Fifteen Jews were among the seamen who went down
with the battleship* Maine *in Havana harbor. Over 5,000
Jews saw service in Cuba, Puerto Rico, and the
Philippines during the Spanish-American War. The famous regiment, the Rough Riders, recruited and commanded by Colonel Theodore Roosevelt, had 14 Jewish
volunteers.*

*In World War I, American Jewry was represented by
250,000 in the Army, Navy, and Marine Corps. Three
Jews were awarded the Congressional Medal of Honor,
Distinguished Service Cross, and six earned the French
Croix de Guerre. One of the most celebrated Jewish
soldiers was Abraham Krotoshinsky, a runner in the
77th Division, who saved the "Lost Battalion" by getting
through enemy lines to inform the command of its plight.*

*When the United States was attacked by Japan at
Pearl Harbor on December 7, 1947, two young Navy en-
signs, Ira Jeffery, who died, and Stanley Kaplan, were
among those whose prompt and heroic action saved
many lives and a number of burning ships. The last
plaintive radio message from the fortress at Corregidor
was sent by Sergeant Irving Storbing just before the
Japanese captured the position. There were a number of
Jews on the "death march" from Bataan.*

*Over 550,000 American Jews served during World
War II, with 10,000 dying in combat. Two Congressional Medals of Honor were conferred and, in addition,
more than 61,000 citations and decorations were awarded.*

*Though no official records were kept of Jewish partici-
pation in the Korean and Vietnam Wars, since a
majority of those who served in those conflcts were
draftees, it has been estimated that well over 500,000
Jews served. There were Jews among the prisoners of
war set free after the 1953 armistice with North Korea.
Twenty POW's freed by the North Vietnamese were*

Jews, and a number are still listed as "missing in action."

An important part of the story of the Jewish military record was its chaplains. The right of rabbis to be chaplains—the last battle for Jewish religious equality in the United States—was first established during the Civil War. President Abraham Lincoln recommended that Congress amend the law to permit their appointment. The first three were commissioned in 1862 in the Union army. They have served in the armed forces in all of the major conflicts since 1862, with seven killed while serving, among them Rabbi Alexander Goode, one of the heroes of the Four Chaplains saga.

URIAH P. LEVY
1792—1862

Monticello, Virginia, the home and burial ground of President Thomas Jefferson, is also the last resting place, one hundred yards away, of Rachel Phillips Levy, mother of a unique figure in American history, Commodore Uriah P. Levy.

Levy, born in Philadelphia in 1792, ran away to sea when he was ten years old. After two years as a cabin boy, his father apprenticed him to a shipowner. So suited was he for the sea that at 18 he was second mate of a brig and at 20 he was a captain and part owner of a ship.

Levy entered the United States Navy as a sailing master during the War of 1812 and served on the *Argus*, which spread terror among British shippers in European waters. While commanding a prize vessel taken by the *Argus*, Levy was captured and spent 16 months in Dartmoor prison.

His entire naval career was marked by a long series of unhappy incidents, most of which grew out of his not being a regular Navy man. His quick and violent resentment of personal insults to his country and his Jewishness resulted in his being courtmartialed six times. Although he climbed to the rank of Commodore, he had difficulty winning active-duty assignments, despite his repeated and passionate pleas.

In the interim he had built up a fortune in New York in real estate, acquiring the mansion of Monticello and 218 acres of the original Jefferson estate after it had fallen on bad times. Levy restored the historic house while he lived there and reclaimed many of the original furnishings which had been sold and widely scattered after Jefferson's death.

In 1855, he was one of 200 naval officers dropped from the service as part of the effort to weed out overage men. He fought his dismissal, objecting bitterly to the secrecy of the proceedings and to the implied slur on his record. There was some feeling that his ouster was based on anti-Semitic prejudice. After lengthy inquiries, during which Levy made a famous and eloquent defense, insisting on the right of Jews to equal treatment in the Navy, not only for their sake but for the national welfare, he and a third of the dismissed officers were reinstated. In 1859, he was given command of the Mediterranean squadron.

112

Levy died in 1862 and is buried in Cypress Hills Cemetery in Brooklyn, New York. Over his grave is a full-length statue of him in full naval uniform with the inscription:

Father of the law for the abolition of the barbarous practice of corporal punishment in the United States Navy.

In his will, he bequeathed Monticello and its land to the American people as the site of an agricultural school for educating the children of deceased naval officers as farmers.

His mother, Rachel Phillips Levy, died at Monticello during the time her son owned the mansion. She was the daughter of the Philadelphia patriot of the Revolution, Jonas Phillips. Her grave, under the deed by which he gave the nation Monticello, must be cared for in perpetuity, is marked as follows:

To the Memory of Rachel Phillips Levy
Born in New York 23 of May, 1769
Married 1787. Died 7 of Iyar (May)
5591, ab. (1831) at Monticello
Virginia, Erected August 15, 1859 By her
son J. P. L. Reerected by her Grandson L. N. L.

The "J.P.L." referred to was Jonas P. Levy, Uriah's brother; "L.N.L." was L. Napoleon Levy, Uriah's nephew.

EDWARD S. SALOMON
1836—1913

Although Edward S. Salomon is best remembered as the Governor of the Washington Territory, he had earlier gained wide fame as a general with the Union forces during the Civil War.

Born in Germany in 1836, he came to the United States in 1854 and settled in Chicago, where he clerked in a general store while studying the law. He gained some minor fame as an early leader in the new Republican party in Chicago while working for the nomination and election of Abraham Lincoln. At the age of 24, he was elected to the City Council— the youngest member of that body.

At the outbreak of the Civil War, Salomon enlisted in the

25th Illinois Infantry and won quick promotions on the battlefield for gallant conduct. His unit took part in the Battles
of Gettysburg and Chancellorsville, and marched with General William Sherman through Georgia. Repeatedly
mentioned in dispatches, he was described by Major-General
Carl Schurz as an officer who "displayed the highest order of
coolness and determination under very trying circumstances."
At the close of the war, he was promoted to the rank of Bre-
vet Brigadier-General, in recognition of meritorious service
and sound judgment in the campaign against Atlanta.

In 1870, President Ulysses Grant appointed Salomon Governor of the Territory of Washington. He served four years in
this post and on his retirement in 1874, the *Pacific Tribune*
wrote in an editorial:

> He mingled freely with the people, identified himself
> with their interests and generously expended his time
> and means to bring hither population and to promote
> our material interest.

After leaving this post, Salomon settled in San Francisco,
where he was District Attorney of San Francisco County and
twice a member of the State Legislature. He also served as
Commander of the Department of California of the Grand
Army of the Republic.

JEWISH ROUGH RIDERS

When Theodore Roosevelt called for volunteers to enlist in
his Rough Riders during the Spanish-American War, 14 Jews
answered the call.

This famous regiment was the first volunteer unit formed,
equipped, and armed during that war, the first to land in
Cuba, and the first to see combat. Although most of the men
were drawn from the ranks of hunters, cowboys, Indian
fighters, and ranchers, the regiment reflected the heterogene-
ous character of the American people. The Jews in the regiment were also a varied lot. Some were sons of pioneer
settlers of the Southwest, several had served in the regular
army, and a few were recent immigrants.

The youngest of this group was Jacob Willensky, a 16-
year-old from Chicago, Illinois, who enlisted under the name
of Jack Berling. He was killed in the first engagement at Las

Guasimas. Samuel Goldberg, another immigrant, was affectionately known as "porkchop" to his comrades because he steadfastly refused to eat non-kosher food. A clerk from Santa Fe, New Mexico, he was wounded at San Juan.

Samuel Greenwald of Prescott, Arizona, was the most celebrated Jew in the regiment. He enlisted as a private with Troop A and was promoted to captain for gallantry in action at San Juan and El Caney, the only Rough Rider to win a battlefield promotion.

Firsthand knowledge of the bravery of the 14 Jewish men who fought with him, motivated Theodore Roosevelt to accept honorary membership in the Hebrew Veterans of the War with Spain, which was later merged with the Jewish War Veterans of the United States. He paid public tribute to his Jewish comrades-in-arms. On June 15, 1903, after he had become President, Roosevelt received members of the B'nai B'rith at the White House. The members had called on the President in connection with the Kishnev pogrom. During the course of the meeting, Roosevelt said:

When in Santiago, when I was myself in the army, one of the best colonels among the regular regiments who did so well on that day and who fought beside me, was a Jew. One of the commanders who in the blockade of the Cuban coast did so well was a Jew. In my own regiment I promoted five men from the ranks for valor and good conduct in battle. It happened by pure accident, for I knew nothing of the faith of any of them, that these included two Protestants, two Catholics, and one Jew. And while that was a pure accident, it was not without its value as an illustration of the ethnic and religious makeup of our nation and of the fact that if a man is a good American that is all we ask, without thinking of his creed or his birthplace.

In Prescott, Arizona, there is the "Bucky" O'Neil Monument, memorializing the Rough Riders. The following Jews' names are inscribed:

Jacob Allaun, Chicago, Illinois
Sol Drachman, Prescott, Arizona
Samuel Goldberg, Santa Fe, New Mexico
Samuel Greenwald, Prescott, Arizona

Joseph E. Kansky, Seattle, Washington
Hyman Lowitzki, San Antonio, Texas
Albin Pollak, San Francisco, California
Henry Weil, Kingman, Arizona
Benjamin Woog, Washington, D.C.

"Bucky" O'Neil was the first man in Arizona to enlist; he was killed leading his men in a charge up San Juan Hill.

PEARL HARBOR

At the *USS Arizona* Memorial at Pearl Harbor, Hawaii, built over the superstructure of the battleship *Arizona* still containing the remains of the 1,102 crewmen who died with their ship during the Japanese attack on December 7, 1941, there is a plaque from the Jewish War Veterans of the United States honoring the Jewish seamen on board. Their names are also inscribed on the Memorial Wall listing all those who went down with the ship.

Among the number of other Jewish military heroes at Pearl Harbor were Commander Solomon Isquith, Brooklyn, New York; Ensign Stanley Caplan, Elmira, New York; and Ensign Ira Jeffrey, Minneapolis, Minnesota.

Isquith, later promoted to Rear Admiral, was in command of the ship *USS Utah* when she was sunk. Through his efforts, most of the crew were saved. He was awarded the Navy Cross.

Only eight months in the Navy, Caplan was aboard a destroyer whose captain had been killed in the first Japanese onslaught. Caplan's skilled seamanship not only saved the ship but enabled his crew to shoot down four enemy planes and sink a Japanese submarine, as he guided the destroyer to safety in open waters.

Jeffrey was killed when he turned himself into an ammunition carrier for the antiaircraft gunners on the battleship *California.*

DAVID "MICKEY" MARCUS
1901—1949

Buried at the historic cemetery of the United States Military Academy at West Point, Colonel David Marcus' epitaph reads: "A Soldier For All Humanity."

Son of a Rumanian immigrant, Marcus was born in 1901 in Brooklyn, New York. He was graduated from West Point in 1924 but resigned from the army after two years to study the law. In 1940, New York's Mayor Fiorello LaGuardia named Marcus Commissioner of Correction, in charge of the city's prison system.

When the country entered the war in 1941, he was appointed a lieutenant-colonel and served in the Pacific on the staff of General George C. Marshall and in Normandy with airborne troops. He accompanied President Franklin D. Roosevelt to Yalta and Teheran, and later went to Potsdam on the staff of President Harry S. Truman.

In the closing weeks of the war, he helped draw up the surrender documents for Italy and Germany. He outlined the program of military government for the occupied areas, and was with the American column that first liberated the Dachau death camp. By V-E Day, Marcus was promoted to full colonel.

Shortly after his return to civilian life in 1947, the Jewish Agency sought his help and smuggled him into Palestine, where he dictated the first military manuals ever to be published in the Hebrew language. He set up officers' training schools and advised the Haganah on the purchase and use of arms. After completing the blueprint and training of the army, he returned home. By April, 1948, he returned to Palestine, this time as Commander of Troops in the Israeli War of Independence.

He was killed while leading his forces on the Jerusalem front on June 10, 1948, just before the Arab-Israeli cease-fire became effective.

Colonel Marcus held the Distinguished Service Cross, second highest American military award, and the Bronze Star Medal, both for gallantry in action.

He was buried at West Point with full military honors.

HYMAN GEORGE RICKOVER
1900—

Hyman Rickover, the father of the American nuclear submarine, was once told by a Navy board that he "does not have enough all-round experience to warrant his advancement to Rear Admiral."

Born in Russian Poland in 1900, Rickover, educated in

Chicago, was graduated from the United States Naval Academy in 1922. He served during World War II in the Navy's Bureau of Ships.

Following the end of the war, he was assigned to the atomic submarine project at Oak Ridge, Tennessee, where he convinced Admiral Chester Nimitz, chief of naval operations, that nuclear sea power was feasible. Rickover directed the planning and construction of the world's first atomic-powered submarine, the *Nautilus*, launched in 1954, and other nuclear-powered ships.

Though his career has been marked by a certain amount of controversy because of his outspoken opinions and unorthodox methods, he was promoted to Rear Admiral in 1953 and Vice Admiral in 1958. He later became chief of the Naval Reactors Branch of the Atomic Energy Commission, and head of the nuclear propulsion division of the Navy.

Noted for his "nuclearrogance," he once stated before a Senate subcommittee that "if the Russians announced that they were sending a man to Hell, there would be at least two government agencies asking for money tomorrow, on the grounds that we should get there first."

CONGRESSIONAL MEDAL OF HONOR

At Valley Forge, Pennsylvania, The Freedom Foundation Medal of Honor Grove, a permanent memorial to the more than 3,300 heroes in uniform who have received the Congressional Medal of Honor, includes the names of a number of Jewish recipients. The citations for each Medal of Honor winner can be seen in the Knox Building. The following Jewish medalists are honored:

CIVIL WAR

Private Benjamin Levy, 40th New York Infantry, who as a drummer boy, age 16, took the gun of a sick comrade, went into the fight, and when the color bearer was shot down, carried the colors and saved them from capture at Glendale, Virginia, June 30, 1862.

Private David Orbansky, 58th Ohio Infantry, was awarded the CMH for distinguished gallantry in action at the Battle of Shiloh, 1862, and the Battle of Vicksburg, 1863.

Sergeant Major Abraham Cohn, 6th New Hampshire Infantry, rallied and reformed, under heavy fire, disorganized and fleeing troops of different regiments at the Battle of the Wilderness, May 6, 1864; and for bravely carrying orders to the advanced line under severe fire at Petersburg on July 30, 1864.

Sergeant Leopold Karpeles, 57th Massachusetts Infantry, who while serving as color bearer, rallied retreating troops and induced them to check the enemy's advance at the Battle of the Wilderness, May 6, 1864.

Henry Heller of Company A, 66th Ohio Infantry, earned the CMH for daring bravery at the Battle of Chancellorville.

WORLD WAR I

Corporal Sydney G. Gumpertz, serving with the 132nd Infantry, 33rd Division, was awarded the CMH while on duty in France where he was assigned with two other men to destroy a German machine gun station which was holding up an advance. When his two companions were killed by bursting shells, he continued on alone in the face of heavy fire, jumped into the German stronghold, silenced the gun, and captured the crew of nine.

Sergeant Philip Katz, of the 363rd Infantry, on learning that one of his comrades had been left wounded in an exposed position from which his company had withdrawn, crossed an area swept by heavy enemy fire to rescue the wounded soldier. He was awarded the CMH for bravery.

Sergeant Benjamin Kaufman of the 308th Infantry, was on a patrol attacking an enemy machine gun that halted his company's advance in the Argonne sector, when he became separated from his group. Before reaching the enemy gun, his arm was shattered by a bullet. He continued his advance alone, throwing grenades with his other hand. He took one prisoner, scattered the rest of the enemy crew, and brought his prisoner back to a first aid station. He left the shelter to bring water to a wounded man caught in a shell hole and was returning for more water when he was killed by a machine gun bullet. He was awarded the CMH posthumously for bravery.

Sergeant William Sawelson, of the 312th Infantry, 78th Division, killed in action in France, was awarded the CMH posthumously for conspicuous bravery.

WORLD WAR II

Sergeant Isadore S. Jachman, serving with Company B, 513th Parachute Infantry Regiment, was awarded the CMH for conspicuous gallantry in 1945 at Flamierge, Belgium. When his company was pinned down by enemy fire which was inflicting heavy casualties, Jachman left his place of cover with total disregard for his own safety, dashed across the open field, seized a bazooka from a fallen comrade, and fired the weapon alone, damaging one tank and forcing another to retire, thus disrupting the attack on his company. He suffered fatal wounds in this action. A drill field at Fort Meade, Maryland, is named for him.

Lieutenant Raymond Zussman, of Detroit, a platoon leader, was killed on September 12, 1944, while leading a unit that captured 92 Germans and killed 18 others in the course of liberating the French village of Noroy de Bourg. The CMH was awarded posthumously. An Army Transportation Center at Inkster, Michigan, is named for him.

WOMEN

The wide-ranging role of women in the American Jewish epic is only now beginning to be recognized as their story emerges from forgotten family records, neglected memoirs and diaries, and yellowing newspaper accounts.

Two of the 23 Jews who landed in New Amsterdam in 1654, as the first permanent Jewish settlers in North America, were women. Jewish women were engaged in commerce and trade in early Colonial America. Mrs. David Hays, whose husband was serving with the Revolutionary forces in Westchester County, New York, was still in bed with a newborn infant when she defied the demands of the British forces to disclose the hiding place of a party of patriots. Abigail Minis, an 80-year-old widow, supplied provisions to American troops when they captured Savannah. Hannah Moses conducted a successful shop in Philadelphia following the end of the Revolutionary War, while Frances Polock continued her deceased husband's far-flung export-import business in Colonial Rhode Island.

There were a number of women among the most prominent Jewish figures of the nineteenth-century. Rebecca Gratz was the founder of wide-ranging philanthropic and Jewish educational institutions, which became prototypes for other religious charitable organizations. Ernestine Rose shocked America with her feminist and libertarian views as she appeared on hundreds of platforms as an exponent of women's rights. It was partially through her efforts that the Wyoming Territory became the first area in America to grant full suffrage to women in 1869.

Annie Nathan Meyer, a cousin of Emma Lazarus, was one of the pioneer advocates of higher education for women. She was one of the founders in 1889 of Barnard College. Her sister, Maud Nathan was an early suffragist leader. Mrs. Frances Wisebart Jacobs, of Denver, Colorado, was one of the first women elected to a state legislature in the 1880's. Mrs. Simon Kander, a volunteer social worker in Milwaukee, wrote the famous Settlement Cook Book, to assist newly arrived Russian immigrants.

Prior to 1880, it was rare to find Jewish women working in factories, but by 1890, thousands of immigrant girls and women were employed in clothing, cigarette, and textile factories, and in stores and offices; many were even peddlers, running fish and poultry pushcarts. In 1909, during the first general strike in the needle trades, 20,000 Jewish factory women walked out, while middleclass Jewish women joined the picket lines after the strikers were routed by club-swinging, mounted police. In the 1911 Triangle Shirtwaist factory fire—a turning point in labor history—most of the 143 women who perished were Jewish. They became martyrs in the successful struggle for major social reforms which improved the working conditions of women and children. Rose Schneiderman was one of the founders and leaders of the Women's Trade Union League, and Belle Moskowitz, later chief political adviser to Governor Alfred E. Smith, were among the leading reformers. Julia Richman, noted for her educational innovations, greatly encouraged many first- and second-generation Jewish girls to enter the teaching profession.

Mrs. Florence Prag Kahn of San Francisco, served in Congress from 1925-1937. Since then, Bella Abzug and Gladys Spellman were also elected to Congress. Hundreds of Jewish women have been appointed or elected to federal, state, and municipal office and have served as judges, mayors, and in the diplomatic corps. Mrs. Anna Rosenberg was Assistant Secretary of Defense, and Rita Hauser was a delegate to the United Nations, Jill Wine-Volner, a member of the legal team that exposed the Watergate scandal, became general counsel to the Department of the Army.

In two of the leading women's issues of the 1960's and 1970's—the women's liberation movement and the enactment of ERA—Betty Friedan emerged as a leader. A high percentage of the delegates to the historic 1977 Women's National Conference in Houston, Texas, were Jews. The movement has also had a decisive impact on the role of women in the Jewish community, with several women serving as rabbis, and elected to high posts in the YM-YWHAs, communal service organizations, the American Jewish Congress, the Jewish Agency, and the American Zionist Federation.

Laura Falk, Florence Heller, Mrs. Felix Fuld, Sophie Irene Loeb, and Claribel Cone were among the foremost philanthropists of the twentieth century. Louise Waterman Wise, wife of Dr. Stephen S. Wise, was a pioneer in social welfare. Dorothy Schiff was the publisher of the New York Post, *and Barbara Walters is one of the country's leading TV personalities. Dr. Rosalyn Sussman Yalow was awarded the 1977 Nobel Prize in the field of medicine.*

Active in every phase of the public and creative life in America, Jewish women emerged from a minority within a minority of impoverished immigrants to a leading role in American affairs.

REBECCA FRANKS
c. 1757—c. 1823

Although most daughters of the American Revolution came from homes where the subject of independence was strongly supported, Rebecca Franks distinguished herself as a Tory sympathizer who fled to England following the end of the war rather than live in the United States.

Born in Philadelphia c. 1757, Rebecca Franks was the daughter of one of the wealthiest and distinguished merchants in the colonies—the ardent Anglophile, David Franks. Reared in an exceptionally cultivated home, she was known to have been a remarkably witty, cultured, and charming woman, trained socially in all the graces which made the Franks' home an intellectual center of Philadelphia.

Her reputation as "Belle of the City" made her the toast of General Sir William Howe, the British Commander, and her home was his social headquarters when he passed through the city. At her soirees she would entertain the British officers and dandies with her wit and doggerel, for which she was known:

> From garrets, cellars, rushing through the street
> The newborn statesmen in committees meet
> Legions of senators infest the land
> And mushroom generals thick as mushrooms stand.

Her written attacks on George Washington, which were published under a pseudonym, were widely circulated and quoted in Loyalist circles:

> Was it ambition, vanity or spite
> That prompted thee with Congress to unite?
> Or did all three within thy bosom roll?
> Thou heart of hero, with a traitor's soul.

When the British fled Philadelphia, David Franks and his family obtained permission to reside in New York, the last Tory stronghold. In 1782, she forsook her religion and married Colonel Henry Johnson, a British officer, who later became a general and a baronet, and lived in England as Lady Rebecca Johnson.

126

In his memoirs, General Winfield Scott mentions his meeting with Lady Johnson in London. In advanced age, she nostalgically reminisced about the American Revolution and said, "I ought to have been a patriot—would to God I too had been a patriot."

REBECCA GRATZ
1781—1869

Rebecca Gratz, the inspiration for Sir Walter Scott's heroine in *Ivanhoe*, was born in Philadelphia in 1781, the seventh of 12 children of Michael and Miriam Gratz. Her father, in addition to being one of the leading merchants of the day, aided in outfitting an American expedition against the British at Detroit and Mackinac, and was a partner of Levi Hollingsworth, a signer of the Declaration of Independence, in the development of the territory now known as Fayette County, West Virginia. Five of her brothers were veterans of the American Revolution.

The Gratz home, a famous gathering for Philadelphia intellectuals, entertained many notables, among them Washington Irving, the artists Sully and Malbone, the actress Fanny Kemble, and the aristocrats of Philadelphia society. Washington Irving once described Rebecca so movingly to Sir Walter Scott that Scott was inspired to create the Rebecca of his immortal *Ivanhoe* after her.

Well known for her philanthropy in Philadelphia, Miss Gratz founded the Female Hebrew Benevolent Society, the first independent Jewish philanthropic agency. This society was a prototype for many of the city's later welfare agencies. She was also the founder, in 1838, of the first Jewish Sunday School in the United States.

She is buried in the historic Mikveh Israel Cemetery in Philadelphia, which dates back to 1738. This cemetery belongs to the Mikveh Israel Congregation, the second oldest in America, and the recipient of the famed letter from George Washington on religious freedom, which he wrote shortly after becoming President.

PENINA MOISE
1797—1880

When Abraham Moise and his family fled their Caribbean island plantation in 1791, they escaped a massacre by slaves of the white settlers. Though Moise had been a slave owner, he was known to have been a humane one, as evidenced by the fact that a group of his slaves assisted the family to the safety of a vessel bound for South Carolina before the insurrection started.

Settling in Charleston, Moise never regained his former wealthy status. When he died in 1809, the family was living in poverty. Penina, the brightest of his nine children, had to leave school to assist in the household duties. Scholarly by nature, she worked days at home at needlecrafts, while her evenings were spent continuing her education by reading.

Charleston, the cultural center of the South in the early nineteenth century, had the largest, most cultivated, and wealthiest Jewish settlement in the United States. Among its prominent members were Lyon Levy, State Treasurer; Jacob de la Motta, a well-known physician and member of the Royal Academy of Medicine in Paris; Solomon Carvalho, artist; and Jacob N. Cardozo, essayist and dramatist. It was in this gracious atmosphere that Penina Moise nourished her intellectual yearnings.

At the urging of her family she began writing articles and essays. Gaining quick acceptance, she became a steady contributor to newspapers in Boston, Washington, D.C., and New Orleans, and to one of the most widely read magazines of the day, *Godey's Lady's Book*. In the early 1830's, following the publication of *Fancy's Sketch Book*, a book of her poetry, Penina Moise's verse appeared in the local newspaper *The Charleston Courier* and later *The Occident*, a Jewish magazine edited by the noted rabbi Isaac Leeser. Deeply moved by the plight of the persecuted Jews of Europe, Miss Moise wrote a number of poems in their behalf. She did not, however, have any literary involvement with any of the urgent issues of her time—slavery and suffrage.

Though she gained some note for her poetry and essays, her most lasting fame was to be in the field of hymns. During the last 25 years of her life, despite total blindness, Miss Moise composed nearly 200 hymns of devotion and faith. Written during the period when the Reform movement in American Judaism was gaining wide acceptance, her English-language hymns were included in the services and in the Prayer Book.

In her last years, she taught at a small school which she and a widowed sister had started. In these humble surroundings, the shy, blinded poetess would discuss the works of the leading writers of the day with her students.

Her last note to her family when she died in 1880 at the age of 83 was:

> Lay no flowers on my grave. They are for those who
> lived in the sun, and I have always lived in the shadow.

ADAH ISAACS MENKEN
1835—1868

Known as the "enchanting rebel," Adah Isaacs Menken, was not only the toast of the theater on two continents, but also a gifted poet and writer.

Born Adah Bertha Theodore in a suburb of New Orleans in 1835, she was able at a young age to master Latin, Hebrew, French, English, and later became fluent in German. In 1856, she eloped with Alexander Isaacs Menken, the black sheep scion of a wealthy Cincinnati family, whom she met on a trip to Galveston, Texas.

Through her husband's social connections, she was able to join an exclusive New Orleans amateur acting society, and in less than a year, she was appearing professionally with a traveling theater group. The provincial audiences would throng to see the performances of the beautiful, vivacious Menken. While appearing in western mining towns such as Virginia City, Nevada, clad only in pink tights, she would shock and startle the lusty Comstock Lode miners. She became their great favorite with her daring performance in the show *Mazeppa*, as she rode across the stage lashed to the back of an unsaddled horse.

Reports of her beauty and performances spread through the mining areas as quickly as news of a new gold strike. Night after night, the miners, crowded in the aisles, cheering her with uninhibited enthusiasm. At the end of a performance, they would often throw gold dust at her feet. One mine was renamed "Mazeppa Mounting Ledge" in her honor, and an entire mining region was dubbed "The Menken." A newly organized mining company printed a likeness of her on their stock certificates. Though she had many devoted fans, the most ardent one in Virginia City was Samuel Clemens.

Despite enjoying her role as the rebellious, emancipated woman with her bobbed hair and semi-nude performances

which shocked Victorian prudery, Menken was also a writer
and poet of great sensitivity. As early as 1857, she had already published poems, essays, and articles in the *American
Israelite*, the famous weekly edited by Rabbi Isaac M.
Wise, one of the founders of the American Reform movement. Her
strong love of Judaism was expressed in her poetry. There
were claims during her short life that she had been born a
Christian and that she embraced Judaism when she married
Menken. She laid all such rumors to rest. In a published letter which appeared in the *New York Illustrated News*, Adah
Menken stated that she was born a Jewess, "and have ad-
hered to it through all my erratic career. Through that pure
and simple religion, I have found greatest comfort and
blessing."

Her greatest triumphs were the performances in London
and Paris, where she became an immediate celebrity, with
royalty in attendance. When she hosted elaborate dinners and
receptions, such personal friends as Charles Dickens, Charles
Swinburne, Alexandre Dumas, and George Sand would mix
with the nobility.

When Adah Menken was only 33, she contracted tuberculosis and died in Paris. She is buried in that city, in the
Jewish section of Montparnasse Cemetery.

ERNESTINE L. ROSE
1810—1892

One of America's greatest pioneer feminists, Ernestine L.
Rose, born in Poland in 1810, was partially responsible for
the Wyoming Territorial Legislature in 1869 granting full
equality to women for the first time in American history.

The daughter of a rabbi, Mrs. Rose studied the Scriptures
and was an observant Jew as a child. At the age of 17 she
left home to become an apostle of humanitarianism.

Soon after her arrrval in America, she became a close associate of Susan B. Anthony in the bitter struggle for
women's rights. She traveled throughout the country speaking
on the evils of the social system, the wickedness of slavery,
and the injustices to women.

Mrs. Rose was elected delegate to the first National
Women's Rights Convention in Worcester, Massachusetts, in
1850. There she met such liberal leaders as Lucy Stone and
William Lloyd Garrison, leading advocates of abolition, reli-

gious liberty, and women's rights. During the Civil War she joined Elizabeth Stanton and Susan B. Anthony to form the Women's National Loyal League, and she was active in collecting signatures to petition President Abraham Lincoln to issue the Emancipation Proclamation.

In the Wyoming Territory, she rode on horseback and stagecoach campaigning for woman's suffrage, and in 1869 witnessed the precedent-shattering legislation which granted suffrage and full equality to women.

Always in the vanguard of the struggle for women's emancipation, she died in 1892, 28 years before Congress passed the Nineteenth Amendment, granting full woman's suffrage.

EMMA LAZARUS
1849—1887

Emma Lazarus, the Jewish American poet, is best known for her sonnet "The New Colossus" which is affixed to the pedestal of the Statue of Liberty in New York City harbor. Yet this paean to liberty and to America as the haven of the oppressed almost went unwritten and, once written, was almost forgotten.

In 1883, the drive to raise $300,000 for the statue's pedestal was foundering. Notable artists and writers were invited to donate works which could be auctioned off for the benefit of the fund. Among those who contributed original manuscripts were Walt Whitman, Mark Twain, and Bret Harte. Emma Lazarus was asked to contribute a poem, and at first she said she had nothing appropriate for the occasion and that she "could not possibly write verses to order." Constance Cary Harrison, who was planning to publish the manuscripts and artwork in a souvenir portfolio, finally persuaded Lazarus to change her mind by writing her, "Think of the Goddess of Liberty standing on her pedestal yonder in the bay and holding the torch out to those refugees you are so fond of visiting at Ward's Island."

Two days later, Constance Cary Harrison received the manuscript of the sonnet "The New Colossus," which was auctioned off for $1,500. The poem was duly published in Harrison's portfolio, and then forgotten.

When President Grover Cleveland dedicated the Statue of Liberty on October 28, 1886, the sculptor, Frederic-Auguste Bartholdi, was among the honored guests. Emma Lazarus, who was critically ill, was not invited. She died of cancer the following year.

In 1903, Georgiana Schuyler, a New York artist, came across a copy of the portfolio in a bookstore. Deeply touched by the sonnet, she had it engraved on a bronze plaque and obtained permission to have it affixed to the base of the statue. (Part of the sonnet is also inscribed in marble at the entrance to the International Arrivals Building at Kennedy International Airport in New York City.)

Emma Lazarus, of Sephardic ancestry, was born in 1849, the daughter of a wealthy sugar refiner. She had achieved minor fame for her verses and essays, which drew praise from Walt Whitman and Ralph Waldo Emerson, and for her translations of medieval Spanish-Jewish and German poets. She was a direct descendant of the patriot of the American Revolution, Reverend Gershom Mendes Seixas, and illustrious members of the family in later generations were Supreme Court Justice Benjamin Cardozo; Robert Nathan, poet and novelist; Annie Nathan Meyer, a founder of Barnard College; and Maud Nathan, a leading suffragist.

Although she was well known in New York for her efforts on behalf of Jewish refugees from Czarist pogroms, some of whom were housed on Ward's Island, Lazarus will always be remembered for her immortal lines:

Not like the brazen giant of Greek fame,
With conquering limbs astride from land to land;
A mighty woman with a torch, whose flame
Is imprisoned lightning, and her name
Mother of Exiles. From her beacon-hand
Glows world-wide welcome; her mild eyes command
The air-bridged harbor that twin cities frame.
"Keep, ancient lands, your storied pomp!" cries she
with silent lips. "Give me your tired, your poor,
Your huddled masses yearning to breathe free,
The wretched refuse of your teeming shore,
Send these, the homeless, tempest-tost, to me;
I lift my lamp beside the golden door!"

The location of the original manuscript of "The New Colossus," which was auctioned off in 1883, is not known. A handwritten draft of the sonnet is one of the cherished possessions of the American Jewish Historical Society, which preserves her autographed notebooks in its archives at Waltham, Massachusetts.

Emma Lazarus's poetry was published posthumously in 1889.

LILLIAN WALD
1867—1940

Known as "the angel among the pushcarts," Lillian Wald, like Jane Addams, came from a cultured and wealthy family, and similarly, both devoted their lives to working among the poor.

Her family came to America from Germany in the migration which followed the rebellion and defeat of the freedom fighters of 1848. The love of liberty and an awareness of injustice were part of Lillian Wald's heritage.

At the age of 22, she entered nursing school, and following her graduation she became a nurse in the New York Juvenile Asylum. Always dispensing more help and attention to her patients than the hospital authorities deemed necessary, she was constantly at odds with her superiors. She left and entered Women's Medical College in 1892, but did not complete her training. Asked to teach a class in home nursing, she encountered an area of New York, the Lower East Side, in which hundreds of thousands of immigrants lived in abysmal poverty. Shocked but not frightened, she began her life work of nursing the poor with great love and compassion. With financial aid from Mrs. Solomon Loeb and her son-in-law, Jacob Schiff, Lillian Wald and her close friend and colleague, Mary Brewster, started their great humanitarian organization, The Visiting Nurses Service.

A founder of the Henry Street Settlement House and the Outdoor Recreation League, she fought for child labor laws, factory safety laws, and improved housing for the poor until her death in 1940.

Lillian Wald was the author of *The House on Henry Street* and *Windows on Henry Street,* two autobiographical works.

EMMA GOLDMAN
1869—1940

Russian-born Emma Goldman came to the United States in 1886. She was later to be known as "Red Emma"—an impassioned feminist and foremost figure in the anarchist movement in America.

Her dreams of political and economic freedom after the harsh conditions of life in Russia soon vanished when she went to work in a clothing factory in Rochester, New York, at wages of $2.50 a week for 63 hours of work, under appalling conditions. Deeply moved by the unjust execution of four anarchists in the Haymarket Square bombing. Goldman committed herself to the radical anarchist movement. This was the start of her long and intense career of anti-government agitation.

She gained quick fame throughout the country for her stirring speeches and her articles in the weekly newspaper, *Freiheit*. It was during this period that Emma Goldman met Alexander Berkman, a fellow anarchist, which was the beginning of their long, ill-fated political and personal relationship.

Goldman and Berkman were thrust into international notoriety during the Homestead Strike of 1892. After writing a fiery manifesto about the steelworkers' struggle, they resolved to kill Henry Clay Frick, chairman of the Carnegie Steel Company, whom they saw as the arch criminal in the slaughter of the strikers. When Berkman's first attempts at making. a bomb were unsuccessful, Goldman took to the streets as a prostitute to obtain money for a gun. Though Berkman was successful in gaining entrance to Frick's office and firing three bullets, Frick sustained only superficial wounds. Berkman was convicted and sentenced to 21 years in jail for this abortive murder attempt.

Emma Goldman's name, inevitably linked with that of Berkman, aroused the press to demand, "How long will this dangerous woman, possessed by a fury, be permitted to go on?" In 1893, "Red Emma" was arrested, tried, and sentenced to one year in prison. On her release, Miss Goldman traveled around the country delivering speeches and organizing small anarchist groups. It was during one of these meetings in Cleveland that she met Leon Czolgosz—the man who was later to assassinate President William McKinley. In his confession, Czolgosz stated that he was inspired and incited to commit the crime by Emma Goldman. The entire country was horrified and demanded that "anarchists must be exterminated . . . Emma Goldman should share the fate of her follower." Although she was arrested for complicity in the crime, no evidence was produced and she was released.

Returning to New York, Miss Goldman, a pariah, could find no lodging or job, and was forced for a time to use an assumed name. It was during this depressed period that she received a letter from Berkman from prison, telling of his loss of faith in the revolutionary effectiveness of anarchism and of individual acts of violence. Shaken by Berkman's letter and the enactment of stringent anti-anarchist laws, Goldman turned her attention to lecturing on birth control, atheism, and women's emancipation.

When the United States entered World War I, Berkman, who had been released after serving 14 years of his sentence, and Goldman made extended lecture tours, speaking out against the war and conscription. They were indicted for conspiracy and sentenced to two years in the Atlanta Federal prison.

After serving their sentence, they were deported to Russia and arrived in Petrograd (formerly St. Petersburg) in December, 1919. After touring the country under the auspices of the new Soviet regime, they slowly became disillusioned by the oppression of the new government. They both left Russia after two years with profound feelings that their faith in the revolution had been betrayed. Berkman drifted to Sweden, Germany, and then settled in France, where he earned a meager living as an editor and translator. Despondent and physically ill, he committed suicide in 1936.

Goldman, without home or country, finally received asylum in England, where she married a British citizen. Though she could not return to live in the United States, she was allowed to enter in the early 1930's for a lecture tour. Before her death in 1940 in Canada, she completed her book *My Disillusionment in Russia.*

HENRIETTA SZOLD
1860—1945

When Henrietta Szold's 80th birthday was celebrated in Jerusalem in 1940, her response to the international honors lavished on her for humanitarian achievements was that she was more aware of the things she had failed to do than of those she had done.

Born in Baltimore in 1860 in the era of Lincoln's Presidency, Miss Szold was the first of eight daughters of

Rabbi Benjamin and Sophie Szold, who had emigrated from Germany the previous year. Rabbi Szold, a passionate believer in human rights, was one of the few supporters of President Abraham Lincoln in Baltimore—a city which had strong Southern sympathies during the Civil War.

Upon graduation from high school, Miss Szold spent the next 15 years teaching liberal arts in an impoverished private school. In addition to her teaching, she was also the Baltimore correspondent for the *Jewish Messenger,* a New York publication.

Her awareness of the Jewish tragedy was heightened on visits with her father to the port of Baltimore to welcome refugees from the Russian pogroms of the early 1880's. Moved by the accounts of the persecution and struggles of these immigrants, she organized evening classes in English and practical vocational subjects to enable them to adjust to their new life. In 1892, she gave up her teaching career to enter a wider educational field. She accepted the post of editor at the Jewish Publication Society, where she brought a wide-ranging knowledge of American and Jewish subjects and considerable literary ability. When she left this position after 25 years, the Society paid tribute to Miss Szold with a citation: "To speak of the literary output of the last 25 years is impossible without remembering her services . . . her great Jewish enthusiasm."

When she enrolled at the Jewish Theological Seminary in New York for further study, her small apartment on West 123rd Street soon became a salon where many of the intellectual elite of the college gathered around her. Drawn from the seclusion of her scholarly interests, Miss Szold was soon deeply involved in the dynamic Zionist movement which was emerging at the turn of the century. After visiting Palestine in 1909, she wrote, "I am more than ever convinced that if not Zionism, then nothing—then extinction of the Jew!" This was written more than two decades before the rise of the Nazi movement in Germany. Convinced that she was too old at age 50 to play an active role in Palestine, she was nevertheless to dedicate the rest of her life to this pursuit.

In 1912, a society was formed with the dual purpose of establishing and maintaining a district system of nursing in Palestine and an educational program to foster Zionist education in America. Miss Szold was elected president of this new group, which called itself "Hadassah"—Queen Esther's Hebrew name.

In founding this organization, Miss Szold displayed a multiplicity of talents and resourcefulness. Always urging "let us stop talking, and do something," she was equal to every demand made upon her. If, as she was to glowingly describe Hadassah many years later, it became "a marvelous flexible, well-oiled machine," it was because she built it with unprecedented precision and skill. Its membership was to rise to 360,-000 in the 1970's, and it was to become one of the largest health delivery and child welfare services in Israel.

In 1916, during World War I, an urgent appeal came to Hadassah for medical help in Palestine, where there were few doctors or drugs to cope with the epidemics that were rife throughout the Middle East. The organization undertook to furnish a complete medical unit. With Miss Szold in command, the group supervised and dispensed the needed help. While observing the medical crisis and the needs of the pioneer immigrants who were plagued with malaria, this small temporary medical unit was the modest beginning of the enormous Hadassah medical organization of today.

Never allowing herself the quiet serenity of old age, Henrietta Szold spent the years between the two wars feverishly organizing a central social service bureau, hospital and health units, and nurses' training schools.

When the clouds of fascism were gathering over Europe in the early 1930's, the indefatigable 73-year-old Miss Szold was to organize one of her greatest humanitarian accomplishments. Disregarding her "tired heart," she established the Youth Aliyah, an organization whose main goal was to rescue Jewish adolescents from the Nazi government. "My new job deals with children—but it is not child's play," she stated when faced with the complicated political and administrative problems. She set about negotiating with the British Mandate Government in Palestine, and the new German government in Berlin. By 1945, her new organization had rescued more than 13,000 adolescents from thirteen countries in Europe and the Middle East. Often she would meet the boats at the port of Haifa to welcome the new arrivals and would on many occasions accompany them to their new settlements to see that they were properly installed.

In her absolute concentration on duty, she sternly denied herself what she wanted most in her old age—to return to her family in America. She died at the age of 84 in her simple lodgings in Jerusalem.

ROSALYN SUSSMAN YALOW
1921—

Rosalyn Yalow went to work as a secretary in 1941, after being told that as a woman she could never enter graduate school to study physics. On October 13, 1977, the Karolinski Institute in Stockholm, Sweden, called Dr. Yalow to inform her that she had been awarded one of the 1977 Nobel Prizes in the field of medicine—the second woman to be so honored.

Born in 1921 in the South Bronx, New York, Dr. Yalow was graduated from Hunter College. Discouraged from seeking admission to graduate school, she went to work as a secretary at the College of Physicians and Surgeons, where they promised she could take some courses if she "behaved herself." She later received an assistantship in physics at the University of Illinois. Since 1950, Dr. Yalow has been associated with the Veterans Hospital in the Bronx, where she is currently chief of nuclear medicine.

In her original research with a co-worker, Dr. Solomon Berson (now deceased), a test was perfected to measure the concentrations of hundreds of hormones, vitamins, viruses, enzymes, drugs, and other substances in the body to help determine changes between normalcy and disease. Dr. Yalow recalled that when they first submitted the findings of their initial research efforts, the editor of a leading medical journal rejected it.

The Nobel citation stated that through this work biologists could measure in the laboratory many more substances than before, which represents "an enormous development in hitherto closed areas of research."

Although the victim of discrimination as a woman, Dr. Yalow said that she did not believe in reverse discrimination for women. "Let them just give us equal opportunity," she stated.

At the end of the formal banquet in Stockholm, Sweden, December, 1977, following receipt of her award, she said, "We still live in a world in which a significant fraction of people, including women, believe that a woman belongs and wants to belong exclusively in the home, that a woman should not aspire to achieve more than her male counterparts and particularly not more than her husband."

Dr. Simon Baruch (*American Jewish Archives*)

David Belasco (*New York Public Library*)

Justice Louis D. Brandeis   Michael Goldwater
(University of Louisville   *(Senator Barry Goldwater)*
Archives)

Samuel Gompers *(AFL/CIO)*

Barnard Gratz *(American Jewish Archives)*

Nat Holman *(Nat Holman)*

Sandy Koufax *(National Baseball Hall of Fame)*

Commodore Uriah P. Levy
(American Jewish Archives)

Adah Isaacs Menken
(New York Public Library)

Dr. Albert A. Michaelson *(U.S. Naval Academy)*

Ernestine Rose *(New York Public Library)*

David Sarnoff *(RCA Photo Library)*

Beverly Sills *(Edgar Vincent Associates)*

Levi Strauss *(Levi Strauss & Co.)*

Judah Touro *(American Jewish Archives)*

Dr. Rosalyn S. Yalow *(Veterans Administration Hospital; Medical Media Production Service)*

Dr. Isachar Zacharie *(American Jewish Archives)*

Irving Berlin *(ASCAP)*

Henrietta Szold *(Hadassah Archives)*

Sir Moses Ezekiel *(American Jewish Archives)*

Chaim Gross *(Forum Gallery, New York)*

David Dubinsky *(B. Berinsky for ILGWU* Justice*)*

Emma Goldman *(New York Public LIbrary)*

Judah P. Benjamin *(National Archives)*

Jonas Salk *(The Salk Institute)*

Rabbi Isaac Mayer Wise *(American Jewish Archives)*

Emma Lazarus *(New York Public Library)*

Aaron Copland *(ASCAP)*

Governor Edward S. Salomon
(Suzzallo Library, University of Washington; Photo by Shaw)

Abraham Jonas *(American Jewish Archives)*

Dr. Cyrus Adler *(Jewish Theological Seminary of America)*

Dr. J. Robert Oppenheimer *(Institute for Advanced Study)*

Dr. Solomon Schecter *(Jewish Theological Seminary of America)*

Dr. Felix Adler *(New York Society for Ethical Culture)*

Rabbi Sabato Morais *(Jewish Theological Seminary of America)*

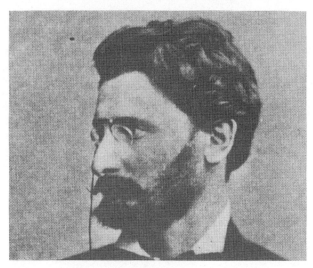

"TO GIVE THE NEWS IMPARTIALLY, WITHOVT FEAR OR FAVOR. REGARDLESS OF ANY PARTY, SECT OR INTEREST INVOLVED"

Adolph S. Ochs *(The New York Times)*

Joseph Pulitzer *(New York Public Library)*

JUDICIAL

Jews have always been a "kingdom of lawyers and a juristic people." They are the only people who have kept a lawbook in the Holy Ark of their temples and provided for reading a segment from it three times a week as a central part of its worship. Nor has any other people set aside a major religious festival to observe the handing down of its statutes.

The Decalogue, handed down to Moses, and the laws of the Hebrew Bible, became the laws of the Puritans, whose legal codes still influence American law. Nourished on the ancient Hebrew moral and juridical traditions, the early New Englanders patterned their legal codes on Hebrew models, which in turn greatly influenced the development of American jurisprudence, beginning with the Bill of Rights and the Constitution.

The inspired Jewish sense of justice reflected in the Old Testament, and particularly in the thunderings of the prophets, has long been the motivating force of Jewish lawyers and religious leaders, who fought against political corruption, defended the downtrodden, and challenged the establishment in support of racial, religious, and economic equality. It is no accident that the five Jews who sat on the United States Supreme Court, the acme of legal authority and legal achievement, were economic liberals and civil libertarians.

The first Jewish judge in America, Daniel Nunez, was a well-regarded citizen of New Brunswick, New Jersey, who was named town clerk and justice of the peace in 1722. In 1727, Isaac Miranda of Lancaster, Pennsylvania, served as deputy judge of the Court of the Vice-Admiralty.

The earliest known Jewish lawyers in the United States were Zalegman Phillips of Philadelphia, a graduate of the University of Pennsylvania Law School, and the brothers Sampson Levy, Jr. and Moses Levy, also of Philadelphia, who were admitted to the bar in 1800. Moses Levy was so well regarded as a lawyer that President Thomas Jefferson first proposed to appoint him

143

United States Attorney General, but was dissuaded. The first Jewish member of the New York bar was Sampson Simson, a graduate of Columbia College Law School, class of 1800, who studied law in the office of Aaron Burr.

Perhaps the first of the many Jewish lawyers who gained fame as counsel to major public investigations, especially by Congressional committees, was Samuel Untermeyer. As counsel for the Pujo Committee probing Wall Street, he drafted the remedial legislation which led to the enactment of the Federal Reserve Act and the first regulatory laws governing the Stock Exchange. Samuel Dash, counsel to the Senate Watergate Committee, carried on in the Untermeyer tradition.

Oscar S. Straus, a lawyer who was better known as a diplomat and Secretary of Commerce and Labor, was the second American appointed to the International Court of Arbitration at The Hague, serving from 1908-1920. Louis Marshall, one of the great constitutional lawyers of the late nineteenth and early twentieth centuries, fought and won many landmark cases before the Supreme Court. He was particularly known for his advocacy of the constitutionality of statutes concerning workmen's compensation, alien immigration, the separation of church and state, and desegregation of blacks.

In addition to the five who served on the Supreme Court, Jews have held some of the highest judicial offices in the land, including the posts of Attorney General and Solicitor-General. They have served as justices of the Federal courts, on state supreme courts, as district attorneys, deans of law schools, and presidents of bar associations.

Prior to the 1930's, professional discrimination limited most Jewish lawyers to private practice in narrow fields of the law, but the New Deal during President Franklin D. Roosevelt's first administration opened new careers in government to them. Their expertise later made them and the next generation of Jewish attorneys more welcome in areas of private practice from which they had been systematically excluded. Young Jewish lawyers also found success as counsels to labor unions and as advo-

cates in the civil liberties field. In recent years they have become prominent in pressing for changes in legal practice and have pioneered in the creation of legal defender programs.

LOUIS MARSHALL
1856—1929

Louis Marshall, the son of German immigrants, born in Syracuse, New York in 1856, was destined to become not only one of the country's leading constitutional lawyers, but an early conservationist and defender of natural resources and wildlife.

After completing a two-year course at Columbia Law School, he settled in New York City, and by 1894 was a nationally recognized authority on constitutional law. For 35 years he argued cases affecting workmen's compensation, alien migration, segregation of blacks, veteran payments, inheritance taxes, and other issues involving basic constitutional principles.

His most famous legal victory was won before the United States Supreme Court, which upheld his contention that an Oregon law denying Catholics the right to send their children to parochial schools was illegal. He fought the Ku Klux Klan and the anti-Semitism of Henry Ford; the auto magnate's public retraction of his anti-Jewish libels was addressed to Marshall. He battled militantly against restrictive immigration laws and intervened with Presidents William Taft and Woodrow Wilson on behalf of Balkan Jewry. He was a key factor in the successful fight in Congress to abrogate the Treaty of 1832 with Russia because of their refusal to recognize the American passports of Jews.

An ardent conservationist, Marshall headed the establishment of the New York State College of Forestry on the campus of Syracuse University. He was the only New Yorker to sit in three of the state's constitutional conventions—1890, 1894, and 1915.

A founder of the American Jewish Committee and its president until his death in 1929, Marshall was a leading spokesman for American Jewry in the two decades before his death.

His unique status as a force in American Jewish life was epitomized by a wit who remarked that American Jewry "was ruled by Marshall law," and he was dubbed "Louis XIX."

146

LOUIS DEMBITZ BRANDEIS
1856—1941

Louis Brandeis, born in Louisville, Kentucky in 1856, was to become the first Jew to be appointed to the United States Supreme Court.

Before he was 40, he had gained nationwide fame as a big business lawyer. The Homestead steel strike of 1892, however, converted him to a zealous opponent of bigness and monopoly in business and industry. For 20 years he fought and won historic legal battles against the nation's corporate giants. His unremitting struggle against railroad monopolies and his defense of the minimum wage and maximum hours legislation brought him the enmity of big business. He was alternately called "the people's attorney" or "the radical lawyer from Boston."

He was nominated to the Supreme Court in 1916 by President Woodrow Wilson, and the appointment touched off one of the bitterest political arguments of the time. Opposition to his confirmation was led by bar associations and leading Americans, among them former President William H. Taft. Amid anti-Semitic overtones, the Senate debated the nomination for five months and finally approved it.

In the 23 years Brandeis served on the bench, he became the symbol of economic and political liberalism. When he retired from the Court in 1939, at the age of 83, he was considered one of the most beloved jurists of all time, having achieved rank with the memorable judges of American history.

Jacob de Haas, editor of the *Boston Jewish Advocate*, excited Brandeis' interest in Jewish history, and he became an acknowledged leader in the American Zionist movement. As a result of Brandeis' influence, President Wilson supported the Balfour Declaration for a Jewish homeland in Palestine.

Brandeis died in 1941. His ashes are buried on the front portico of the Law School of the University of Louisville.

BENJAMIN NATHAN CARDOZO
1870—1938

A direct descendant of Abraham de Lucena, who arrived in America in 1655, and Gershom Mendes Seixas, patriot minister of the American Revolution, Cardozo was born in

1870 in New York. Tutored in his youth by Horatio Alger, he practiced the law for 22 years and was known as a "lawyer's lawyer." He had been a judge of the New York State Supreme Court for only a few weeks in 1913 when he was elevated to the Court of Appeals and served as Chief Justice of the Court of Appeals from 1927-1932. He was appointed an associate justice of the United States Supreme Court by President Herbert Hoover in 1932, to fill the vacancy left by the retirement of Oliver Wendell Holmes.

Cardozo came to the Supreme Court with a towering reputation. His decisions on the federal bench made legal history, and his opinions have been acclaimed as models of English legal writing. He was the foremost spokesman of sociological jurisprudence, and his views on the relation of law to social change made him one of the most influential of American judges. Cardozo is ranked along with Marshall, Story, and Holmes as among the ten greatest judges in American history.

He is buried at Union Fields Cemetery in Brooklyn, New York, near his illustrious relative, Emma Lazarus.

FELIX FRANKFURTER
1882—1965

"This man Laundry must be a very rich man because he has so many stores." This was an observation made by Felix Frankfurter in 1894, a 12-year-old immigrant to the United States from Austria. Forty-six years later he was appointed to the Supreme Court by President Franklin D. Roosevelt— the only appointee with no previous judicial experience.

Frankfurter attended City College in New York City and was graduated from Harvard Law School in 1906. He was considered a legal prodigy and was one of the few Jewish law school graduates to be engaged as a clerk in a major New York law office before World War I. He became Assistant United States Attorney in New York and in 1914 he started a 25-year tenure as law professor and dean of Harvard Law School.

He worked for the release of Sacco and Vanzetti and was a founder of the American Civil Liberties Union. His opinions on the Sacco and Vanzetti trial were unpopular in Massachusetts, especially at Harvard, where there was talk of his resigning. His reaction was, "Let [President] Lowell resign."

Frankfurter was appointed to the Supreme Court in 1939, where he served until 1962. He was regarded as an intimate adviser of President Roosevelt's and an important member of what was known as the New Deal "brain trust" before his appointment to the bench. Those government appointees he recommended were dubbed "New Deal hot dogs."

A long-time Zionist, Frankfurter was a member of the Zionist delegation to the Versailles Peace Conference in 1917. Through the well-known British Arabist and writer, T. E. Lawrence, he met Emir Feisal, head of the Arab delegation. In 1919 Feisal wrote to Frankfurter stating that his delegation regarded the Zionist proposal as "moderate and proper," and that he wished the Jews "a most hearty welcome home." He further stated that the "two movements complete one another" and "neither can be a success without the other."

Frankfurter was awarded the Presidential Medal of Freedom by President John F. Kennedy.

ARTHUR JOSEPH GOLDBERG
1908—

Arthur J. Goldberg, born in Chicago, Illinois in 1908, the youngest of eleven children of Russian immigrants, was destined within a short time span of five years to be a cabinet member, an associate justice of the Supreme Court, and an ambassador.

After completing Northwestern Law School in 1929, Goldberg practiced law in Chicago, where he gained a national reputation as a labor lawyer. It was said that his love of labor was a labor of love.

During World War II, he served in the Office of Strategic Services as a contact man with the European underground labor movement.

As general counsel of the CIO, Goldberg helped draft the historic agreement merging the AFL and the CIO in 1955. President John F. Kennedy appointed him Secretary of Labor in 1961, and in this post, he succeeded in raising the minimum wage law and federal unemployment benefits. In 1962, President Kennedy named him to the United States Supreme Court to succeed Felix Frankfurter when the latter resigned.

Goldberg left the Supreme Court in 1965 at the insistence

of President Lyndon B. Johnson, who appointed him senior
United States delegate and Ambassador to the United Nations. He resigned this post after serving two years to become
president of the American Jewish Committee. In 1970, Goldberg ran for Governor of New York on the Democratic
ticket, but was defeated by the incumbent, Nelson Rockefeller.

He was appointed by President Jimmy Carter in 1977 as
United States envoy to the Belgrade Conference on Human
Rights.

ABE FORTAS
1910—

On that fateful Friday, November 22, 1963—the day
President John F. Kennedy was assassinated—a call was put
through from Dallas, Texas, to the Washington law firm of
Arnold, Fortas, and Porter. That call, from the new President
of the United States, Lyndon B. Johnson, was to Abe Fortas.
The message was terse: "Abe, stand by!" The President asked
Fortas to be his personal liaison with Mrs. Jacqueline Kennedy. He handled many of the arrangements for the funeral
of the fallen President, and formulated plans for the investigation of the assassination.

Born in Memphis, Tennessee, in 1910, the son of an immigrant cabinet-maker, Fortas received his law degree from
Yale University in 1933 and was appointed to the Yale law
faculty. After serving in a number of New Deal agencies during the Presidency of Franklin D. Roosevelt, he was named
Under Secretary of the Interior in 1942. He was one of the
advisors to the American delegation to the San Francisco
Conference in 1945, which founded the United Nations.

In 1946, Fortas entered private practice. A number of his
criminal cases are considered legal landmarks. He was responsible for the Federal District Court adopting new standards for the criminally insane.

President Johnson appointed Abe Fortas to the United
States Supreme Court in 1965, and in the summer of 1968,
the President nominated him to the post of Chief Justice, to
succeed the retiring Earl Warren. However, before he could
be confirmed by the Senate to this high office, he was forced
to resign on the charge that he had accepted lecture fees

from a charitable foundation while on the bench. He resigned
in May, 1969, and returned to private law practice.

One of President Johnson's closest friends, Fortas wrote a
number of historic decisions while on the Supreme Court
bench.

SCIENCE AND MEDICINE

In the course of the past century, American science, technology, and medicine have revolutionized life to an extent far greater and more significant than any other period in the history of man. This period has seen the advent of the Atomic Age, the age of jets, of satellites lifting man to the moon. It saw the advent of streptomycin and other life-saving and life-giving substances, and the development of an anti-polio vaccine, to mention a few.

While nowhere in the annals of American science are the names of its achievers broken down by religion or race, the American Jewish scientist did play a leading role in these dramatic events. The names of Abraham Jacobi, Albert Sabin, Jonas Salk, Albert Einstein, Selman Waksman, Isidor Rabi, J. Robert Oppenheimer, Edward Teller, Leo Szilard, and many others, were all part of the tremendous expansion of the momentous scientific developments of this period, and they were all primarily second- and third-generation descendants of the Jewish immigrant to America.

Although little of their medical and scientific tradition was inherited, the European scientific climate did produce Freud, Ehrlich, Schick, and Wasserman. For the most part, however, Russian and Polish Jews were limited to the perimeter of the shtetl, where they had to create their own educational facilities through the study of Hebrew and the Talmud.

As they emerged from their status as immigrants in America, they had to overcome the handicap of being latecomers. Many studied nights and worked days for years until they became renowned in their fields.

It is this Jewish exodus from the shtetl and emancipation to the world of freedom that brought forth the remarkable flowering of Jews in American science and medicine.

ISAAC HAYS
1796—1879

Isaac Hays, one of America's early medical pioneers in the field of ophthalmology, was also one of the foremost medical writers of his time and a co-founder of the American Medical Association.

Son of a wealthy Colonial merchant and a nephew of Rebecca Gratz, Hays was graduated from the University of Pennsylvania School of Medicine.

Specializing in the diseases of the eye, he quickly gained recognition for his early studies in the causes and effects of color blindness, and for the perfecting of lenses for the correction of vision impairments.

Turning his attention to writing, Hays became the editor of the *American Journal of the Medical Sciences*, and by broadening its scope, secured the cooperation of researchers throughout the country. The high level of the journal prompted one medical historian to write that if all other medical literature of the period were destroyed, the real contribution of medical science would be preserved in Hays' publication.

While continuing his medical practice, he edited and enlarged upon Sir William Lawrence's *Treatise on Diseases of the Eye*—a work that advanced substantially American knowledge in this field. At the time he was elected president of the Ophthalmological Society of Philadelphia, he was also interested in general science and natural history. It was during this period that he brought out a new edition of Alexander Wilson's *American Ornithology*, revised a basic sourcebook in physics, and published a new edition of *Dictionary of Medical Terms*.

As the study of medicine grew in skill and prestige in the United States, Hays recognized the need for a permanent national organization which would act as a forum for the exchange of ideas and the establishment of standards in the profession. Although he was instrumental in bringing about a national conference in 1847 for this purpose, the idea was rejected. It would take another generation to incorporate his ideas in the charter of the Congress of American Physicians and Surgeons. As a committee chairman, Dr. Hays drafted the ethical principles for the guidance of the membership. In recognition of his tireless efforts as founder and organizer, Hays was elected an officer of the American Medical Association.

His numerous activities in diversified fields brought him recognition in the world of scientific research. Elected a member of the Medical Society of Hamburg, the Université d'Ophthalmologie of Paris, and the American Philosophical Society, he helped organize the Franklin Institute and was president of the Academy of National Science of Philadelphia.

A fellow medical researcher summed up Isaac Hays' career; "The name of Isaac Hays is always associated with that which is well written and worth reading in American medical literature. Handsome, tall, benevolent, a bland and dignified gentleman of the old school, with courteous manners and a warm heart."

SIMON BARUCH
1840—1921

In an issue of *Modern Medicine* in 1903, an article stated ". . . Certainly there is not a man in the medical profession today whose services have been of greater worth than those of Dr. Simon Baruch."

Born in Posen, Germany, in 1840, Baruch emigrated to Camden, South Carolina, at the age of 15. He worked for a time as a clerk in a general store before enrolling in the South Carolina Medical College in Charleston. When the school was closed shortly after the outbreak of the Civil War, he completed his studies at the Medical College of Virginia. He joined the 3rd South Carolina Battalion as an assistant surgeon, and saw his first action in the Second Battle of Manassas. He served throughout the war in General Robert E. Lee's Army of Northern Virginia, with the exception of two intervals when he was taken prisoner while tending the wounded in field hospitals. As a prisoner at Fort Henry, he assisted Union Army doctors in treating their wounded, and it was during this time that he wrote an essay, "Bayonet Wounds of the Chest," which is still the standard authority on the subject.

Following the end of the war, he returned to Camden, where he was to practice medicine for the next 15 years. It was during the difficult years of the Reconstruction period that Baruch briefly became a secret member of General Nathan Forrest's original Ku Klux Klan.

As one of the most prominent doctors in the state, he was elected president of the South Carolina Medical Society and later chairman of the State Board of Health.

In 1881, he moved to New York with his wife and four sons. One son, Bernard, was to attain fame as a wizard of finance and as an adviser to Presidents from Woodrow Wilson to Harry S. Truman. Another son, Herman, was to become Ambassador to the Netherlands and to Portugal.

In New York, Dr. Baruch pioneered in malarial research and diagnostic medicine. He was responsible for the successful surgical treatment of a ruptured appendix. At a meeting of the New York Academy of Medicine in 1894, a colleague reported that "the profession and humanity owe more to Dr. Baruch than to any other man for the development of the surgery of appendicitis."

He devoted his later years to the principles and practice of hydrotherapy—the internal and external medical use of water—and was responsible for the establishment of free municipal bath houses for the indigent in more than 100 cities.

In recognition of his great contributions to physical medicine, the Simon Baruch Research Institute at Saratoga Springs, New York, carries on the research he started in public health and cardiac therapy.

A painting of Simon Baruch at New York University-Bellevue Medical Center pays tribute to his memory with the inscription: "Simon Baruch, father of physical medicine, a great humanitarian."

EMILE BERLINER
1851—1929

Largely forgotten and unsung, Emile Berliner was the inventor of the microphone and developer of a transmitter which made Alexander Graham Bell's telephone possible.

Born in 1851 in Hanover, Germany, Berliner had to end his formal education at the age of 14 to help his father support the large family of 11 children. Starting as a printer's devil, he then became a clerk in a dry goods store. There, while handling fabrics, he constructed a weaving machine, although he had never had any scientific training.

Hanover in 1866 was taken over by the militaristic state of Prussia, and when a visiting family friend from America offered Berliner a job, he eagerly accepted the opportunity to emigrate. After clerking in a men's furnishing store in Washington, D.C., and then working at odd jobs in various parts of the country, he came to New York, where he found work analyzing sugar in the laboratory which subsequently discovered the method of manufacturing saccharin out of coal tar. His evenings, spent in the scientific library of Cooper Union which had collections of material on acoustics and electricity, were to become the great influence of his life.

Berliner, intrigued by the idea of the telephone, grappled with the shortcomings of Alexander Graham Bell's invention. In its early, primitive stage in 1876, the telephone was hardly more than a device largely used by neighbors for talking to each other through the walls of their apartments.

By experimenting in the bedroom of his boarding house, Berliner invented two improvements which transformed the telephone into a practical device with vast commercial potential. The first was a microphone, which was capable of receiving and transmitting the voice through a wire; the second was a transformer to prevent the sound from fading out. When an agent for the struggling new enterprise, the Bell Telephone Company, saw a demonstration of Berliner's invention, they negotiated and acquired his patent, and he was appointed to an important research job with the company.

Berliner now turned his attention to the talking machine. Thomas Alva Edison had experimented with phonographs and was marketing soft wax cylinders which crudely reproduced the human voice. Discarding Edison's early method, Berliner invented the flat disk, which moved a reproducing needle in a groove of even depth and turning direction. The disk, which was made of a composition of hardened rubber, could be mass-produced cheaply. Berliner's gramophone was later developed into the Victor Talking Machine, which was to provide cheap home entertainment and pleasure to the entire world.

Berliner applied his scientific talent to medical research when his infant daughter almost died of an intestinal disorder. With an awesome infant mortality of 300 out of 1,000 infants in the closing years of the nineteenth century, he was convinced that such diseases as typhoid fever, scarlet fever, and diphtheria were caused by the ingestion of raw milk.

Organizing the Society for the Prevention of Sickness, Berliner started a widespread campaign to urge the public to scald milk before use. Due to his tireless efforts, the Department of Agriculture formulated milk standards in 1907, and the pasteurization of milk received Federal endorsement despite the skepticism of the medical profession.

Until his death in 1929, Berliner continued his scientific work in acoustics and the motion picture projector, and together with his son, Henry, designed three different models for helicopters which made successful flights from 1919 to 1926.

In a testimonial to Berliner on his 75th birthday, the speaker noted, "But for him, scientific facts might have remained unnoticed for a long time."

JOSEPH GOLDBERGER
1874—1929

Joseph Goldberger, a medical researcher, was the father of the science of nutrition.

Born in Austria in 1874, he came to the United States at the age of six. He was graduated from Bellevue Medical College in New York City and joined the United States Public Health Service, specializing in preventive medicine, infectious diseases, and nutrition.

In the course of his research on pellagra, a disease prevalent in the South at the turn of the century, he demonstrated with volunteer prisoners that the disease was not contagious, as had previously been assumed, and that the cause was due to a nutritional deficiency in niacin.

Dr. Goldberger continued his research in yellow fever, typhoid, typhus, malaria, and diphtheria—at times experimenting on himself.

His major contribution, however, was in the field of nutrition. More than anyone else, he laid the basis for the science of nutrition, calling for a balanced diet for the preservation of health.

SIMON FLEXNER
1863—1946

At the time Simon Flexner became director of the Rockefeller Institute for Medical Research, he had already achieved world fame as a pathologist.

Born in Louisville, Kentucky, in 1863, the son of a Bohemian immigrant, Flexner received his medical degree in 1889 at the University of Louisville.

Following the ceding of the Philippines to the United States at the end of the Spanish-American War in 1899, Flexner was sent there to report on the medical conditions of the area. On the journey out, he also studied a form of the plague which was then virulent in Hong Kong, and from Manila brought back cultures of an active form of dysentery—now known as the "Flexner" type of dysentery bacillus.

On this return, he was appointed to a professorship of pathology at the University of Pennsylvania. He had barely begun his duties at the university when he was asked by government health officials to investigate reports of cases of the plague in San Francisco. Confirming these cases, he was able to promptly isolate them and set up a successful program for the extermination of the rat infestation causing it.

On the establishment of the Rockefeller Institute for Medical Research in 1901, Dr. Flexner was invited to join, not only as a director of the laboratory but also as an active researcher. The following year, when an epidemic of fatal cerebrospinal meningitis swept New York, Dr. Flexner conducted experiments inoculating its causative bacterium into animals, developing a serum which retarded the progress of the disease and in many cases cured it. This serum was used for more than three decades until the advent of sulfa drugs.

When the National Research Council initiated their fellowships in the physical and biological sciences, the plans for this program were developed by Flexner. He was a member of a commission organized by the Rockefeller Foundation to establish the Peking Union Medical College. When the group returned from China in 1915, Flexner said, "We must create the Johns Hopkins of China. We must give superior medicine to China."

He served the Rockefeller Institute from 1903 to 1935, the last fifteen years as its director, and was Eastman professor at Oxford University.

Though he is best known for his experimental work in epidemiology, he was also one of the early pioneer researchers in the causes and cure of poliomyelitis.

The Armed Forces Medical Museum in Washington, D.C., has an extensive collection of material relating to the medical contributions of Flexner. At the Smithsonian Institution's Hall of Medical Sciences Bacteriological Research Laboratory, there is a portrait of Simon Flexner, his microscope, and other articles used in his experiments.

Simon's brother Abraham was another distinguished member of the Flexner family. A graduate of Johns Hopkins University, he was a member of the Carnegie Foundation. Known as the "father of modern medical education," he wrote the report which hastened much-needed reforms in the standards, organization, and curriculum of medical schools. He was also a director of the Institute for Advanced Study at Princeton, New Jersey, from 1930 to 1939.

Another brother, Bernard, was a distinguished lawyer and a member of the American Red Cross mission to Rumania. A Zionist, he was the first president of the Palestine Economic Corporation when it was organized in 1925.

JULIUS ROBERT OPPENHEIMER
1904—1967

J. Robert Oppenheimer, one of the world's great physicists, was to become head of America's successful ultra-secret atomic bomb project during World War II, only to be then denied access to all classified documents as a security risk— all within the span of eleven years.

Born in New York City in 1904, the son of a prominent businessman, Oppenheimer was graduated from Harvard in 1925. He continued his research in physics at Cambridge University, and received his Ph.D. from the University of Göttingen, Germany, in 1927. He was a member of the faculties of the University of California and California Institute of Technology until 1942.

He was appointed director of the atomic energy research project at Los Alamos, New Mexico, in 1942, where he made important contributions to the development of atomic energy for military purposes.

Following the use of the atomic bomb against Japan, Oppenheimer became one of the foremost proponents of civilian and international control of atomic energy. The success of the Los Alamos project filled him with despair. "In some crude sense," he said after the war, "which no vulgarity, no humor, no overstatement can quite extinguish, the physicists have known sin, and this is a knowledge which they cannot lose."

Named chairman of the General Advisory Committee of the Atomic Energy Commission, Oppenheimer continued to influence policy. He strongly opposed the development of the H-bomb on "moral" grounds and became embroiled in a controversy with scientist Edward Teller and Lewis Strauss, Chairman of the Atomic Energy Commission; this resulted in his suspension from the Atomic Energy Commission as a security risk. The case stirred wide controversy, with the right-wing press denouncing him as a villain, and the liberal press calling him a martyr to the hysteria of the Cold War period.

Notwithstanding all this controversy, he was the recipient of one of government's highest awards, the Fermi Award, in 1963, for his contribution to nuclear research. On receiving the award, he said, "Most of us look to the good opinion of our colleagues and our government. I am no exception."

At the time of his death in 1967, he was director of the Institute for Advanced Study at Princeton, New Jersey.

CASIMIR FUNK
1884-1967

One of the great biochemists of the twentieth century, Casimir Funk, born in Poland in 1884, was the discoverer of vitamins.

Receiving his Ph.D. in 1904 at the University of Bern, Switzerland, Funk worked for a time at the famous Lister Institute in England, named for the British surgeon who brought the principle of antisepsis to surgery.

Funk came to the United States in 1915, and while working on a cure for beriberi, a degenerative disease of the nervous and digestive systems, he discovered that a compound derived from yeast was useful in the cure of this disease. He believed that the compound belonged to the amines class of chemicals and added the Latin word for life, *vita.*

When his paper was published in 1912 on vitamin deficiency diseases such as scurvy, pellagra, and rickets, it stirred wide international medical interest. He was able to identify the existence of Vitamins B1, B2, C, and D. His later research contributed greatly to the knowledge of the hormones of the pituitary and sex glands.

JONAS EDWARD SALK
1914—

Born in New York City in 1914, the son of a garment center worker, Jonas Salk was to become not only one of the nation's most celebrated medical researchers, but was to rid the world of poliomyelitis.

Salk studied medicine at New York University and commenced his medical research at the University of Michigan, where he experimented with influenza vaccines. In 1947, he joined the staff of the University of Pittsburgh, and it was as the director of the Virus Research Laboratory of the School of Medicine that he began his research in developing an anti-polio vaccine.

In 1955, after a six-year battle against "the crippler," the quiet researcher dramatically announced, "The vaccine works." The publicity-shy scientist became a hero, and the world rejoiced. When asked who owned the vaccine's patent, he quietly replied, "The people . . . Could you patent the sun?"

He continues his research in virus-related diseases at the Salk Institute in La Jolla, California.

He was the recipient of the Presidential Medal of Freedom in 1977.

BUSINESS AND BANKING

When Barnard Gratz, a Jewish merchant in Philadelphia, wrote to his brother in London in 1758, he specified the conditions for success in the Colonies: "This place requires honesty, industry, good nature, and no pride."

The early Jewish settlers of the seventeenth century earned their livelihood chiefly as fur traders and butchers. By 1700, Jewish merchants were beginning to make their influence felt in all of the Colonies where they were pioneers, and in ocean and coastal shipping. Hayman Levy was a leading merchant in Colonial New York. Newport merchants were a leading factor in whale oil and candle-making enterprises. Jacob Franks was chief purveyor of goods to the British forces during the French and Indian Wars, and Isaac Moses owned ships that plied the American coast from Montreal to Savannah. Moses and Samson Simson, shipowners, were among the founders of the New York Chamber of Commerce in 1768. Ephraim Hart helped charter the Stockbrokers Guild in 1792 which later became the New York Stock Exchange.

At the time of the Jewish immigration from Germany and Poland in the late 1820's, most of the old-line Jewish families in New York, Philadelphia, Richmond, and Charleston, were engaged in retail business, manufacturing, the professions, and as artisans. The new immigrants who were not artisans or professionals turned overwhelmingly to petty trade and peddling. These risk-taking backpack peddlers, who played a considerable part in the opening of the West, were to become the founders of great mercantile and industrial enterprises.

From peddling it was an easy step to retailing, importing, wholesaling, and manufacturing, and then into real estate, banking, and industry in the expanding economy

167

of the post-Civil War period. Some of the best-known Jewish names in business and banking to emerge during this time—Lehman, Guggenheim, Filene, Seligman, Straus, Altman—started modestly as peddlers.

When the massive movement of East European immigration began in the 1880's. German Jews already dominated the men's clothing and tobacco industries, and had major footholds in whisky distilling, home furnishings, furs and leather goods. They were also widely represented in the women's ready-to-wear field as it began to replace custom and home-made apparel.

Although many of the early immigrants from Russia and Poland found employment in the clothing industry, some were artisans who were able to work as carpenters, painters, glazers, and plumbers. A far smaller proportion of these post-1880 immigrants took to peddling than was the case among their German predecessors, because the changing economy had narrowed the market for their wares. Some, however, did become pushcart peddlers, converting large Jewish areas of the major cities into street bazaars.

The thrifty sweatshop worker, peddler, junk dealer, and petty tradesman pyramided tiny accumulations of capital into successful clothing manufacturing, real estate, and mercantile businesses. By 1917, Jews were well established in the printing, paper products, watchmaking, and millinery industries, and in the 1930's they were preeminent in such new business areas as rubber products, plastics, electronics, steel, and construction. In almost every major city Jews were, and still are, prominent in the building of residential housing and commercial structures.

Until the late 1960's and 1970's, Jews were rare in the executive suites of corporate American business and industry, but of late, more and more leading companies have Jewish executives in top positions. The appointment of Irving Shapiro as chairman of the board of the Dupont Company, and later as head of the prestigious Business Round Table, indicated that the American Jew had finally arrived in the upper precincts of American business.

JOSEPH SELIGMAN
1820—1880

Horatio Alger may well have gotten his inspiration for his "rags to riches" books while employed as a tutor in the home of Joseph Seligman, a penniless immigrant who struggled against adversity to gain honor and wealth.

A steerage passenger to America from Bavaria, Seligman arrived at the height of the Great Depression of 1837. Working as a peddler, he gained a reputation for honesty and ambition, and was soon able to send for his seven younger brothers—William, James, Jesse, Henry, Leopold, Abraham, and Isaac. With hard work and enormous energy, they opened dry goods stores in Lancaster, Pennsylvania, Greensboro, Alabama, and Watertown, New York. It was at Watertown that Jesse and Henry became personal friends of Ulysses S. Grant, a young lieutenant stationed at Sackett's Harbor.

During the Gold Rush of 1848, Jesse and William went to California, where they were very successful in a clothing business when their brick building was the only one to escape destruction during the great 1851 fire in San Francisco. Never involved directly in prospecting for gold, they nevertheless made a fortune by steady hard work and a reputation for dealing fairly with the miners. Respected members of the community, they joined the Vigilantes to combat the lawlessness of the city and were members of the volunteer fire brigade. When Grant was sent to the city to quell the violence, the brothers had the opportunity of renewing their friendship with the future President.

When the brothers returned to New York in 1857, they joined with Joseph Seligman in establishing the banking house of J. & W. Seligman, although they continued operating their clothing business. When mass recruitment commenced at the outbreak of the Civil War, the Seligmans became one of the largest clothing suppliers of the Union army. In a demonstration of their patriotism, they extended $1 million in credit to the beleaguered government. Joseph Seligman, however, is best remembered during this period of American history for his ability to sell $200 million in United States bonds to Germany at a time when French and British financial institutions favored the Confederate states. The well-known historian,

169

W.E. Dodd, stated that the accomplishment of Seligman in floating this loan was as helpful toward winning the war as the Battle of Gettysburg.

Prominent in the Capital during the war, Joseph was instrumental in persuading President Lincoln to appoint General Grant commander-in-chief of the Union army. When Grant was elected President, he offered Joseph Seligman the post of Secretary of the Treasury, but he declined. It was through the Seligmans' efforts that Congress voted a pension for the widow of Abraham Lincoln after she was found to be living in poverty in Germany.

Joseph Seligman's firm stand on Jewish rights is part of the history of the struggle for equality. When he was refused accommodations at the fashionable Grand Union Hotel in Saratoga Springs, New York, on the grounds that the new owner, Judge Henry Hilton, did not welcome "Israelites," the incident created a sensation in the press. The Reverend Dr. Henry Ward Beecher denounced this act of anti-Semitism from his pulpit in 1877 in his famous sermon, "Jew and Gentile."

Prominent in the Republican party, Joseph Seligman was elected vice-president of the famed Union League Club. Once president of New York's Temple Emanu-El and a founder of the New York Hebrew Orphan Asylum, he was one of the chief supporters of Felix Adler's Society for Ethical Culture. He took the lead in mobilizing public opinion against the Rumanian persecution of Jews in 1870 and persuaded President Grant to appoint Benjamin Peixotto as United States Consul-General to Rumania, a special emissary charged with studying the status of persecuted Jews and with bringing them aid.

The Seligman firm was one of the first to espouse a waterway to connect the coasts of the United States, and to this end headed an American syndicate to take over the ill-fated De Lesseps Company, which originally conceived the idea of the Panama Canal.

The town of Seligman, Montana, founded in 1881, honors Joseph Seligman, whose company financed a branch line of the main railroad in this area. In 1884, Mrs. Joseph Seligman donated a fund toward the construction of the town's Union Church.

When Joseph Seligman died in 1880 at the age of 60, he

was not only one of the country's leading financiers and men of affairs, he was one of the most eminent Jews in America.

DAVID LUBIN
1849—1919

When David Lubin died in Rome on January 1, 1919, a colleague wrote:

> . . . He was the father of the "first" League of Nations, a League that held fast through the period of the World War . . . The one tie that held through the military conflicts and darkness of the war, was the force brought into existence under the leadership of this great California Jew.

Lubin, born in Klodowa, Poland in 1849, came to the United States with his family in 1853, following a Czarist pogrom in the town. After attending school until the age of 12, he was employed as a gold plate polisher, and for the next ten years worked at odd jobs across the country as a lumberjack, salesman, gold prospector, and merchant. In Sacramento, California, he established the first "one price" general store in western America.

In 1884, Lubin went to Palestine—a trip which was to have a profound effect on his life. In the Holy Land, his observations led him to conceive of the small land-owning farmer as the basic factor in a democracy. Following his stay abroad, he was to make his life's mission the preaching of the idea that the world's regeneration would come through agriculture. On his return, he bought a farm in California and set out to master the subject of agrarian economics.

In applying the same native shrewdness and good judgment that had gained him success as a merchant, Lubin soon became an expert wheat farmer and fruit grower. He organized the Fruit Growers Convention which established one of the first western farm cooperatives, and led the Convention's fight against prohibitive freight rates. He convinced the railroads that lower rates would bring greater revenues through increased tonnage and wider markets. The Convention which he had created led to the founding of the California Fruit Growers' Exchange, which opened a new chapter in the economic history of the West as well as in the marketing of farm produce.

As a wheat grower, Lubin found that ocean freights and tariffs maintained prices of grain artificially, and that over-production could ruin farmers in one country while crop failures caused starvation in others. He proposed a government subsidy in the form of a bounty on agricultural exports which would reduce shipping costs on farm products sent abroad and equalize the protection enjoyed by industry. He stumped the country in behalf of his bounty plan which became known as "Lubinism," and it became a national issue in the political battle of 1896. Though a bill was introduced in Congress, the legislature was defeated. Parts of "Lubinism," however, were to be adopted in New Deal legislation during Franklin D. Roosevelt's administration.

Undaunted, Lubin, the ardent crusader for farmers, turned his attention to the international agricultural scene. Obsessed with the idea that farmers needed a world chamber of agriculture, Lubin urged the United States to lead the way in bringing agricultural nations together in an effort to solve global food supply problems. His innovative plan was turned down by every country with the exception of Italy. He received an invitation from King Victor Emmanuel III to meet with his ministers to develop a program for the organization. Three months later, royal authority was given to invite representatives of various governments to form an international body—nonpolitical in its aim—to gather essential agricultural information and promote trade in agricultural products.

On May 25, 1905, representatives of 40 countries met in Rome and formed the International Institute of Agriculture, which was later to be merged with the United Nations Food and Agricultural Organization. In 1906, the United States joined, and President Theodore Roosevelt appointed David Lubin as its first representative. In 1908, when the Institute moved to its permanent headquarters in a beautiful building donated by King Victor Emmanuel, Lubin was named director and served in this capacity until his death 11 years later.

Samuel Gompers, in paying tribute to Lubin in his autobiography *Seventy Years of Life and Labor*, wrote, "Lubin insisted upon forcing on all with whom he came in contact his pride in his Jewish ancestry. He stated upon any and all occasions that it was his greatest glory that he was a Jew."

In 1936, the city of Rome paid posthumous honor to this

practical visionary by dedicating a street to him—the Via David Lubin.

PAUL M. WARBURG
1868—1932

Paul Warburg, a name famous in banking and philanthropy, was the founder of the Federal Reserve System.

Born in Hamburg, Germany in 1868, he was graduated from gymnasium at 18 and went to work at the family banking house of M.M. Warburg. After spending several years in the financial centers of England and France, he returned home with his wife, the daughter of Solomon Loeb of Kuhn, Loeb & Co., to become a partner in the family firm. When he was offered a partnership in his father-in-law's company, the Warburgs settled in New York.

As a member of the Kuhn, Loeb firm, Warburg, together with E.H. Harriman, took part in the reorganization of the Union Pacific Railroad. When Senator Nelson Aldrich headed a commission to recommend legislation aimed at controlling bank manipulations and stock speculators, he sought help from Warburg, who had gained a reputation for sound banking practices. Warburg reported on the precarious condition of over 20,000 state, national, and private banks which operated independently without supervision.

Based on his report to the commission, Aldrich introduced a bill to establish a large privately owned central bank with 15 branches. The bill, however, was defeated by a Democratic-controlled Congress, which opposed this centralization. Warburg was to continue his campaign for a central bank, which he compared to such successful institutions as the Bank of England and the Banque de France, until 1913, when the Glass-Owen Federal Reserve Act was passed. Its preamble reflected most of Warburg's recommendations:

> To provide for the establishment of Federal Reserve Banks, to furnish an elastic currency, to afford means of rediscounting commercial paper, to establish a more effective supervision of banking in the United States.

The vision that Warburg had brought to fruition was to provide a powerful commission which was able to cope with the nation's unprecedented monetary demands during World War I. In recognition of Warburg's services in drafting the

Act, President Woodrow Wilson named him a member of the
first Federal Reserve Board in 1914, and he served the Board
in other capacities until 1926.

When Warburg returned to private life, he devoted his time
to philanthropic and cultural institutions, among them the
Tuskegee Institute, the Juilliard School of Music, the National
Child Labor Committee, and the Academy of Political
Science.

On his death in 1932, *The Nation* published the following
eulogy:

> No one in a similar influential position excelled Mr.
> Warburg in his feeling of responsibility to the public.
> Never was there a man who recognized more keenly the
> principle that wealth, like nobility, obliges. His generos-
> ity was without stint . . . A patron of the arts, he never
> ceased to do what he could to advance the cultural de-
> velopment of the United States . . . A leader among
> American Jews, it can truthfully be said of him that he
> set for his race in America an unsurpassable example of
> public service.

DAVID SARNOFF
1891—1971

David Sarnoff, who couldn't read the newspapers he
peddled as a boy on the Lower East Side in New York City,
rose to become head of one of the largest radio and television
corporations in the world.

Born in Russia in 1891, he came to the United States at
the age of nine. As was the custom among newly arrived immigrants, he was sent out on the streets to peddle newspapers
to help supplement the family's meager income. At 15, he
had to quit formal school when his father died, going to work
at such part-time jobs as butcher boy or delivery boy; he also
sang in a synagogue choir and attended classes at the Educational Alliance—the famous pioneer Jewish Community
Center and Settlement House which helped Americanize
three generations of immigrants.

While working as a clerk at the American Marconi
Corporation, Sarnoff bought a telegraph key and taught himself the Morse Code. He worked directly with Marconi, developer of wireless telegraphy, who patiently taught him the
"theory of the propagation of electromagnetic waves!" In

1912 he became a wireless operator at a new radio station in New York, where he made radio history by picking up the first shocking message from the *SS Titanic*: "Ran into an iceberg, sinking fast." Sarnoff stayed on duty for 72 hours without sleep to keep the world up-to-date on news of the tragedy. President William Taft ordered all other stations off the air so that the messages could be clearly interpreted by Sarnoff. Rescue efforts were coordinated with the aid of his wireless.

He rose quickly in the company, and when it was absorbed by RCA in 1919, he became general manager and, in 1930, its president.

His early belief in the development of a radio as a household essential and his commitment to the possibility of successful research in a radio which could also see as well as hear—television—attest to his preeminent leadership and genius in the field of communications. As a result of Sarnoff's efforts, there were other major electronic developments which played an important role during World War II.

He held a commission of Brigadier-General during the war and was responsible for organizing the intricate communications system of General Dwight D. Eisenhower's headquarters. He was awarded the Legion of Merit for his wartime service.

When interviewed about the failure of RCA's efforts in the color television field and in data processing, he said he had his share of garlands and garbage, but he never let the garbage obscure his vision.

Known as "the General," David Sarnoff died in 1971 at the age of 80.

PHILANTHROPISTS

Historically, detractors of Jews have always decried the Jews' ability to make money. Seldom have these critics pointed out their immeasurable generosity once they made it. Nor has it been noted that such a relatively small community in a vast country has made such tremendous financial contributions to those in need.

The immigrant Jews came with little and found refuge from persecution. When they were no longer uncertain about their acceptance in the new land, they set about working for economic security. As their fortunes grew, they simultaneously began to carry out the biblical precepts of charity, benevolence, and social responsibility. Wealth was not exclusively for self-gratification. It was to be put to use for the less fortunate. Their philanthropy was always relevant, as they responded to every plea and petition when disasters, famines, and especially the persecutions of other Jews called on their resources.

At the turn of the century, when it became mainly the burden of American Jewry to care for the refugees from the excesses of the Czar, they responded with a dedication that has seldom been paralleled. When the State of Israel came into being, they gave lavishly with unprecedented magnitude.

Those remarkable families—the Schiffs, Warburgs, Lehmans, Strauses, Rosenwalds, Hirshhorns, Guggenheims—who brought new meaning to the word "philanthropy," left lasting memorials to the splendor of giving.

JUDAH TOURO
1765—1854

Bunker Hill Monument in Boston, one of America's hallowed shrines, would never have been completed but for the generosity of Judah Touro.

From the time General Lafayette laid the cornerstone in 1825 until 1840, the monument remained unfinished due to lack of funds. A Boston merchant, Amos Lawrence, agreed to donate $10,000 if another citizen could be found to match his offer. Half a continent away, in New Orleans, Judah Touro, remembering his happy days in Boston, sent a matching check for the completion of the monument.

At the dedication on June 17, 1843, President John Tyler, Daniel Webster, and Oliver Wendell Holmes paid tribute to Touro. Webster and several others, including ex-President John Quincy Adams, were commissioned to prepare an inscription for a plaque on the monument. A verse read at Faneuil Hall marking the dedication is part of the American epic:

Amos and Judah—venerated names,
Patriarch and prophet, press their equal claims,
Less generous coursers, running neck and neck,
Each aids the work by giving it a check.
Christian and Jew, they carry out one plan,
For though of different faiths, each in heart a man.

When Judah Touro arrived in New Orleans in 1802, he found a number of Jews living there, among them Ezekiel Salomon, son of Revolutionary patriot Haym Salomon. Prior to that time, the Black Code of 1724 excluded Jews from the entire territory and banned the practice of Judaism there, although some Jews who were involved in trade were tolerated.

Touro came from Boston just before New Orleans was ceded by Spain to France. Son of the prominent Dutch-born minister of the famous Rhode Island Synagogue, Isaac Touro, he prospered in brokerage and shipping under American rule after 1803.

Touro expanded his fortune in real estate, and was a leader in the civic affairs of the city. Badly wounded during the Battle of New Orleans during the War of 1812, his heroism and zeal was described by General Andrew Jackson in his book *Narrative of the Defense of New Orleans.*

One of America's earliest and most generous philanthropists, he gave away $500,000, an enormous sum in his time, to Jewish and non-Jewish causes in various parts of the world. A great cultural influence in early New Orleans, Touro founded the Touro Free Library, the first public library in the country.

When he died in 1854, *The Bee,* the leading newspaper of New Orleans, reported that Judah Touro's funeral was "the largest assemblage of citizens we have ever beheld . . . the funeral train was immense, almost every carriage in the city being filled."

His obituary read, "In death, Touro became what he had never been nor ever wanted to be in life—a local and national hero, a leader of men, a dignitary, a man of inspiring presence, an exemplary Jewish philanthropist."

In his will he left bequests to orphan homes, Christian welfare agencies, churches, a new alms house, property for a new hospital, relief for Jews overseas, and sums to 17 Jewish congregations throughout the United States.

Originally buried in the Dispersed of Judah Cemetery in New Orleans, Touro's remains were removed to the Old Jewish Cemetery in Newport, Rhode Island, one of the oldest Jewish burial grounds in the United States. This cemetery and the Touro Synagogue, founded in 1658, are part of the early history of Rhode Island. In 1947 the synagogue became the only Jewish house of worship to become a national historic shrine.

MEYER GUGGENHEIM
1828—1905

Meyer Guggenheim, a Swiss immigrant, parlayed an investment of $25,000 in two supposedly worn-out silver and lead mines in Colorado into one of America's largest fortunes. From this modest beginning, Guggenheim and his seven sons became the mining and smelting kings of Colorado and later extended their "empire" to South America, Africa, and Canada.

Born in Langnau, Switzerland, in 1828, Guggenheim came to America in 1847 with his father, Simon, and the family. Settling in Philadelphia, father and son became peddlers, with

Meyer specializing in polish for iron stoves. Realizing that the manufacturer made sizeable profits on his product while he earned pennies, Meyer developed his own formula, which brought sufficient earnings to enable him to expand into various other items and to give up the backpack for a horse and wagon.

Meyer, now married, with a growing family of his own, constantly sought new sources of income. When he gained sole distributorship of an English caustic alkali which was cheaper than the lye used in the manufacture of soap, a large salt company bought him out. He was also successful when he extended his interest to the complexities of the stock and bond market.

When lace and embroideries became very popular in America, Guggenheim sent three of his sons to Switzerland to learn the manufacture and marketing of this product. He might have remained in this profitable business had it not been for an incident which ultimately catapulted the lace merchants into one of America's wealthiest families.

Charles Graham, a Pennsylvania speculator urgently in need of money to further an investment in a silver and lead mine in Colorado, asked Meyer Guggenheim for a loan. Graham described the mine's potential in such glowing terms that Meyer agreed to the loan in exchange for a partnership in the mining venture.

When Guggenheim went to Leadville, Colorado, all that could be seen of the mine was a deep shaft filled with water. The mine's engineer assured him that with sufficient capital a big strike could be made if he could pump the water and hire miners to continue digging. Guggenheim returned to Philadelphia consumed with doubt and grew more skeptical with each telegram demanding more money for operational costs. At a time when he was determined not to cast more money down the shaft, a telegram arrived announcing, "Rich strike—15 ounces silver—60 percent lead." After computing what the mine could produce a day, he knew he had achieved great wealth. Guggenheim, however, was to learn that the profits were in the smelting of the ore, rather than in mining. Undaunted, he organized and built his own smelting plant.

No longer lace merchants, the Guggenheim family, now numbering seven sons and three daughters, devoted their energies to the mine, with Daniel Guggenheim assuming directorship as his father gradually retired from active participation. When the American Smelting and Refining Company was formed by the Rockefellers and H. H. Rogers, the Guggenheims were invited to join. Guggenheim, disapproving of his family becoming part of a large corporation, opposed any merger, opting to remain independent. With astute management and a relatively good relationship with labor, they were able to outmaneuver their competitors. In 1901, the Guggenheims assumed control of American Smelting and Refining Company, receiving a majority of stock valued at $45 million.

Within a generation, the Guggenheims controlled much of the precious metals and ores in the world. They extended their holdings from the tin mines in Bolivia to the gold lodes of the Yukon territory. At the invitation of King Leopold II of Belgium, they became his partners in the diamond fields in southern Africa. Always enlarging their interests, they extracted nitrates in Chile and ran rubber plantations in the Belgian Congo. Such giant enterprises as Kennecott Copper Corporation, Nevada Consolidated, the Esperanza Gold Mine in Mexico, and the Chile Copper Company were launched by them.

When Meyer Guggenheim died in 1905 at the age of 77, he had only been in the mining business 17 years. In that short time span, the Guggenheim family had become one of the richest in the United States.

When World War I started in 1914, the Guggenheim enterprises were the primary source of essential metals for the Allies, and later to their own country. When America entered the war in 1917, the family was represented in the armed forces and on boards and committees which initiated policies and programs in the war areas and the home front.

The sons, with a deep sense of responsibility of wealth, distinguished themselves as benefactors in many areas. Solomon established a foundation to increase public appreciation of art. He donated the Solomon R. Guggenheim Museum in New York City and its controversial Frank Lloyd Wright building, together with a valuable collection of nonobjective art. Simon was elected to the Senate from the state of Colorado, but served only one term. In memory of his son, he established the $10 million John Simon Guggenheim Memorial Foundation, which since 1940 has given thousands of fellowships to artists, writers, scholars, and scientists. Daniel's field of philanthropy was aeronautics. He established a number of schools in this field throughout the country. It was at the Guggenheim residence, Hempstead House, in Sands Point, New York, that Charles A. Lindbergh found refuge after his historic flight in 1927. Daniel's son, Harry, was one of the chief supporters of the rocket and astronautic experiments of Dr. Robert Goddard.

JACOB HENRY SCHIFF
1847—1920

Although Jacob Schiff was one of the nation's most powerful and influential bankers, he was also one of its greatest philanthropists.

Jacob Henry Schiff was born in 1847 in Frankfurt, Germany, to a learned family which traced their ancestry back to the fourteenth century. At the age of 17, he left his religious school studies to enter the business world. Emigrating to the United States in 1865, he secured a job as a clerk with a brokerage house. Within two years, he had a sufficient knowledge of the field to open his own firm. At 28, he was invited to join the large international banking firm of Kuhn, Loeb & Company. This affiliation was the beginning of Schiff's astounding career as an innovative financier who was to spur the rapid development of the country's growth and industry in the post-Civil War period.

At 38, when Schiff became head of Kuhn, Loeb, he was to commit the resources and power of his firm to the vision he had of America. He backed the building of the great national railroad systems which became a major factor in opening vast areas of the West to settlement, commerce, and agriculture. In 1906, after his firm helped float loans to Japan totaling $400 million, he became the first private westerner to be received by the Emperor.

Deeply stirred by the Czar's pogroms against the Jews, Schiff consistently refused to extend urgently needed loans to Russia. In 1911, during the Taft Administration, he headed a successful private and Congressional effort to have the commercial treaty between the United States and Russia abrogated because of that country's discrimination against Jews holding American passports.

Though renowned in the financial world, it is for his bountiful philanthropies and his hopes for America that Jacob Schiff is known. His charities were extended to all. His gifts to the Knights of Columbus, the Red Cross, the Salvation Army, and the YMCAs were magnanimous. The benefactor of scores of educational institutions, he presented Harvard University with the Semitic Library and Museum for the study of ancient and modern civilizations of the Near East.

Intensely involved in health care and social work, Schiff supported the Montefiore Home and Hospital. Visiting weekly, he knew many of the patients personally. Lillian Wald and her new creative ideas in social work captured his attention, and his large contributions made possible the great traditions of the Henry Street Settlement House.

A devout Jew, Schiff was concerned about the survival of Judaism amid the upheavals of the Czarist pogroms in Russia and the religious schisms brought about by the Reform movement in America. To these ends he raised $1,500,000 for aid to the victims of the Kishnev pogrom of 1903. Among the many institutions he helped found were: The Jewis. Theological Seminary of America; the Industrial Removal Office, which assisted in the settlement of new immigrants; the YMHA in New York; the Hebrew Union College; the Jewish Publication Society; the National Jewish Welfare Board; and the American Jewish Committee.

In 1897, the New York Public Library was the recipient of a large gift from Schiff for the purchase of Semitic literature, which later became the famed Jewish Division of the Library.

To the Library of Congress, he gave one of the world's great collections of Hebraic books, manuscripts, documents, and pamphlets. Although the Library had been collecting works in Semitic languages from its inception in 1800, it was not until 1914 that a separate Hebraic section was established by an Act of Congress. Schiff's original gift consisted of nearly 20,000 books, which he later enlarged with 10,000 additional volumes.

A leader of American Jewry with great pride in his heritage, Jacob Henry Schiff died in 1920 at the age of 73. He left an unparalleled record of generosity and civic leadership. Many of the institutions which are thriving today owe their existence or their establishment to his philanthropy.

NATHAN STRAUS
1848—1931

Nathan Straus was one of the three illustrious and remarkable sons of Lazarus Straus of Talbotton, Georgia. Impoverished by the Civil War, Lazarus moved his family to New York, where he launched the business that ultimately became R. H. Macy's. His son Oscar, a lawyer by profession, was appointed U.S. Minister to Turkey in 1887 by President Grover Cleveland, and was the first Jewish member of a Presidential Cabinet, Secretary of Commerce and Labor, during Theodore Roosevelt's administration. His other son, Isidor, was to become a noted philanthropist who lost his life in the sinking of the *Titanic*.

Nathan Straus, a businessman and philanthropist, had an abiding interest in public health. After attending a convention in Europe where Louis Pasteur, the famed French bacteriologist, demonstrated a process of treating milk with heat to kill harmful bacteria—a process which bears his name, pasteurization—Straus returned home and in 1892 launched the first movement in America to provide pasteurized milk for the poor.

The Straus Milk Fund established over 300 milk stations in 36 American cities and eventually was credited with saving the lives of thousands of infants. In addition to milk depots for needy children, Straus organized and sponsored tuberculosis prevention centers to stem the disease caused largely by milk from infected cows. During the panic of 1893-94, he initiated a chain of groceries to distribute coal and food to the needy, and later served as president of the New York Board of Health.

Deeply interested in Palestine, he became a Zionist after a visit there and founded the Pasteur Institute, a health center, and food stations which ministered to the needs of Jews and Arabs.

President William Taft summed up Nathan Straus' life when he said, "Nathan Straus is a great Jew and the greatest Christian of us all."

JULIUS ROSENWALD
1862—1932

Julius Rosenwald's fame rests not on the accumulation of one of America's great fortunes, but on the giving away of much of his wealth for the benefit of mankind through conceived acts of generosity.

A self-made man of humble beginnings, Rosenwald left his native Springfield, Illinois, when he was 17, for a clothing salesman's job in New York. In 1885 he settled in Chicago as a salesman. One of his accounts was an up-and-coming mail order house, Sears, Roebuck & Co. In little more than a decade, he bought out the founders.

Rosenwald sought to aid groups and masses rather than individuals. He gave away $63 million—most of it placed strategically where it created maximum public benefit. The Rosenwald Fund was established in 1917 and was completely liquidated 25 years later.

Rosenwald was responsible for the construction of 5,357 schools, homes, libraries, health clinics, and YMCA's for blacks in 883 counties in 15 southern states. The Y's had a profound effect on rural communities and were a major factor in improving race relations. In his far-reaching efforts to improve the conditions of blacks, Rosenwald braved bitter prejudices and risked major business losses when his competitors spread the rumor that he was really black. His birthday was celebrated and his photograph hung alongside those of Lincoln and Booker T. Washington in thousands of black homes and schools. In one school, an arithmetic problem was taught: If Mr. Rosenwald had six dozen eggs and if Mr. Rosenwald bought four more eggs, how many eggs would Mr. Rosenwald have?

In addition to his interest in improving black education, he supported Jane Addams' Hull House in Chicago, became a principal contributor to the University of Chicago, aided Jewish immigrants from Russia, and assisted in the establishment of agricultural experimentation stations in Jerusalem. In 1916 he made philanthropic history by giving $1 million to the Jewish War Relief drive and pledged up to $10 million in matching donations.

Although politically conservative, he defended Jane Addams against charges of radicalism, contributed to the Sacco-

Vanzetti defense fund, and helped make possible publication
of the record of the Sacco-Vanzetti and Mooney-Billings
cases.

He was described as "the little man who carries on his
broad shoulders the love of all Chicago," and as "the man
who did more for Negroes than anyone since Lincoln."

FELIX WARBURG
1871—1937

Felix Warburg, one of the country's most powerful financiers, enjoyed an international reputation as a philanthropist
and champion of social causes.

Born in Hamburg, Germany, in 1871, he received his education in that city, and acquired a knowledge of finance as a
young man through employment in a banking institution. In
1895, he married the daughter of Jacob H. Schiff, Frieda,
and settled in New York.

One of the earliest social enterprises with which he became
associated was the Henry Street Settlement. Its founder, Lillian D. Wald, had sought his help in providing playgrounds
for children in the Lower East Side tenement districts of New
York City. He also gave generously to the growth and development of the Educational Alliance.

In 1902, Warburg was appointed a commissioner of the
New York Board of Education by Mayor Seth Low, where
he introduced such reforms as the placement of nurses in
schools and special schooling for mentally handicapped
children. The organization of the first Children's Court was
due in part to his assistance. In 1907, Warburg was appointed
one of the first two State Probation Commissioners by Governor Hughes.

In 1915 he was elected treasurer of the newly formed Joint
Distribution Committee and later became its chairman. During World War I, at the request of Herbert Hoover, Warburg
directed a survey of the food supply of New York City as
part of the problem of handling the nation's food during the
war emergency.

For many years he was president of the 92nd Street
YMHA, and when the National Jewish Welfare Board was
organized in 1917, Warburg was one of the members of its
advisory committee. He was a prime mover in and first
president of what is today the Federation of Jewish
Philanthropies.

In 1926, President Calvin Coolidge appointed Warburg a member of the Thomas Jefferson Centennial Commission. Prior to this appointment, Warburg had given substantial support to the maintenance of Jefferson's home, Monticello.

Among the other causes and institutions which claimed Warburg's support were the American Museum of Natural History, Teachers College of Columbia University, Hebrew Union College, the Fogg Art Museum of Harvard University, and the New York Philharmonic Society.

While not a Zionist, he was always interested in Palestine. His interest was fanned following World War I, through the relief work of the Joint Distribution Committee. He contributed substantially in 1929 to the establishment of the Hebrew University in Palestine.

Several years after his death in 1937, Mrs. Frieda Warburg presented their six-story mansion on Fifth Avenue to the Jewish Theological Seminary for the establishment of the Jewish Museum. She said that she was making the gift as "a tribute to the men of my family—my father, my husband, and my brother Mortimer, who each in his own way has done so much to build up the Seminary toward its present effective usefulness."

THE ARTS
AND JOURNALISM

In the history of America's cultural arts, leading contributions were made by Jewish writers, artists, composers, musicians, architects, journalists, and producers. In literature, the stage, opera, concert halls, ballet, screen, radio, television, comedy, journalism, book publishing, painting, and sculpture, every generation has seen the emergence of Jewish men and women of talent and skill who not only epitomized the issues of the times, but stirred the imagination and intellect of their contemporaries.

The world of music has been, and remains, an arena in which Jewish instrumentalists, singers, composers, and conductors have attained unique distinction.

Pianist Louis Gottschalk, the most outstanding Jewish musical figure of nineteenth-century America, was succeeded by an incredible gallery of violinists who made Yiddle with the Fiddle a catch phrase, and they numbered among the leading piano virtuosi of the world. Jerome Kern, Irving Caesar, Gus Kahn, Harold Arlen, Richard Rodgers, and Burt Bacharach, are but a few of the tunesmiths who have kept America humming for generations.

Notable among American orchestra conductors are Eugene Ormandy, Otto Klemperer, Arthur Fiedler, Pierre Monteux, Artur Rodzinski, Serge Koussevitsky, William Steinberg, Eric Leinsdorf, Andre Kostelanetz, and Fritz Reiner.

Some other well-known names in the field of music are Emanuel Feuermann, cellist; Samuel Chotzinoff, NBC musical director; Benny Goodman, clarinetist; and Sol Hurok, the impresario. Beverly Sills, Jan Peerce, Robert Merrill, Alma Gluck, Regina Reznik, Richard Tucker, Leonard Warren, Rosa Ponselle, Roberta Peters, Julius Rudel, Leopold Godowsky, and Rudolf Bing are celebrated in the operatic field.

In the last three decades, Jewish writers have become prominent in contemporary American letters. As popular authors on the bestseller lists, they have been accorded acclaim and honors from critics and readers, including the Pulitzer Prize, the National Book Award, and the Nobel Prize. Many, if not most, have written on Jewish themes.

In the 1930's and early 1940's, authors such as Meyer Levin, Henry Roth, Ludwig Lewisohn, Mike Gold, Ben Hecht, and Budd Schulberg struggled for recognition of their novels on themes about the generational conflict, the search for identity, the alienated Jew, and Jews trying to achieve the "American dream." Their successors made the breakthrough that elevated an extraordinary group of Jewish writers to literary fame. Their books depicted the American Jewish milieu as an integral element of American life, with its Jewish roots blossoming into a unique literary flower garden.

Contributors to this Jewish literary renaissance included not only novelists but poets, critics, editors, publishers, and playwrights.

Just a partial list of eminent authors of the second half of the twentieth century reads like a mini-Who's Who of modern American literature: Irwin Shaw, Elie Wiesel, Fannie Hurst, Philip Roth, Dorothy Parker, Jerome Weidman, S. N. Behrman, Bernard Malamud, Isaac Bashevis Singer, Herbert Gold, Edna Ferber, Norman Mailer, Saul Bellow, Herman Wouk, Wallace Markfield, Irving Wallace, Laura Hobson, Leon Uris, Grace Paley, Chaim Potok, S.J. Perelman, Joseph Heller, and Bruce Jay Friedman. Karl Shapiro, Muriel Rukeyser, Howard Nemerov, Kenneth Fearing, Maxwell Bodenheim, Harvey Shapiro, and Allen Ginsberg are noted poets.

As critics, Philip Rahv, Lionel Trilling, Harold Rosenberg, Leslie Fiedler, Irving Howe, Alfred Kazin, Paul Goodman, Norman Podhoretz, and Robert Silver, helped shape American literary taste.

Sir Moses Ezekiel, the renowned nineteenth-century American-born sculptor, set the stage for generations of Jewish painters and sculptors of world repute. Among these are Sir Jacob Epstein, Jo Davidson, Jacques Lipschitz, Ben Shahn, Enrico Glicenstein, William Zorach,

Joseph Tepper, Chaim Gross, William Auerbach-Levy, Louise Nevelson, Abraham Walkowitz, Mark Rothko, Larry Rivers, and Moses and Raphael Soyer.

In the field of architecture, Dankmar Adler, a partner of the eminent Louis Sullivan, had much to do with changing the skyline of Chicago at the end of the nineteenth century, as did Albert Kahn in Detroit. Julian Levi, Arnold Brunner, Louis Kahn, Percival Goodman, Eric Mendelson, Victor Brenner, and Eric Portman were important figures in American architecture. Max Abramowitz was the co-designer of the United Nations' building and Lincoln Center, both in New York City.

The founders of the American motion picture industry such as Jesse Lasky, William Fox, Adolph Zukor, Louis B. Mayer, and Carl Laemmle, have been succeeded by a new breed of Jewish moviemakers who are the top executives of the multinational conglomerates who now own the studios. It is men like Mike Medavoy, Ned Tanen, Daniel Melnick, Frank Yablans, and hundreds of other Jewish producers, directors, writers, and composers who dominate the industry.

Of special interest is the growing number of popular Jewish movie stars, most of whom have retained their original names. Formerly, many of them had to accept new glamorous names conjured up by the studio publicity departments. These include such performers as Dustin Hoffman, Mel Brooks, Madeline Kahn, Barbra Streisand, Richard Benjamin, James Caan, Richard Dreyfuss, Marty Feldman, and Woody Allen. Walter Matthau, Shelly Winters, Paul Newman, Rod Steiger, Lorne Greene, Peter Falk, Kirk Douglas, Lauren Bacall, and Tony Curtis, all older box office stars, continue to enjoy wide popularity.

In the early years of television, Sarnoff, Paley, Flamm, and Goldenson dominated this medium. During the 1970's, such names as Norman Lear, Barbara Walters, Henry Winkler, Sander Vanocur, Bernard and Marvin Kalb, Abe Vigoda, Mike Wallace, and Edward Asner are but a few who are familiar to the viewing public.

MUSIC

LOUIS MOREAU GOTTSCHALK
1829—1869

Louis Gottschalk was one of the first American composers to achieve international recognition.

Born in New Orleans of English-French parents in 1829, Gottschalk was an American citizen by reason of the Louisiana Purchase, which had formerly been a colony of both France and Spain.

As a child prodigy he soon became the sensation of Europe, not only for his pianistic virtuosity, but also for his compositions. He was hailed by Chopin and Berlioz as the future "king of pianists." His piano pieces represent one of the first attempts to introduce native popular and folk music into classical music. He utilized Negro music as early as 1845 in his *Ballade Créole* and *Chanson Nègre*. The use of this folk music was long scorned by composers until Anton Dvorak gave it further impetus fifty years later in his *New World Symphony*. Stephen Foster drew much of his inspiration from Gottschalk's music.

Though there were many hymn and song writers during the Civil War, Gottschalk's reputation as one of America's foremost composers of the period was not challenged until Edward MacDowell began composing.

Gottschalk died in Rio de Janeiro on December 18, 1869.

LEOPOLD DAMROSCH
1832—1885

Leopold Damrosch, one of the leading figures in the annals of music, had a profound effect on the musical taste of America.

Born in Posen in 1832, Damrosch displayed an early talent for the violin. His parents, however, disapproved of a musical career as a dilettantish pursuit, and insisted he study medicine. After graduating from the University of Berlin with honors, he attempted to practice medicine, but returned to the study of the violin and music.

His unique musical gift impressed Franz Liszt, who appointed him first violinist in the ducal orchestra at Weimar, and later director of the City Theater of Posen. At the age of 30, following his appointment as conductor of the Philharmonic Orchestra of Breslau, Damrosch, together with Liszt, became enthusiastic supporters and performers of the music of contemporary composers.

In 1871, Damrosch was invited to the United States to become the musical director of the New York Arion Society, a choral group dedicated to promoting Neo-German music in America. He later organized the Oratorio Society and became conductor of the Philharmonic Society, predecessor of the New York Philharmonic Orchestra.

As conductor of these musical groups, he scored such triumphs as Berlioz' *Requiem*, Rubinstein's *Tower of Babel*, and Handel's *Messiah*.

When Damrosch accepted the directorship of the Metropolitan Opera House for the 1884-1885 season, he was impelled by the opportunity to bring German opera, chiefly the music dramas of his friend Richard Wagner, to the American public. His son, Walter Damrosch, later wrote of his father, "Money matters were to my father always so insignificant as far as he was concerned that I think he would have signed a contract in which he bound himself to pay the Metropolitan Opera House for the privilege of performing Wagnerian opera there."

His greatest accomplishment and triumph was the introduction of Wagner's music to the American opera repertoire which, until that time, had been dominated by Italian opera.

His distinguished career came to an end in 1885 when he was stricken during a rehearsal of Verdi's *Requiem*.

When he first arrived in the United States 14 years earlier, the state of musical appreciation in the country was limited and often neglected, and it was the talent and genius of Leopold Damrosch that helped to elevate America to a music-loving nation.

GEORGE GERSHWIN
1898—1937

George Gershwin, one of the most imaginative composers of popular music of the 1920's and 1930's, was born in

Brooklyn, New York, on September 26, 1898. He wrote his first songs while working as a pianist with a music publishing firm. His first great hit, "Swanee," sung by Al Jolson in the revue *Sinbad*, caused a national sensation. Gershwin wrote the scores for *Scandals, Lady, Be Good!, Funny Face, Girl Crazy*, and *Of Thee I sing*, as well as composing the tone poem *An American in Paris*, and the Piano Concerto in F.

Commissioned by Paul Whiteman to compose a jazz symphony, Gershwin wrote *Rhapsody in Blue* for piano and orchestra. It was first performed in New York in 1924, with Gershwin as the soloist. It was acclaimed for its rich melodic and rhythmic sense steeped in the American idiom.

His most ambitious and enduring work, the folk opera *Porgy and Bess*, had its first performance in 1935 in Boston, with an all-black cast. *Porgy and Bess* established Gershwin as a pioneer in a new type of American opera. The libretto for *Porgy*, written by DuBose Heyward, was rich with primitive aspects of American life, which Gershwin, with his spontaneous genius, captured with fidelity in his score. He was lauded by critics for bringing opera down to earth, with singable melodies which appealed to the "man in the street." No work to date has been written to challenge the secure place of *Porgy and Bess* in the history of American opera.

It was his last work in a pathetically short life. Gershwin died in Beverly Hills, California, on July 11, 1937, at the age of 39.

IRVING BERLIN
1888—

A rare combination of genius and melodious saccharine, Irving Berlin is a living legend.

Born in Temum, Russia in 1888, Irving Berlin (Isidor Baline) came to the United States with his family at the age of four. His father, a part-time cantor, died four years later, and the young Berlin went out on the streets to sing for pennies. While still in his teens he worked as a "busker" (song plugger) and as a singing waiter in a Bowery cafe. Herbert Bayard Swope, famed journalist on the *World*, gave Berlin his first press notice in a small feature story about the singing waiter who refused a tip from Prince Louis of Battenberg. His first published song was "Marie from Sunny Italy." It was at the cafe that Berlin wrote "Alexander's Ragtime

Band," his first outstanding song hit, which was to become the prototype for ragtime pop music.

From 1913 to the present, Berlin was to compose over 1,-000 songs. Among his classics which are still played today are: "A Pretty Girl is Like a Melody," "Cheek to Cheek," "This is the Army, Mr. Jones," and "The Girl That I Marry." He was probably the only Jewish songwriter to compose two of the most popular tunes associated with Christian holidays—"White Christmas" and "Easter Parade." Jerome Kern once remarked that Berlin's music is "the nearest thing to a native folk song since Stephen Foster."

His greatest triumph, which was to become a "second national anthem," was composed during World War I as the finale of a musical he wrote while serving in the army. "God Bless America," written for the show *Yip, Yip, Yaphank,* was never performed and was shelved for more than 20 years. In 1939 when he was asked to write a patriotic song, he recalled the *Yaphank* finale. When the popular singer Kate Smith introduced it, it became an instant hit, and was referred to as the "Hymn of World War II."

AARON COPLAND
1900—

Called the "dean of American composers," Copland has been composing ever since he first became interested in music at what he calls the "rather late age of 13."

Born in Brooklyn, New York, in 1900, his Russian parents entered the country as Kaplan, but through an immigration officer's error, it became Copland. At the age of 15, he decided to become a composer and studied with Rubin Goldmark, and Nadia Boulanger in Paris. He recalled that his first composition was too European in inspiration, and in looking for American themes, he started introducing the jazz idiom into his work.

In an effort to reach the new musical public which had grown up around the radio and phonograph, Copland turned to American folk sources, and in this period his *Billy the Kid, Rodeo, The Tender Land,* and his major work *Appalachian Spring,* put him in the forefront of contemporary American composers. He won the Pulitzer Prize and the New York Music Critics Circle Award in 1944, and the Academy Award for his film score for the motion picture *The Heiress.*

Returning to more classical composition, his *Third Symphony*, which he wrote in 1946, was acclaimed as "the greatest American Symphony," for which he received another New York Music Critics Circle Award.

LEONARD BERNSTEIN
1918—

Leonard Bernstein, born in Lawrence, Massachusetts, in 1918, has been called an "egoist with empathy," an "optimist with anxiety," and a "professor who is never absentminded."

"Lennie," as he is affectionately known, was graduated from Harvard in 1939 where he impressed such notables as Dmitri Mitropoulos and Aaron Copland. He studied conducting at the Curtis Institute with Fritz Reiner, and became Serge Koussevitsky's protégé at Tanglewood. When he was appointed assistant conductor of the New York Philharmonic Orchestra in 1943 under Artur Rodzinski, he was well on his way to becoming America's music idol.

He has appeared as conductor and piano soloist with the world's major symphony orchestras and was the first American to conduct at La Scala in Milan. Bernstein taught at Brandeis University from 1951–1956. Among his major scores were *Jeremiah Symphony, Age of Anxiety;* such musicals and ballets as *On the Town, West Side Story, Fancy Free, Wonderful Town;* and *Trouble in Tahiti,* an opera. In 1958 he became the musical director of the New York Philharmonic Orchestra.

This highly versatile artist—conductor-pianist-composer-teacher-author—added a new dimension to his talents when he became a musical commentator on television, turning the whole country into his classroom.

BEVERLY SILLS
1929—

In the short span of eleven years, Beverly Sills has become one of the great operatic stars of the world. Although she is the star of many international opera houses, she is probably one of the few performers to have two home companies—the Metropolitan Opera and the New York City Opera.

Born in Brooklyn, New York, in 1929, she first sang in public at the age of three, when she won a Beautiful Baby Contest.

After studying voice privately and appearing with a number of companies, her reputation as a leading performer of *bel canto* roles was assured after her success in the coloratura role of Cleopatra in Handel's *Giulio Cesare* at the New York City Opera. In exploring the *bel canto* repertory, she extended her roles to more than seventy operas, including revivals of the Donizetti trilogy about British monarchs, *Roberto Devereux, Maria Stuarda,* and *Anna Bolena,* and her subsequent recordings of them constitute a quasi-historic document in operatic terms. Though passed over for a number of years by the Metropolitan Opera in favor of such sopranos as Joan Sutherland and Maria Callas, she made her long-delayed debut there in 1975, at the age of 45, in the *Siege of Corinth.*

A prolific recording artist, she has completed sixteen full-length operas and several solo recital disks. As a member of the Council of the National Endowment for the Arts, Miss Sills is an effective advocate for the arts, believing that "art is the signature of a civilization." She has emphasized the "need to see more American singers take their places in the operatic sun. There are big talents out there, and we've got to use them, build them up."

In her role as a national chairman of the March of Dimes, she appears widely on its behalf and has helped raise more than $50 million since her association began in 1971.

She made her entrance into television "specials" via the "Sills and Burnett at the Met" show in 1976, and her own program, "Lifestyles with Beverly Sills," which is a weekly feature over a national network.

In January, 1978, when she announced she would retire as a singer in the fall of 1980 to become co-director of the New York City Opera, she said, "Window dressing I'm not—I have strong opinions about our opera company. I'll be 51 years old when I quit. I have no more operas I want to sing in, no more roles I want to do. There are no more opera houses I haven't sung in. I will have recorded everything I ever dreamed of recording. I'll put my voice to bed and go quietly and with pride."

WRITERS

MORRIS ROSENFELD
1862—1924

Morris Rosenfeld, beloved poet laureate of the Lower East Side ghetto of New York City, was born in Poland in 1861, to a humble family of fishery workers. After attending religious school *(cheder)*—the only school allowed the ghetto Jew—he left Poland, first for Amsterdam, then to England, where he eked out a living at tailoring, and finally, in 1886, to New York.

In his flight from religious persecution, starvation, and pogroms, Rosenfeld, like the millions of East European Jews who came to America, found the conditions of life bitter. Though they had religious freedom and civil rights, their lack of skills forced them into a new form of slavery—the sweatshop.

Arriving penniless, with his belongings wrapped in a bundle, Rosenfeld settled on the Lower East Side of New York, where he was quickly recruited into the piecework labor system which later evolved into the sweatshop—an economic trap which many of his fellow immigrants were never to escape from.

Rosenfeld, too, worked the long hours, witnessing the exploitation of women, children, and the aged. He saw their plight as a desperate struggle for survival where complaints went unanswered, because the next wave of immigrants would gladly take their places at the machines.

Although Rosenfeld had written verses as a young man, he now commited all of his indignation and yearnings to writing poetry about a life around him which he felt was devoid of hope and beauty.

> Year after year, like this is goes
> Generation rots, generation grows
> Without a purpose, without hope
> Only through grief and fears to grope.

His early poetry, though simple and direct, was published in small Yiddish-language newspapers. His poetical themes,

with their intense appeal, gained the immediate acceptance of
an audience of fellow-workers, who shared his expressions of
despair.

When *Liederbuch*, a small edition of Rosenfeld's poetry
was published, it attracted wide attention, including that of
Professor Leo Wiener of Harvard University, who translated
the poetry into English, under the title *Songs of the Ghetto.*

Rosenfeld, receiving recognition and acclaim, was invited
to poetry readings at the leading universities of the United
States and abroad, and his works were translated into twelve
languages. No longer dependent on his factory job, he devoted his later years to writing articles and poetry which were
published in the *Jewish Daily Forward* and other newspapers
and periodicals.

Rosenfeld died in 1929 at the age of 62, having witnessed
the abolition of the infamous sweatshop. Though the labor
leaders and the unions are generally credited with its demise,
it was the poet of the Jewish masses from "his corner of pain
and anguish" who enriched their lives.

SHOLOM ALEICHEM
1859—1916

Sholom Aleichem (peace be upon you) was the pen name
of the great Yiddish writer and humorist, Sholom Rabinowitz.

Born in the Ukraine in 1859, Aleichem exhibited as a
youngster a remarkable talent for mimicry and caricature.
After attending a government school, he secured a job as a
tutor at the age of 17. Following an ill-fated business venture,
he dedicated himself to writing. Although Aleichem wrote
hundreds of stories, novels, and plays in Yiddish, he is best
known for his humorous tales of life among the poverty-rid-
den and oppressed Russian Jews of the late nineteenth and
early twentieth centuries.

When he settled in the United States, he became a member
of the Educational Alliance, while continuing his writing. In
1906, Aleichem and Mark Twain appeared together at the Alliance and it was here that he was introduced as the "Jewish
Mark Twain," to which Twain replied, "I am the American
Sholom Aleichem."

His autobiographical writings include the *Adventures of
Mottel* and *The Great Fair.* His *Tevye's Daughters,* depicting
the loving and despairing world of the Jewish *shtetl* of Rus-

sia, were movingly translated and adopted into the internationally successful musical *Fiddler on the Roof*.

When he died in 1916, he was buried at Cyprus Hills Cemetery, a pantheon for outstanding figures in Yiddish literary circles.

Before he died, he asked that the poem he wrote for his tombstone be inscribed beneath his name:

> Here lies a simple-hearted Jew
> Whose Yiddish womenfolk delighted;
> All the common people, too
> Enjoyed the stories he recited.
> Life to him was but a jest,
> He poked fun at all that mattered;
> When other men were happiest,
> His heart alone was bruised and shattered.

SHOLEM ASCH
1880—1957

Though Sholem Asch was an eminent Yiddish novelist and playwright, he achieved his widest audience and fame for his biographical novels on the great figures of Christianity—*The Nazarene, The Apostle,* and *Mary.*

Born in Kutno, Poland, in 1880, Asch settled in the United States in 1909. His early writings, in both Hebrew and Yiddish, were published through the assistance of Ab Cahan, editor of the *Forward.* His first success in the theatre, *The God of Vengeance,* was produced by Max Reinhardt in Berlin in 1910. When it was produced in New York in English, the play, concerning the operation of a brothel, was compared with George Bernard Shaw's *Mrs. Warren's Profession.* Attacked as scandalous, it was closed by the police and its leading star, Rudolph Schildkraut, was jailed.

Among his other well-known works, available in English translation, are *Mottke the Thief* (1917), *Uncle Moses* (1920), *Three Cities* (1933), *One Destiny* (1945), *East River* (1946), and *A Passage in the Night.*

Although many of his early works depicted Jewish life in Europe and the United States, his later writings on the early figures of Christianity reflected his views on the common spiritual heritage of Jews and Christians. When *The Nazarene* was published, Asch was severely criticized by his co-religionists, who regarded this book as a sign that he had lost his Jewish identity. In his last book, published in 1955, two years before his death, he returned to the Jewish theme in *The Prophet,* a biographical novel about Isaiah.

DOROTHY PARKER
1893—1967

Short story writer, poet, playwright, and critic, Dorothy Parker, member of the famed Algonquin "Round Table," would often draw blood with her caustically critical two-liners.

Born in West End, New Jersey, in 1893, she received critical praise when her first books of witty, often sardonic, prose and verse were published: *Enough Rope* (1926), *Death and Taxes* (1931), *and Not So Deep as a Well* (1936). Though she claimed that the only thing she learned in school was "if you spit on a pencil eraser, you can erase ink," she had a notable career as a writer and teacher.

As a drama critic for *The New Yorker* and *Vanity Fair,* she could often close a show with her brief reviews. In referring to the talent of a particular actress, she wrote, "She ran the gamut of emotions from A to B." As literary critic, she wrote of an author, "The only 'ism' he believes in is plagiarism."

Dorothy Parker's short stories of social satire appeared in *Laments for the Living* and *Here Lies,* and her collected works were published in *The Portable Dorothy Parker* in 1944. an enlarged edition of which was brought out in 1973.

Before she died in 1967, she suggested the one-liner "Excuse My Dust" for her epitaph.

LOUIS UNTERMEYER
1885—1977

No history of the literature of the United States can ignore the contributions of Louis Untermeyer—critic, poet, and anthologist—who exercised a significant influence over American letters for half a century.

Born in New York City in 1885, Untermeyer was the son of a prosperous jeweler. After dropping out of school at 17, he joined the family business but lacked sufficient interest, resigning after several years to devote full time to writing.

First as a contributor of light verse to the Franklin P.

Adams column "The Conning Tower," and later when his short poems began to appear in *The Forum*, his reputation grew and in the years before World War I, he was a contributing editor to *The Liberator* and *The Masses*.

Untermeyer was one of the first literary figures to recognize the importance of the anthology as a device for critical survey. His first collection, *Modern American Poetry*, which included selections from Emily Dickinson, Stephen Vincent Benét, Robert Frost, Carl Sandburg, and Ezra Pound, represented the best of American poetry up to the post-World War I period. Following the publication of *Modern British Poetry*, the two books became basic texts in many classrooms. His two-volume collection of the poetry of Heinrich Heine is still considered the standard work on this poet. His ability to turn out such anthologies led to it being said that he was "an author ready to deliver a book if a publisher could think of a title."

When he published an anthology on the poetry of his close friend Robert Frost, a critic wrote, "The profound talents of the poet and a critic have gone to make a book which should hold a place in American literature." In addition to the Frost anthology, Untermeyer published the personal letters he received from the poet, and he considered this the fruit of his lifelong friendship with Frost.

Although it was his anthologies which brought him fame, Untermeyer wrote over a thousand poems in his lifetime, and in 1956, he received the Poetry Society's Gold Medal.

In 1961, when he was named a consultant in English poetry for the Library of Congress, he remarked, "As I understand it, I'm meant to act as a poetic radiator. I think I'm supposed to radiate the love of poetry over as many square miles as possible, and at least as far as Alexandria, Virginia."

Of himself, he said, "I have been an aspiring composer, a manufacturer of jewelry, a part-time journalist, a full-time editor, a lecturer, a teacher, a radio commentator, and from time to time, a poet."

While berating his audiences that "the poet is reflecting a more and more complicated simplicity," his own poetry was simplicity itself:

> We love the things we love
> In spite of what they are.

ISAAC BASHEVIS SINGER
1904—

Isaac Bashevis Singer, bless the name! A writer to drive one crazy if one has the ear for the underlying melody, the meaning behind the meaning . . . above all, there is love, a bigger, broader love than we are accustomed to reading about in book.

—Henry Miller

Isaac Bashevis Singer, hailed as one of today's most gifted writers, was born in Poland in 1904, the son and grandson of a rabbinical family. He began writing prose and poetry in Hebrew at the age of 15, at the age he decided not to continue his studies at a rabbinical seminary.

He emigrated to the United States in 1935 and was associated with the *Jewish Daily Forward* since that time. Written in Yiddish, his books encompass the experiences and traditions of the *shtetl* of Eastern Europe. He has been described as "a modern writer carrying the burdens of his time: estrangement, unfulfilled passions, and awareness of terrible ironies."

Among his most notable books are *Gimpel the Fool,* a volume of short stories; *The Slave,* a moving story of a seventeenth-century devout, captive Jew who falls in love with his master's daughter; and *The Magician of Lublin,* a fantasy tale of man's struggle with evil and sensuality. *The Magician of Lublin* was awarded an international prize by French critics as "the best foreign novel of 1960."

Heralded as one of this century's remarkable American authors, Isaac Bashevis Singer was the 1970 recipient of the National Book Award for Children's Books, and is a member of the National Institute of Arts and Letters, to which he was elected in 1965. In 1974, he was co-winner of the National Book Award for Fiction.

A number of his books are dedicated to "the blessed memory" of his brother, I. J. Singer, author of *The Brothers Ashkenazi* and *Yoshe Kalb,* "who helped me to come to this country and was my teacher and master in literature. I am still learning from him and his work."

ART

MYER MYERS
1723—1796

American art historians have cited Myer Myers as one of the first native-born artists in Colonial America.

This gifted silversmith, whose works bear the hallmark of MM or Myers, was born in New York in 1723. His father, Solomon Myers, having emigrated from Holland, became naturalized with other Jews under a special act of New York's Colonial legislature. This extension of full citizenship entitled the younger Myers to be apprenticed to a master silversmith. After completing seven years of work, which was required by law, he opened his own workshop.

The beauty of his work was soon recognized, and many of the leading families of Colonial New York, such as the Livingstons, Murrays, and Schuylers, frequented his shop. Though the English aristocracy in the Colonies could easily have imported their silver service from London, many preferred the work of Myers. The records indicate that he designed pieces for Sir William Johnson and the Earl of Loudoun.

In addition to his art, Myers became well known as a patriot and community leader. He was devoted to Judaism and was president of the famed Congregation Shearith Israel in New York—the oldest in the United States. He was elected chairman of the Gold and Silver Society and, like his fellow silversmith Paul Revere, was a member of the Masonic order.

In 1776 Myers left New York for Connecticut, together with the Reverend Gershom Mendes Seixas and other Jews, rather than remain under British rule when the city was captured. While in Connecticut, he lent his skill to the army in refining ore from the Middletown lead deposits for bullets. Following the end of the war, Myers' fame and wealth grew. He was the owner of property in New Hampshire, Vermont, and Connecticut.

Though a devout Jew, Myers accepted commissions for ritual objects, such as baptismal bowls and alms basins, from churches. One of his most noted works, however, are the pomegranates, crown, and silver bells that decorate the old Torah scrolls of Touro Synagogue in Newport, Rhode Island.

Today, Myers' work can be seen on display at many of the notable American museums which maintain colonial silver collections.

SOLOMON NUNES CARVALHO
1815—1894

Solomon Nunes Carvalho, born in Charleston, South Carolina, in 1815, was to become the first photographer of the Great Plains.

The son of one of the founders of the first Reform congregation in America, Carvalho was a close friend of General John C. Frémont, who was also raised in Charleston.

Carvalho, a successful artist with studios in Philadelphia and Baltimore, had a considerable reputation in the new photographic method of . daguerreotyping. Frémont, conqueror of California and the Republican party's first Presidential nominee, was conducting his fifth and last expedition of exploration in Utah. In 1854, he invited Carvalho to be "the artist of an exploring expedition across the Rocky Mountains." In this role, Carvalho became the first man to photograph the West and the first official photographer ever attached to an exploration undertaking. In his book *Incidents of Travel in the Far West with Colonel Frémont,* which was based on the journals Carvalho kept during the expedition, he relates the only contemporary account of one of the great adventures of nineteenth-century western exploration. The book was originally written by Carvalho as a contribution to Frémont's Presidential campaign.

After suffering the dangers of unknown country, hunger, hostile Indians, and freezing weather, the expedition stumbled into Parowan, a small Mormon settlement in Utah, five harrowing months after leaving St. Louis. It was Carvalho's letter from Parowan that gave the world the first news that Frémont and his comrades were alive.

After recuperating in the home of a Mormon, Carvalho moved to Salt Lake City with a Mormon wagon train. There he turned artist again and painted the portraits of several Mormon dignitaries, including Brigham Young. Two of these paintings, including the one of Young, are in the Salt Lake City Museum of the Daughters of the Utah Pioneers. The daguerreotypes, which he risked his life again and again to take, have never been found.

In Salt Lake City he made friends with the Mormon leaders and was well liked by them, although he made no effort to hide his disapproval of polygamy. Carvalho was once invited by Brigham Young to open a ball by dancing with one of his three wives.

He eventually went to California where he became one of the founders of the famous Cedars of Lebanon Hospital in Los Angeles.

SIR MOSES JACOB EZEKIEL
1844—1917

Knighted by the emperor of Germany, the king of Italy, close friend of Franz Liszt and King William II of Wuerttemberg, Moses Jacob Ezekiel in his day was compared to Michelangelo.

One of the great sculptors of the late nineteenth and early twentieth centuries, Ezekiel was born in Richmond, Virginia, in 1844. His father, Jacob Ezekiel, born in Richmond in 1812, had fought vigorously for civil rights for Jews. He carried on a correspondence with President John Tyler on the propriety of describing the American nation as a "Christian people."

The younger Ezekiel studied at Virginia Military Institute and served with the V.M.I. cadet battalion in 1864 in the famous Battle of Newmarket during the Civil War. He was a personal friend of General and Mrs. Robert E. Lee.

In 1869, he enrolled at the Royal Academy of Art in Berlin, Germany, where he created his famous statue *Washington,* which won him membership in the exclusive Berlin Society of Artists.

After opening his own studio, he executed his bas-reliefs *Israel* and *Adam and Eve,* for which he won the coveted Michel Beer Prix de Rome in 1873—the first American to receive this prize.

While living in Rome, he was asked to return to the United States and was commissioned to execute a statue for the celebration of the centennial of American independence. For this occasion Ezekiel executed the heroic statue *Religious Liberty,* now in Philadelphia's Fairmont Park. This was the first piece of sculpture dedicated to this theme in America.

Unveiled on Thanksgiving Day, 1876, it had been commissioned by B'nai B'rith as a gift to the American people. On the front of the pedestal is this excerpt from the Constitution:

> Congress shall make no law respecting
> the establishment of religion or
> prohibiting the free exercise thereof.
> 1776—1876

Among his other works are busts of Longfellow, Liszt, Shelley, Jefferson, Lee, and Stonewall Jackson. His bust of Lord Sherbrooke is in Westminster Abbey.

His other statues can be seen at the Corcoran Gallery, Washington, D.C.; Cornell University, Ithaca, New York; Johnson's Island, Ohio (*The Outlook*, a Confederate war monument on the site of a Civil War prison camp where 15,-000 Southerners were held); University of Virginia, Charlottesville, Virginia; Lexington, Virginia; and Charleston, West Virginia.

Ezekiel died in Rome in 1917, but because of the war, his body was not returned to America until 1921. When the United Daughters of the Confederacy, donors of the monument at Arlington, asked to have him buried at the foot of the monument, his family agreed. The burial service was held in the Arlington Memorial Amphitheater on March 30, 1921. The monument at whose base Ezekiel lies was dedicated by President Woodrow Wilson on June 4, 1914.

SIR JACOB EPSTEIN
1880—1959

When Jacob Epstein was knighted by Queen Elizabeth II in 1954, Abraham Walkowitz, the artist, remarked to Jacob's brother, "I see Jake is Sir Jake now." *"Pfui,"* his brother retorted, "Jake was knighted at 103 Hester Street, where he found his first models among pushcart peddlers."

Born in New York City in 1880 of Polish parents, Epstein first studied art at the Educational Alliance, on the Lower East Side in New York. He attended the École des Beaux Arts in Paris, where he studied with Auguste Rodin, the great French sculptor.

In a revolt against the ornate and pretty in art, Epstein produced forms striking in effect—massive creations in stone and bronze which stirred enormous controversy.

In 1907 he was commissioned by the British Medical Association to execute 18 marble statues for their new building. Their modernity created such a scandal that they were eventually removed as offensive. His other works appear in Hyde Park, London, and Fairmont Park, Philadelphia. One of his most famous sculptures is the Oscar Wilde Memorial in Père Lachaise Cemetery in Paris. Some of the more notable busts he has done are studies of the Duke of Marlborough, Joseph Conrad, Albert Einstein, and Jawaharlal Nehru.

Epstein, who had resided in England since 1906, died in 1959.

BEN SHAHN
1898—1969

Ben Shahn, one of America's great artists, is best known for his preoccupation with social themes and the condition of human beings in their political and personal environments.

Born in Lithuania in 1898, he came to the United States in 1906. After an early apprenticeship in lithography, he studied at the National Academy of Design. It was during this period that he developed the mastery of line and tone, and the visual shorthand which characterizes his later paintings.

During the Depression years of the 1930's, he executed his famous murals and posters under the WPA (Works Progress Administration). His style crystallized during this period in a series of paintings on the famous Sacco-Vanzetti trial.

He used his unique talent in a uniquely precarious period as a personal statement of protest and indictment of what he considered injustices of the time, the horrors of Germany of the thirties, and against the McCarthy era.

When asked about the source of his subject matter, he replied that he always painted things he loved or hated.

He lived modestly in Roosevelt, New Jersey, until his death in 1969.

MAX WEBER
1881—1961

More than a quarter of a century has passed since Max Weber's retrospective show at the Whitney Museum of American Art in New York. At that time the noted art critic Lloyd Goodrich said, "His work between 1912 and 1919 places him among the pioneers of abstract art, not only in America but anywhere." This view has been reinforced by critics, museum directors, and collectors.

Born in Russia in 1881, Weber came to the United States in 1891 and studied art at Pratt Institute. In 1905, he went to Paris where the new modern movement—fauvism—in which form and color were used purely as elements of design and emotional expression, had just been launched.

Weber's love of primitive art—African, Mayan, and Aztec—was incorporated in the sculptural massiveness of his painted figures with their unnatural proportions. In developing an independent art form, Weber gradually moved away from the new movements of his day—fauvism, cubism, and futurism. In another medium—sculpture—his style ranged from a freely representational to the complete abstraction of *Spiral Rhythm*. From 1916 through 1919, his oils and gouaches became more realistic and intimate—domestic life, and specifically Jewish domestic life.

In the years following 1919, Weber was in the forefront of the international art movement, creating original personal developments of style. In America, he was considered the most versatile and inventive exponent of abstract art. After a decade of experimenting, his style and viewpoint again underwent fundamental changes with a transition to paintings with more poetic and religious undertones. In his still lifes, he achieved an uncomplicated sensuous beauty and concentrated richness of color.

In the late 1930's, contemporary social themes began to emerge in his paintings, with many of them depicting refugees fleeing with their possessions, scenes of terror and flight that were among his most moving works.

Though many of his early paintings were inadequately understood in their time, Weber is considered one of America's great painters—an artist of genuine vitality and achievement.

CHAIM GROSS
1904—

Chaim Gross, a world-famous artist, is credited with the reawakening of American interest in wood sculpture.

Born in the Carpathian mountains of Galicia in 1904, he came to the United States in 1921. His first love of wood came from memories of his early childhood, as he recalled how "delicious the pungent smell of newly cut wood" was.

Enrolling in the art school of the Educational Alliance in New York City, he was drawn to the sensuous properties of wood—pleasant to the touch, vibrant and alive. It was to be his medium for more than 30 years.

Fascinated by the human body in action, Gross would often use circus figures as subjects. One-fourth of his thousand or more sculptures are of acrobats, dancers, and jugglers. When not depicting the lively world of the circus, his studies are mainly of mothers and children. His famous sculpture, *My Sister Sarah: In Memoriam,* a sensitive study with gentle flowing lines, commemorates his sister who perished with her children in a Nazi death camp.

Though mainly working in wood, Gross mastered other materials—sandstone, lithium stone, alabaster, onyx, marble, and eventually he expanded his scope to plaster pieces, which were later cast in bronze.

During his summers in Provincetown, Massachusetts, he enlarged his artistic process and techniques to the field of drawing and painting. At a retrospective exhibition at the Jewish Museum in New York in the fall of 1977, 186 pieces—sculpture, drawings, watercolors, prints, and tapestries—were assembled from 40 leading private and public collections.

At 73, Gross said, "I am going through a change." The "change" is his surging interest in biblical characters. He has completed a nine-foot sculpture entitled *Isaiah,* and contemplates creating other prophets on an equally monumental scale.

The recipient of many prizes, Gross was given the Award of Merit for Sculpture from the American Academy of Arts and Letters in 1963. The following year he was inducted as a member of the National Institute of Arts and Letters.

JOURNALISM

JOSEPH PULITZER
1847—1911

Joseph Pulitzer, crusading editor and publisher whose innovative methods in newsgathering changed American journalism, is respectfully remembered by the hundreds of recipients of Pulitzer Prizes for achievement in the arts.

Son of a Jewish father and Catholic mother, Pulitzer was born in Mako, Hungary in 1847. He came to the United States in 1864 and served with the Union forces during the last year of the Civil War.

Mustered out in July, 1865, Pulitzer went to St. Louis, where he found work at odd jobs, including gravedigging and burials during a cholera epidemic in the city. After a chance meeting in a public library with Carl Schurz, the editor and statesman, Schurz offered him a job as a reporter on the *Westliche Post,* a German-language newspaper. As a young idealistic reporter, in pursuit of facts, Pulitzer was responsible for exposures of political corruption in the city during the difficult years of the Reconstruction period.

In 1878, Pulitzer made his first move toward creating a newspaper empire when he acquired the failing St. Louis paper, the *Dispatch,* at auction for $2,500 and merged it with the *Post,* another unsuccessful paper. It was during this period that Pulitzer initiated radical changes in American reportage. Urging his reporters to write about poverty, crime, and fraud in language which usually shocked the readership, he believed that his writers should "think when taking part in the news machine," and "look for what is original, distinctive, dramatic, curious, humorous, and apt to be talked about."

In 1883, when he bought the *New York World* from Jay Gould, he commenced his hard-hitting aggressive method of building up the paper with exposures of social evils and demands for reform. The paper's circulation soared. One of his more popular crusades involved raising money to build a pedestal for the Statue of Liberty. When Pulitzer started this campaign after Congress had failed to appropriate the needed money, thousands of contributions poured in from *World* readers—some in pennies—to complete the base.

Pulitzer's success led to a heated rivalry with Charles A. Dana of the *New York Sun,* with each editor engaging in insults and denunciations. Although Pulitzer never considered himself Jewish, nor did the Jews consider him one of them, Charles A. Dana did not hesitate to call him a "renegade Jew." His greatest competition, however, came from William Randolph Hearst, who had inherited a fortune in gold mining stocks and was already the owner of the *San Francisco Examiner* when he founded the *New York Journal* in 1895 to vie with Pulitzer's paper in sensationalism and circulation. The ensuing contest, with its banner headlines, lavish pictures, emotional exploitation of news—in short, "yellow journalism"—reached notorious heights before and during the Spanish-American War.

Following the loss of his sight, Pulitzer retired from active direction of his papers and spent most of his last years cruising around the world on his yacht.

He left funds to found the School of Journalism at Columbia University in New York City at a time when most publishers scoffed at the idea of journalism classes. But Pulitzer predicted that "before the century closes, schools of journalism will be generally accepted, like schools of law or medicine."

His most enduring contribution, however, was the establishment of the Pulitzer Prizes, which are awarded annually by the trustees of Columbia University for outstanding contributions in the fields of journalism, literature, and music. Pulitzer directed that the winners should be judged by their study of the "social, political, and moral conditions of the people and the character and principles of the foreign press."

There is a memorial bust of Pulitzer by the great French sculptor Auguste Rodin at Columbia University, and a large tablet inscribed with one of his quotations:

Our Republic and its Press will rise or fall together. An able, disinterested, public-spirited press, with trained intelligence to know the right and courage to do it, can preserve that public virtue without which popular government is a sham and a mockery. A cynical, mercenary, demagogic press will produce in time, a people as base as itself. The power to mould the future of the republic will be in the hands of the journalists of future generations.

ADOLPH S. OCHS
1858—1935

Adolph S. Ochs, who built an enduring memorial in *The New York Times,* was called "An Honorable Titan" by his biographer.

Born in Cincinnati in 1858, Ochs was the son of Julius Ochs, who originally settled in Knoxville, Tennessee, in 1845, and Bertha Levy Ochs of Nashville. The Civil War found Ochs' parents with divided loyalties. Mrs. Ochs was a staunch Confederate sympathizer, while Julius Ochs enlisted in the Union army's 52nd Ohio Infantry.

Following the end of the war, they settled in Knoxville, where the father ran a failing drapery business. He reluctantly permitted Adolph to go to work at the age of eleven, and more reluctantly allowed Mrs. Ochs to advertise her services as a teacher of fancy needlework.

Adolph Ochs started his newspaper career as a printer's devil and compositor on *The Knoxville Chronicle.* Moving to Chattanooga, he launched the *Daily Dispatch* and later merged it with the Chattanooga *Times,* which became one of the most influential newspapers in the post-bellum South.

In 1896, Ochs came to New York, after losing part of his money in the panic of 1893, to discuss the possible purchase of the *Daily Mercury.* It was at this time that Ochs learned that *The New York Times* was in serious financial difficulties. He was invited to reorganize the company, and in 1899, Ochs became its owner. His slogan, "All the news that's fit to print," won the *Times* the reputation of being the greatest organ of American public opinion, with its unrivalled and complete coverage of world news and its rigid separation of news from opinion.

Ochs, a prominent leader of Reform Judaism, donated a vast tract of land on the site of the Civil War Battles of Chicamauga and Missionary Hill at Chattanooga, for a park and museum to house the historical documents of the period. Ochs also donated $500,000 to the endowment fund of the Hebrew Union College, and underwrote the preparation of the monumental *Dictionary of American Biography.*

In September, 1976, the United States Post Office issued a commemorative stamp honoring Adolph S. Ochs.

ABRAHAM CAHAN
1860—1951

To many, Ab Cahan, the man who built the *Jewish Daily Forward* into the largest and most influential newspaper in the Jewish world, was the symbol of the Lower East Side in New York City.

Born in Vilna in 1860, he came to America at the age of 21. One year later he sold his first article about Jewish life on the Lower East Side to the *New York Sun*. Encouraged, he was soon contributing to such famous publications as the *Atlantic Monthly, The Century, Harper's, Scribner's,* and *The Sun*.

In 1902, he became editor of the *Forward*. He continued in this post until 1951, a time span in which the paper rose to great influence on the tidal waves of immigration. Its circulation rose from 6,000 readers to a paid circulation of 200,000. He was responsible for one of the most successful journalistic human interest features, "A Bintel Brief" (Bundle of Letters), which carried letters describing the problems of the East European Jewish immigrants. Under his editorship, the newspaper became a major weapon in the rise of the Jewish labor movement and in the Americanization of two generations of immigrants. A successful writer in English, he helped America learn about the Jewish immigrant, and as a Yiddish journalist and Socialist organizer, he taught the immigrant about America. As a mediator between the two cultures, he helped infuse the one with the other and thus had a share in creating a Jewish American culture.

He published simple lessons in civics, history, and American government. On one occasion when some of his Socialist colleagues objected to editorials urging mothers to keep their children supplied with clean handkerchiefs, Cahan asked, "Since when is Socialism opposed to clean noses?"

He was the author of *The Rise of David Levinsky*, one of the most widely read novels about the Lower East Side.

WALTER LIPPMANN
1889—1974

Walter Lippmann's column "Today and Tomorrow," which appeared in over 200 newspapers in the United States and abroad, had such a powerful influence on domestic and foreign policy that its author was sometimes referred to as "the other State Department."

Born in New York City in 1889, the son of a successful clothing manufacturer, he was graduated from Harvard University in 1910. Among his classmates were Heywood Broun, John Reed, and T. S. Eliot, whom Lippmann once described as "men who are orthodox even though they are young."

He became an associate editor of *The New Republic* in its early days from 1914–1917, and at the outbreak of World War I, he left to become Assistant Secretary of War, later helping to prepare data for the peace conference.

From 1921 to 1931 he was on the editorial staff of the *New York World,* and in 1931 he began his widely read column in the *New York Herald Tribune.* When the *Tribune* folded, his column was syndicated by the *Washington Post.*

Although an early supporter of Franklin D. Roosevelt and the New Deal policies, Lippmann became disillusioned and his political stance became one of moderate detachment. He won wide recognition, as a farsighted and incisive analyst of foreign policy.

In 1958 a special Pulitzer Prize citation praised his powers of news analysis, which he demonstrated in his books *United States War Aims, The Cold War, Isolation and Alliances,* and *The Communist World and Ours.*

THEATER

BORIS THOMASHEVSKY
1866—1939

Boris Thomashevsky—actor, playwright, and theater manager—was the matinee idol and hero of thousands of young Jewish sweatshop girls at the turn of the century.

Generally credited as the founder of the Yiddish theater in America, Thomashevsky was born in Kiev, Russia, in 1866, and after arriving in New York at the age of 15, found employment in a cigar factory. As a member of a synagogue choir, he persuaded a saloonkeeper, who was a trustee of the synagogue, to bring over a Yiddish theater troupe from London.

Joining to produce *Koldunya* (The Witch), Thomashevsky was one of the first to bring to the immigrant audiences Yiddish entertainment and drama. Combining genius and *schmaltz*, he starred in leading roles and even, because of the scarcity of Jewish actresses at that time, played female parts. After managing a number of theaters in Chicago, Thomashevsky returned to New York in 1893, and for a short time was associated with the People's Theater. During the 1895-96 season, he formed a company with the actor Jacob P. Adler and the tragedian David Kessler, but the intramural rivalry was too keen for this combination to survive.

Always a showman *par excellence*, his lifestyle of garish splendor was to provide a prototype for Hollywood movie stars 25 years later. A huge photograph of his corpulent figure, resembling that of a wrestler, in pastel tights with bare chest, adorned the lobby of his National Theater. Sporting a cape, silk hat, and cane, he took his salary in gold, which he kept in a money belt. Employing a Japanese valet, he was the first star to have a chauffeur-driven limousine among the luminaries of the Yiddish stage.

As one of the most popular actors at the turn of the century, he played to swooning standing-room-only audiences, and at the end of a performance, there was scarcely a dry eye in the house. One account described him as a "young fat man, with black curly hair, languorous eyes, and a rather ef-

220

feminate voice, who is thought very beautiful by the girls of the ghetto." Playing *Hamlet* in Yiddish, he seemed to fit Shakespeare's description of his tragic hero in the much disputed passage, "He is fat and scant of breath."

Thomashevsky, in his devotion to the Yiddish theater as an art form, was always willing to produce or star in new or untried plays, and was responsible for bringing to the United States many actors who were later to gain fame, including Joseph and Rudolph Schildkraut.

Before his death in 1939 in New York City, Thomashevsky had gone through a number of fortunes, and his last years were spent entertaining audiences in East Side night clubs.

This great popular figure, adored by the young women of the sweatshop, lived to see the decline of the folklore dramas of Yiddish theater as the waves of immigrants became Americanized and flocked to the newest art form—the motion picture.

DAVID BELASCO
1853—1931

David Belasco is a producer of much skill, infinite patience, enormous industry and true relish for the theater.

—Alexander Woollcott

David Belasco, one of the notable figures of the American theater, was born in San Francisco in 1853, the son of Abraham Humphrey Belasco, an English circus performer. Although he was later to claim that he had been educated in a Canadian monastery, this pretense was part of the flamboyant reputation Belasco carefully nurtured.

Appearing in amateur productions in his teens, he worked the entire gamut of theatrical experiences: acting, playwriting, beating a drum, and directing. At 19, he became the stage manager of the famed Baldwin Theater in San Francisco. His first venture as a playwright was in 1880, when he adapted *Hearts of Oak*, a melodrama. He later adapted and produced 14 plays from novels and French literature, and wrote 13 dramas in collaboration with other writers. Belasco also created such memorable dramas as *Madame Butterfly* and *The Girl of the Golden West*, which Puccini was later to use for opera librettos.

Invited to New York in 1882 by the great producer Charles Frohman, they formed an association which was to last until 1895, when Belasco became an independent producer. From the years 1890 to 1914, theater in America was dominated by what has been called "Belascoism," a cult of drama which attained extraordinary popularity with its spectacular sets which meticulously reproduced reality. Belasco was the first to introduce Edison's incandescent electric lighting on the stage.

The care he lavished in developing new stage personalities made stars of Mrs. Leslie Carter, David Warfield, Blanche Bates, Lenore Ulric, and Frances Starr. He gave the child actress Mary Pickford her early start.

When he died in 1931, an obituary summed up his amazing career:

> . . . a self-styled genius, charlatan, poseur, call him what you will—who nonetheless managed to write an important page in the history of the American theater.

CLIFFORD ODETS
1906—1963

In a preface to a collection of his first six plays, Clifford Odets wrote, "My belief, is that the plays will say whatever is to be said; most of them have bones in them and will stand up unsupported."

Born in Philadelphia in 1906, Odets was brought up in New York City, and after graduating from high school he sought a career as an actor. After appearing with the Theatre Guild, he turned his attention from acting to playwriting. He joined in founding the Group Theater, and their production of his first one-act play, *Waiting for Lefty,* in 1935, catapulted him to fame as a gifted social protest dramatist. The play, with its somewhat Marxian theme of the awakening and insurgency of the impoverished working class, is now regarded to be typical of the 1930's.

In the same year, *Awake and Sing,* his first full-length play, considered to be his best work, compassionately portrayed the struggles and rebellion of a financially destitute Jewish family. This was followed by *Till the Day I Die,* one of the first dramas about the new Nazi regime in Germany.

In the production of *Golden Boy* in 1937, Odets used the

sport of boxing to extend his theme of human deterioration in an urban competitive society, with its story of a young talented Italian-American violinist who is forced into the brutality of prizefighting.

Among his other plays, the best-known are *Rocket to the Moon*, a story of a Bronx dentist who tries to find happiness in a belated love affair, and *Night Music*, a love tale of a lower-income couple. In his later plays, *The Big Knife* and *The Country Girl*, Odets turned from social drama to studies of individual conflict.

In summing up his early work, Odets said, "When these plays were written, it was almost impossible for me to do more or differently with them. Much of them was felt, conceived and written out of a personal need . . . let them stand, crudities and all, as a small parade of a young talent discovering and shaping itself."

CURIOSA AND
ECCENTRICS

Every societal group in America has had its quota of eccentrics, rebels, nonconformists, and dissenters from the mores of the establishment, and American Jewry has had its share.

The earliest eccentrics were several veterans of the Revolutionary War. Abraham Simons of Thomson, Georgia, requested that he be buried standing up with his musket at his side. Abraham Mordecai, the first white settler in Montgomery County, Alabama, was a loner who built a crude coffin for himself and used it as a dining table during his lifetime.

The best known eccentric, however, was "Emperor Joshua Norton" of San Francisco, a colorful character of the Gold Rush era of California. One of his more notable decrees prophetically directed the city government to build a bridge across San Francisco Bay—a project which was finally completed 62 years later in 1937.

Elias Abraham Rosenberg, adviser to King David Kalakaua of Hawaii, was also the court astrologer and seer. Lewis Charles Levin, a member of Congress from 1845 to 1850, was one of the leaders of the "Know Nothing Party" and the temperance movement. He achieved notoriety as an organizer of the violent anti-Catholic riots of 1844 in Philadelphia.

Mordecai Manuel Noah, a well-known politician and journalist, attempted to buy Grand Island in the Niagara River in 1825 as a city of refuge for the Jews of the world. Naphatali Herz Imber, an alcoholic vagabond poet, wrote the Jewish national anthem "Hatikvah" more than half a century before Israel became a state. Daniel Bandman, an itinerant actor, toured the western mining camps performing Shakespeare in German. He was usually denounced as a rascal and drummed out of town by mine owners after he organized benefit performances for striking miners.

227

Gary Davis, son of the noted bandleader Meyer Davis, was a pacifist during World War II. Declaring himself a citizen of the world, he issued his own passport and was jailed by a number of countries as he sought vainly to enter and spread his message of peace.

Jerry Rubin and Abbie Hoffman were the self-styled "Yippie" leaders of the violent student protest movements of the 1960's, and Allen Ginsberg, always in the public eye, was once the guru of the "beatnik" era and is now a highly acclaimed poet.

Though many of these individuals deviated from the established pattern of Jewish life by their odd or whimsical behavior, or by playing a part in an unusual incident, each exhibited a strong individuality and independence of action.

ABRAHAM SIMONS
c. ?—1824

Abraham Simons of Thomson, Georgia, a Jewish soldier in the American Revolution, was described as a "Jew of strong plain sense." Somewhat of an eccentric, he requested upon his death that he be buried in a standing position with his musket at his side so that he could shoot the devil. The coffin was accordingly placed on end, which necessitated the digging of the grave twice the usual depth.

His widow, Nancy Mills Simons, member of an aristocratic Christian family, remarried in 1827, three years after Simons' death. Her second husband was the Reverend Jesse Mercer, a well-known Baptist clergyman who used the fortune Abraham Simons had accumulated to establish Mercer University, a Baptist institution in Macon, Georgia.

In reviewing Mercer University's history, Dr. H.R. Bernard, auditor of the mission board of the Georgia Baptist Church, said, "Mercer University is largely indebted to the skill and enterprise of a Jewish financier for much of the larger part of its life and power. A copious Providence this which founds a Christian college on Jewish cornerstones."

Simons' grave, a short distance from Thomson, is marked with a Daughters of the American Revolution plaque.

ELIAS ABRAHAM ROSENBERG

When the Hebrew Military Association of the Territory of Hawaii was to hold High Holy Days services in 1913, they had to borrow a Torah from the royal family of Hawaii. How the Torah came into the possession of the royal family is the incredible story of a rascal named Elias Abraham Rosenberg, a self-styled rabbi.

In 1887, Rosenberg arrived in Honolulu and ingratiated himself with King David Kalakaua by his chanting and so-called occult powers. He soon became the King's soothsayer and astrologer, acquiring such power over the monarch that the Hawaiian press bitterly denounced him as a "Holy Moses." Rosenberg taught the King some Hebrew and was persuaded to appoint him appraiser of customs. He was given quarters in the Iolani Palace, where he practiced magic, read the stars, and chanted Bible stories in Hebrew.

Several months after Rosenberg's *chutzpah* won him the King's favor, a revolution limited much of the King's power and marked the swift end of Rosenberg's career. Before Rosenberg sailed back to San Francisco in June, 1887, he received from the King an inscribed silver cup, a gold medal, and $260. The Torah Rosenberg had brought with him was left with the King, together with a handsome silver Torah pointer (*yad*). It has been suggested that the two Judaica articles were left behind as security for the $260, which may have been a loan to enable Rosenberg to leave the islands quickly.

Later the same year, the King exhibited some royal curios at a charity bazaar, including the pointer and the Torah Scroll. The Scroll was unrolled and profanely draped around the inside of a tent. When Kalakaua died in 1891, his sister, Queen Liliukalani, inherited the Judaica. In the Archives of the Territory of Hawaii, there is a note in the Queen's handwriting, penned while still a princess, concerning the Torah exhibited at the bazaar.

In 1899, the Torah and pointer came into the possession of David Kawananakoa, Liliukalani's nephew, and later was inherited by Princess Abigail Kawananakoa, David's widow.

Between 1900 and 1945, these items were lent to the Jews of Honolulu for religious services. The pointer was eventually given to Honolulu's Temple Emanu-El in 1959. The Torah, however, seemed to have vanished.

It was not until August, 1972, that Samuel Landau, a Honolulu attorney and member of Temple Emanu-El, informed Rabbi Julius Nodel that one of his clients, Homer Hayes, had a Hebrew manuscript that had been in his family for many years. Hayes was prepared to donate it to the Temple. When Landau brought the "manuscript," Rabbi Nodel quickly saw that it was a Torah Scroll, but the rollers at each end were missing.

JOSHUA A. NORTON
1817—1880

"Emperor" Norton I, one of the most colorful eccentrics of the post-Gold Rush era of California, pyramided $40,000 to a quarter of a million and then lost his fortune in an attempt to corner the rice market. Son of an English businessman, he came to California in 1849 and became a popular leader. He was a member of the Vigilantes who helped tame the lawlessness of San Francisco.

After emerging from a long period of seclusion following the loss of his fortune, he sent a notice to the *San Francisco Bulletin* in which he declared himself "Emperor Norton I, High Ruler of the United States and Protector of Mexico." Clothed in a shabby uniform and military cap, with a small sword dangling at his side and a stick from his blue cotton umbrella in his hand, Norton became a familiar figure on the street and the city's favorite ward.

From time to time he issued "imperial" funds for "His Majesty's wardrobe." His most prophetic proclamation was the proposal to build a bridge across San Francisco Bay.

The "Emperor" was permitted to eat, drink, and amuse himself without cost and to draw checks up to the sum of fifty cents on San Francisco banks. The checks were always honored, and Norton added to his funds by selling fifty-cent bonds and levying and collecting "taxes" from his "subjects."

A bronze bas-relief plaque on the wall of Cliff House was dedicated to Norton on February 23, 1939, memorializing this Jewish eccentric and his two constant companions, his dogs, "Bummer" and "Lazarus," with these words:

Pause traveler and be grateful to Norton, 1st Emperor of the United States, protector of Mexico, 1859–1880, whose prophetic wisdom conceived and decreed the bridging of San Francisco Bay, August 18, 1869.

JOSEPHINE MARCUS EARP

Josephine Marcus had the rare distinction of having been not only one of the few Jewish dance hall girls in the pioneer West, but also, eventually, the wife of one of the most famous gunfighters and marshals of that time.

Josephine, daughter of Henry and Sophie Marcus of San Francisco, California, ran away from home in the 1880's and joined a troupe of dancing girls touring the Arizona Territory.

It was at Tombstone, Arizona, that she met Wyatt Earp, the legendary former sheriff who brought law and order to Dodge City, and the then sheriff of Tombstone. There she fell in love with Earp and they were married.

They moved to San Francisco, where he died in 1929. He

is buried in the Hills of Eternity Jewish Cemetery in Colma, California, which is owned by San Francisco's Congregation Sherith Israel.

Josephine Marcus Earp is buried beside him.

ABRAHAM KOHN
1818—c. 1883

Abraham Kohn, president of Kehilath Anshe Mayriv, Chicago's oldest Jewish congregation, dating from 1847, was a militant foe of slavery. When he was elected City Clerk of Chicago in 1860, his Democratic opponent branded him as "one of the blackest Republicans and abolitionists."

Introduced to Abraham Lincoln after the latter's nomination for the Presidency in Chicago in 1860, Kohn conceived of the idea of giving the future President a unique message of encouragement just before his inauguration in 1861.

When Lincoln stopped in Chicago en route to the capital, Kohn presented him with a silk replica of the American flag, the work of his own hands. Its folds contained Hebrew characters exquisitely inscribed in black with four verses from the biblical Book of Joshua.

Lincoln's letter of acknowledgment of this unusual gift has been lost, and the whereabouts of the flag cannot be traced, although it was mentioned in Admiral George Preble's *History of the Flag of the United States*, and at a later date by Governor William McKinley in an address he made at Ottawa, Kansas.

In a letter to the *Jewish Record* from John Hay, Lincoln's secretary, he described the flag, and ended the letter with, "It has been in the Executive Mansion ever since the President's Inaugural."

Abraham Kohn was on the citizen's committee that represented the city of Chicago at Lincoln's funeral in Springfield. When Lincoln's body lay in state in the Chicago courthouse, it rested under a canopy inscribed with the Hebrew lament, "The beauty of Israel is slain upon the high places."

ISSACHAR ZACHARIE
c. 1827—c. 1889

One of the curious and close friendships President Lincoln had was with Dr. Issachar Zacharie, an English chiropodist.

Beginning in 1861 when Zacharie was called in to treat the President, Lincoln was impressed by his intelligence and loyalty. In 1863, Zacharie was entrusted with an espionage mission to New Orleans to interview local leaders and report on conditions under the military occupation by General Nathaniel Banks. Returning to Washington, he reported directly to the President, who found the information useful in formulating policies for governing areas taken from the Confederacy.

In this new role, Zacharie put forth the possibility of arranging a meeting with leaders of the Confederacy in Richmond, "to terminate the war." The President referred him to Secretary of State William Seward, who had doubts about the mission, which the Cabinet opposed.

Zacharie was, however, sent to Richmond on a semi-official mission in October, 1863, where, under a flag of truce, he conferred with Jefferson Davis and Judah P. Benjamin.

When news of the mission was published in the *New York Herald*, Zacharie assured Lincoln that he had not "lisped a word respecting this matter." The *Herald*, in a long editorial, satirized the President and his "corn" doctor, under the headline "The Head and Feet of the Nation." It depicted Zacharie as a "wit, gourmet, and eccentric with a splendid Roman nose, fashionable whiskers, a dazzling diamond breastpin, great skill in his profession, and an ingratiating address." The mocking editorial ended with, "What is needed is someone to operate on the head and remove the corns from the brain of Dr. Zacharie."

The *World* editorial declared that Dr. Zacharie "has enjoyed Mr. Lincoln's confidence perhaps more than any other private individual. He has visited the cotton states, armed with letters from the President. He was courted, feted, flattered by high officials because he was regarded as standing so high in the graces of the President who has often left his business apartment to spend his evenings in the parlor of the famous bunionist."

Zacharie exerted some influence on the President in securing a pardon for a young Jewish Confederate soldier.

The father of the condemned officer, a member of a prominent family in South Carolina, had contributed the first gift to the Confederacy of $10,000 when that state seceded from the Union. Lincoln, in freeing the soldier on the condition that he remain neutral for the rest of the war, said, "I am glad to be able to serve my enemy."

LEVI STRAUSS
1829—1902

When Bavarian-born Levi Strauss went to California in 1850, he went with the same adventurous spirit as other prospectors who had been spurred on by the tales of instant wealth shortly after the news spread across the continent of the discovery of gold at Sutter's Mill. Though he was to strike it rich in the West, it was not through the pick and pan, but with a pair of pants.

One of 33,000 immigrants to come to California during the Gold Rush, Strauss had two fortuitous encounters—with a miner and tailor—which were the start of his great success as the early founder of a great industry of international renown.

Strauss had brought with him as his stock-in-trade a bundle of tough heavy fabrics which he thought could be sold for tents and wagon covering. When a miner castigated him for bringing fabrics and not pants, which were badly needed for digging, Strauss took the miner to a tailor who converted the fabric into trousers. The elated miner went through town proudly proclaiming the durability of his new pants and shouted that they were made by Levi. The name Levi, now over 125 years, stuck, as other miners, loggers, and rail workers sought him out.

Strauss, however, was not able to solve the problem of the torn pockets on his Levis which the miners would stuff with specimens and tools, until a tailor, Jacob W. Davis, took the pants to a harness maker and had the pockets riveted at the corners. Davis discussed his solution with Strauss, who had already set up the firm of Levi Strauss and Company, and they agreed to have the idea patented. The patent was granted in 1873, and from that time Levi Strauss and Company advertised their riveted clothing as "so tough even a team of plow horses could not tear them apart." The two-horse logo became one of the company's most famous trade-marks.

In his later years, Strauss, one of the most prosperous pioneer merchants of San Francisco, devoted most of his time to charitable societies and organizations. His business advice was sought by many, and throughout his career he served as a director of a bank, insurance company, and a utility, and was a charter member of the San Francisco Board of Trade. In 1897, he donated 28 perpetual college scholarships to the University of California, which are still in effect today.

On the day of his death, September 26, 1902, the *San Francisco Call* devoted three front-page columns and a large photograph to his obituary. The headline over the obituary read, "His life devoted not only to fostering the highest commercial conditions, but to the moral, social, and educational welfare and development of the young men and women of the State."

SPORTS

In the United States, Jews first participated in organized sports in the 1840's and 1850's. The Jews who fled central Europe had no early involvement with the American rough-and-tumble frontier-type of sports, but they had participated in noncompetitive sports such as ice skating, boating, and horseshoe pitching.

There were a number of English Jewish pugilists who visited the United States in the 1850's and 1860's and were later to become the first professional boxing instructors in the United States. Before the Civil War, the nation's leading jockey was Jacob Pincus of Baltimore, and in 1866 Lipman Pike of Brooklyn, New York, was baseball's first professional player. Lucius Littauer, later to gain fame as a philanthropist and patron of Jewish scholarship, was Harvard's first football coach in 1881. August Belmont, Sr., the banker, was the first president of the American Jockey Club, and a leading horse breeder.

The German Jews who first joined the German and Bohemian turnvereins in America in the 1840's and 1850's later organized the young men's literary and social clubs in which physical training became an important feature. Out of these associations grew the first YMHA's before the Civil War, and these in turn became the fertile ground for some of the earliest American-born Jewish amateur athletes of standing.

In the mid-nineteenth century, Y's inherited the recreational facilities of the Jewish social clubs when the latter disappeared or became the nuclei of the first Jewish townclubs, with their lavish indoor athletic equipment. As the Y's acquired their own buildings, most of them added athletic programs and facilities. New York's 92nd Street Y, the oldest in existence, had an athletic circle as part of its cultural and recreational program when it was founded in 1874.

Jewish athletics achieved national and international fame as members of the United States Olympic teams in

239

1900, 1904, and later and as national titleholders in a number of sports. Before the turn of the century, the first American-born, college-educated generation of German Jews made their debut in intercollegiate sports, including football, rowing, boxing, and basketball.

Although the East European immigrant parents frowned on athletics as the pastime of loafers, their children took to sports with avidity. In the settlement houses and the Y's, they acquired sports skills and played in team competition for the first time. In the streets they became adept at punchball, stickball, and stoopball, with garbage can covers used for bases and peach crates affixed to warehouse doors as basketball nets. The more exotic sports such as tennis, golf, squash, and rowing, which required expensive equipment and money for fare to the courts, held no interest for these first-generation immigrants.

Many ghetto youngsters learned to box to defend themselves against street gangs. They became professional fighters when they found it was an easy road to fame and fortune. Out of this milieu came such stellar champions as Abe Attell, Benny Leonard, Ruby Goldstein, and Barney Ross. Today the professional Jewish boxer is almost extinct in the United States.

The big city ghettos also produced some of the early basketball stars, among them Nat Holman and Barney Sedran, who later became top professional coaches. George Stone of the St. Louis Browns was the American League batting champion, and Myer Prinstein and Hugo Friend were Olympic track team medalists.

When the masses of Jews left the big city ghettos during and after World War I, Jewish youngsters began to appear in lineups of high school sports' teams and were to star in track, hockey, lacrosse, and swimming.

Prejudice against Jewish athletes, amateur and professional, however, manifested itself in many ways and in varying degrees, with some professional athletes changing their names to avoid discrimination. The country clubs openly excluded Jews. Until they opened their own clubs, few Jews played golf and tennis.

In professional sports, Jewish stars were greatly sought after because they were heroes in the Jewish community and thus box office assets. The success of Jewish boxers brought Jewish fans to the arenas and impelled the Yiddish press to begin covering sports events.

When Andy Cohen was signed by the New York Giants and Hank Greenberg was elected to baseball's Hall of Fame, a milestone was reached in the history of Jews in American sports. When Greenberg refused to play on Yom Kippur, it made front-page news. However, by 1963, the fans were not surprised when the pitching rotation was changed to accommodate Sandy Koufax's observance of the High Holy Days.

Two generations of American Jews became sports fans and participated in various sports in the military camps of World Wars I and II and returned to civilian life as sports enthusiasts. The shift of the Jewish population to the suburbs following World War II greatly stimulated the growth of Jewish country clubs, with first-rate golf courses, tennis courts, pools, and boat marinas.

Jewish parents, who once disapproved of competitive sports as not respectable or a waste of time, now encourage their children to compete in major and minor sports and are not unhappy when athletic prowess yields college scholarships.

In the Olympiads from 1896 to 1976, over 100 Jews were selected to represent the United States, participating in 20 different events. They won a total of 27 gold, 11 silver, and 16 bronze medals in these competitions.

BENNY LEONARD
1896—1947

Arthur Brisbane, noted Hearst editor, once said of Benny Leonard that he had "done more to conquer anti-Semitism than a thousand textbooks."

Brisbane was referring to the Lower East Side boy who had to fight to survive gang wars and fought so well as an adult that boxing authorities rate him as one of the greatest lightweights of all time and the best Jewish boxer in history.

Leonard was born on the Lower East Side of New York in 1896, the son of parents who came from Russia in the first great wave of immigration in the 1880–1890 decade. Without the knowledge or consent of his parents, he became a professional boxer to augment the family income. He earned $4 for his first bout, which he lost at the age of 15.

After being knocked out in his first important fights in 1912 and 1913, Leonard was never knocked out again in 209 bouts during 13 years of an active career in the sport.

In 1917, he won the lightweight title from the Englishman Freddie Welsh. Leonard defended his title 14 times in 1917 before joining the United States Merchant Marine in World War I. Earlier, he had visited the training camps at his own expense to teach boxing and to stage exhibits for war bond drives.

The Jews on the Lower East Side found in Leonard the first major Jewish sports luminary, a hero who won respect for all Jews and gave them pride in a genuine celebrity.

His family, particularly his mother, had constantly urged Leonard to quit the ring, even though he had earned $1 million dollars. He finally acceded to her wishes in 1925 when she became critically ill.

During the Depression of the 1930's, Leonard lost everything and sought to recoup by returning to the fight ring after leaving it seven years before. In his last fight, in 1932, he was knocked out and his comeback was over. This ended the career of the man famed as a gentleman in a sport not known for its exemplary characters.

In the prime of his career, Leonard had said, "I'll be in boxing until I breathe my last." In 1943 he had become a boxing referee, and four years later he died of a heart attack while officiating at a bout.

Just before his death, the New York Boxing Writers Association awarded him its coveted Edward J. Neil Trophy, and later he was voted into boxing's Hall of Fame.

HENRY "HANK" GREENBERG
1911—

We shall miss him in the infield,
and we shall miss him at the bat,
But he's true to his religion,
and I honor him for that.

This poem by Edgar Guest and the Happy New Year headline in Hebrew and English in the *Detroit Free Press* were both prompted by the possibility that "Hammering" Hank Greenberg, the first baseman of the Detroit Tigers, might not play in a pennant game on Rosh Hashanah.

The question was heatedly debated, not only in the Jewish community but throughout the country. A Detroit rabbi advised Greenberg to decide for himself; another found a Talmudic reference to ballplaying on the Sabbath over 900 years ago. The dilemma of Greenberg's loyalty to his team and also to his Jewish traditions was solved by attending holiday services in the morning and hitting two winning home runs in the afternoon. When a similar situation occurred the following year, on Yom Kippur, Greenberg did not play and his team lost.

Born in the Bronx, New York, in 1911, of Rumanian immigrant parents, Greenberg started playing baseball at James Monroe High School, where he attracted big-league scouts. A New York Yankee scout visited the Greenberg home on a Friday evening and offered Greenberg's father a contract for Hank, who was still a minor. The older Greenberg, an Orthodox Jew, was outraged by this Sabbath desecration, and refused to discuss the matter. Several months later, he signed with the Detroit Tigers.

Greenberg, a 6' 4", 215-pounder, distinguished himself in the minor leagues before playing with the Tigers in 1933. Terribly awkward as a fielder, he overcame this weakness by long hours of diligent practice before and after the game, and by taking dancing lessons to make his feet behave. In 1934, after he had boosted his batting average, the Tigers won the pennant for the first time since 1909. During the World

Series of 1934, the Cardinals called Greenberg "pants presser Greenberg."

Twice voted the American League's most valuable player and winner of three home-run championships, Greenberg injured his wrist and did not play again until 1937.

His name became a household word in 1938 when he made a dramatic but unsuccessful effort to top Babe Ruth's record of 60 home runs in a season.

Greenberg was drafted early in 1941—the first big-leaguer to go into the service. Later that year he was discharged under the law allowing men over 28 to return to civilian life. After Pearl Harbor, he enlisted and served four years in the Air Force, commanding a B-29 plane in the China-Burma area, and took part in the first land-based bombing of Japan in 1944.

In 1956, Greenberg became the first Jew elected to baseball's Hall of Fame. When his active playing days ended after 17 years with the Tigers, he became general manager of the Cleveland Indians and later part-owner of the Chicago White Sox.

RICHARD SAVITT
1926—

Following the end of World War II, a writer, commenting on the extent of anti-Semitism in American sports, noted, "In tennis, the best man wins if he is free, white, and gentile."

In the years just following the end of World War II, leading tennis clubs in the country barred both Jews and blacks. It was during this discriminatory period, however, that Richard (Dick) Savitt, excluded from the prestigious West Side Tennis Club at Forest Hills, was to capture the coveted Wimbledon Cup.

Dick Savitt, born in New Jersey in 1926, started playing tennis as a boy in the public parks, where he entered local tournaments. When his family moved to El Paso, Texas, he dropped tennis for the more scholastic sports of football and basketball. He played basketball at Cornell University, but was eliminated from the team when he injured his knee. He returned to tennis and reached the quarter finals of the National Junior Championships, achieving the rank of 26th nationally in 1949; the following year, he was rated sixth. During a tour of Australia in 1951, Savitt defeated the best on the Australian Davis Cup team and won the title. The same year, he captured the most prized amateur tennis crown, the Wimbledon-All England Championship, defeating another Jewish tennis ace, Herbie Flam.

Aiming at the triple crown (Australia, England, and Forest Hills) Savitt played at the West Side Tennis Club and won all his preliminary matches, but lost in the semi-finals. Though he was regarded as a top choice for the United States Davis Cup team in 1951, he was bypassed and another player of lesser rank was named. Though Savitt never discussed this rebuff, many tennis authorities believed that anti-Semitism had kept him from participating on the team in international championship matches.

After Savitt won the national indoor singles title for the third time—the first player to achieve this honor in 25 years—he left tennis for the business world.

SANDY KOUFAX
1935—

Sanford (Sandy) Koufax is perhaps the only great professional athlete who began his career in one sport, basketball, but went on to win his laurels in another, baseball.

Born in Brooklyn, New York, in 1935, he attended Lafayette High School where he starred in basketball at the Jewish Community Center and at high school competitions. He won a basketball scholarship to the University of Cincinnati, where he planned to study architecture.

As a college freshman, he started pitching and chalked up a spectacular strikeout record. When a number of big-league scouts offered him a contract, he opted for the Brooklyn Dodgers in 1955. When they signed the contract for his first year salary of $6,000 with a bonus of $14,000, he had only pitched 15 games in sandlot and college play. By 1958, his baseball record was considered only fair.

In 1958 he went into the Army for several months and returned to the team in 1959. This was the year he made his mark with the most strikeouts in a single game—18. With 13 strikeouts from the previous game, he established a new record of 31 for two consecutive games. The next few years did not produce the promise of his earlier games, but in 1961 he created a new National League strikeout record of 269.

It was in 1963 that Koufax reached his prime, setting two

new pitching marks; he was named the National League's Most Valuable Player. He received the Cy Young Award as the major leagues' outstanding pitcher, the Babe Ruth Award as the outstanding performer in the World Series, and the Hickok diamond belt as the year's outstanding professional athlete.

A manager once created an uproar by scheduling the Jewish star for the mound on Yom Kippur, but quickly made a change when Koufax let it be known he would be in synagogue that day with his parents. Thereafter the Dodgers' manager kept a Jewish calendar on his desk.

In 1972, Koufax was voted into baseball's Hall of Fame, five years after his retirement. He retired in 1967 after he developed incurable arthritis in his arm.

Following his retirement from baseball, he became a TV broadcaster in Los Angeles.

NAT HOLMAN
1896—

To familiarize German youth with the American game of basketball, the sports authorities of Nazi Germany, who had barred Jews from all athletic competition used a book, *Winning Basketball*, by the Jewish author Nat Holman, otherwise known as "Mr. Basketball."

The son of Russian-Jewish immigrants, Holman was born in New York City in 1896. He grew up on the Lower East Side where he learned to play basketball at the Educational Alliance and the Henry Street Settlement.

Although he starred in other sports, he became the basketball coach of City College of New York at the age of 23, the youngest coach in the country. He remained with this team for 36 years. From 1923 to 1950, the team was ranked among the top five in the United States.

While coaching at City College, Holman also played on a pro team. In 1921, he joined the original Celtics, the wonder team of pro basketball, still regarded by experts as the greatest team of all time. He remained with the team until it was disbanded in 1929.

It was Holman who devised the pivot play a strategy that revolutionized basketball. Every game in which the Celtics appeared was a virtual basketball clinic, to which college coaches flocked to observe the finesse with which Holman feinted an opponent out of position. The genius he exhibited as a pro, Holman applied to his coaching at City College, making him one of the few to reach the pinnacle both as a player and coach.

Holman's career as a player ended in 1930, when he was 34, but he remained a coach until the late 1950's. He is the author of four books on basketball, which have been translated into several languages; they are used to teach the game to thousands at home and abroad.

At the request of the United States State Department, Holman made many trips to a number of countries around the world to spread the gospel of basketball. He was largely responsible for promoting basketball into a major sport in Israel. As coach, teacher, and adviser, he visited Israel often, and also persuaded many non-Jewish basketball stars from the United States to coach Israeli teams. He was president of the National Collegiate Basketball Coaches Association for nine years.

Holman was in his late seventies when he assumed the presidency of the United States Committee for Sports in Israel—the organization that provides sports experts and equipment to Israel and sponsors American participation in the Maccabiah Games.

At City College, the Nat Holman Gymnasium keeps his name remembered among new generations of students—"Mr. Basketball," the peerless player and unrivalled coach.

MARK SPITZ
1952—

Minutes after Arab terrorists had murdered eleven Israeli athletes in the 1972 Olympic Games in Munich, Germany, American and German security agents secretly hustled Mark Spitz, the American swimming star, out of the country.

Born in 1952, in Sacramento, California, his parents devoted years to enable him to receive the best coaching possible. At the 1968 Olympiad in Mexico City, Spitz was expected to capture a number of gold medals, but he failed badly. Up until that time he had set or tied five American records and was considered one of the outstanding swimmers of the world. Arguments with his coach, a number of anti-Semitic remarks by his teammates, and an inability to adjust to the high elevation and the cold combined to make the 1968 games a failure for him.

Spitz, who had been swimming since he was 8 under professional instruction, winning his first medals at 11, entered Indiana University as a pre-dental student. At Indiana, he set nearly three dozen collegiate and AAU swimming records, and was counted on to win a number of gold medals for the United States at the forthcoming Munich games. He won seven gold medals—unprecedented in Olympics History.

Following the Olympics, he was named the 1972 sportsman of the world by the United Press International and rated the world's top male athlete by the French news agency, Agence France Presse.

Within a year after his remarkable achievement, Spitz left college and accepted the remunerative offers for TV commercials and magazine ads that made him a millionaire by the age of 22.

Spitz first appeared in international competition at the Maccabiah Games in Israel in 1965, where he won five medals. He repeated this feat at the same games in 1969. When he accepted the chairmanship of a campaign to raise funds to send American Jewish athletes to the 1973 Maccabiah Games, he said that the experience he had gained in the so-called Jewish Olympics was a major factor in his sweep of the swimming awards at Munich.

The tragedy that surrounded the 1972 Olympics and Spitz's swift departure from Munich combined to give him a bad press following the games. He was often criticized by sportswriters, some of whom resented the commercialization of his athletic prowess. This ill feeling has long since abated, and Spitz is now considered a successful businessman.

He remains active in the Jewish community in California, where he was a pupil in the religious school of Temple B'nai Israel in Sacramento.

Of all the honors that came to him, Spitz is proudest of a resolution adopted by both Houses of Congress, commending him for his achievement in the Olympics and hailing him as "the outstanding Olympian of modern times."

THE NOBEL
LAUREATES

The preeminence of Jews among Nobel Prize winners is another facet of the Jewish contribution to all fields of human achievement. The record of Jews is particularly impressive in relation to other Americans who have received this prize.

Since the first Nobel Prizes were given in 1901, the awards have gone to 460 men, women, and institutions in all parts of the world. Among the laureates, 73 were Jews or of Jewish descent.

The first American to receive the Nobel Prize was Dr. Albert Michelson, a Jewish graduate of the United States Naval Academy and a physicist. He received the award in 1905 for his discovery of the speed of light. Since then, 138 Americans have received the award, 38 of them Jewish. American Jews have achieved this honor in all categories.

American Nobel Awards

	Total American Awards	Total Jewish American Awards
Medicine	50	17
Physics	37	13
Chemistry	21	2
Peace	15	1
Literature	8	1
Economics	7	4

See also: Roslyn Yallow, p. 138. Other American Jewish Nobel Laureates are: Leon N. Cooper (Physics, 1972), Max Delbruck (Medicine and Physiology, 1969), Dennis Gabor (Physics, 1971), Burton Richter (Physics, 1974), William Howard Stein (Chemistry, 1972), Howard M. Temin (Medicine and Physiology, 1975), Eugene Paul Wigner (Physics, 1963), and George Wald (Medicine and Physiology, 1967).

JULIUS AXELROD
1912—

Julius Axelrod, a pharmacologist, was awarded the Nobel Prize in Physiology and Medicine in 1970, together with Bernard Katz and Wolf Von Euler. Born May 30, 1912, in New York City, Dr. Axelrod was educated at the College of the City of New York, New York University, and George Washington University. He has specialized in the fields of biochemistry, and drug and hormone actions. Among his principal contributions are the discovery of 15 enzymes in hormone metabolism and the description of biochemical actions in the pineal gland. Dr. Axelrod has been Chief of the Pharmacological Section of the National Institute of Health since 1955.

DAVID BALTIMORE
1938—

Born in New York in 1938, Dr. Baltimore received his Ph.D. from Rockefeller University in 1964. He has taught experimental virology and biochemistry at Einstein University, and the Massachuetts Institute of Technology. He has also been engaged in research at the Salk Institute and the American Cancer Research Center.

He was a co-recipient of the Nobel Prize in Physiology and Medicine in 1975 for his work in the interaction between tumor viruses and the genetic material of the cell.

SAUL BELLOW
1915—

Born July 10, 1915, in Lachine, just outside of Montreal in Canada, the fourth and youngest child of Abraham and Liza Bellow, Russian immigrants from St. Petersburg, Bellow acquired four languages as he grew up: English, French, Yiddish, and Hebrew. The family moved to Chicago, where Bellow attended the University of Chicago and Northwestern, completing his degree in anthropology and sociology.

Bellow received the National Book Award three times, the International Literary Prize in 1965, the Croix de Chevalier des Arts et Lettres in 1968, and the B'nai B'rith Jewish Heri-

252

tage Award. In 1963, he became a member of the National Institute of Arts and Letters.

He was awarded the Nobel Prize in Literature in 1976 "for the human understanding and subtle analysis of contemporary culture that are combined in his work."

FELIX BLOCH
1905—

Born in Zurich, Switzerland, in 1905, Dr. Bloch came to the United States in 1934 after the Nazis came to power. He taught mathematics and physics at Stanford University.

In 1940, with Dr. Luis D. Alvarez, Dr. Bloch was the first experimental physicist to determine the magnetic moment of the neutron. During World War II, he conducted research projects at Los Alamos Laboratory and at Stanford University. In 1952 he was the co-recipient of the Nobel Prize in Physics with Dr. Edward N. Purcell for their experiments in the precise measurement of nuclear magnetic moments.

KONRAD BLOCH
1912—

Born in Germany in 1912, Dr. Bloch came to the United States in 1936. He received his doctorate at Columbia University in 1938, in the field of biology. After 1941, Dr. Bloch taught biochemistry at the University of Chicago and later at Harvard University. He was the co-recipient, with Feodor Lynen, of the Nobel Prize in 1964 in the field of Physiology and Medicine for the discovery of the mechanism and control of cholesterol metabolism.

BARUCH SAMUEL BLUMBERG
1925—

Born in New York City, educated at Union College, Columbia University, and Oxford University, Dr. Blumberg received the Nobel Prize in 1976 in the field of Medicine and Physiology. Though he has his degree in medicine, he has become somewhat of a medical anthropologist. His research has taken him to remote areas seeking blood samples from the Eskimos of the Baffin Islands and the natives of Surinam and India in his efforts to develop a vaccine against a severe form of hepatitis. He found one of his clues—the so-called Australian antigen—among the aborigines of Australia.

Dr. Blumberg, an associate director of the Institute for Cancer Research in Philadelphia, was awarded the Nobel Prize for his research that led to a test for hepatitis viruses in donated blood and to an experimental vaccine against the disease.

MELVIN CALVIN
1911—

Born in St. Paul, Minnesota, in 1911, Dr. Calvin received his doctorate at the University of Minneapolis in 1935 in the field of biochemistry. He joined the faculty of the University of California at Berkeley and was director of the bio-organic division of the Lawrence Radiation Laboratory. He worked on the Manhattan Project (atomic fission) in 1944-1945, was the United States delegate to the Geneva Conference on peaceful uses of atomic energy, and was a member of the President's Science Advisory Committee. He received the Nobel Prize in 1961 in the field of Chemistry for establishing the chemical reactions that occur during photosynthesis.

GERALD MAURICE EDELMAN
1929—

Born in New York City in 1929, Dr. Edelman received a medical degree from the University of Pennsylvania in 1954. He was associated with the Massachusetts General Hospital and spent two years as a captain in the United States Army Medical Corps before joining the Rockefeller University. He was the recipient of numerous honors and awards for his pioneering research in immunology and related fields.

In 1972 he received the Nobel Prize in Physiology and Medicine for his research in protein chemistry and immunology basic to a deeper understanding of the treatment and prevention of cancer.

ALBERT EINSTEIN
1879—1955

Albert Einstein, physicist and mathematician, was only 26 when he published his theory of relativity that ushered in the atomic age, supplanted Newtonian physics, and caused the greatest revolution in science since Galileo.

Born in Germany on March 14, 1897, Einstein lived to see his theories outlawed by the Nazis and himself deprived of his German citizenship. In 1939, he became a citizen of the United States.

As a child, he was slow to speak and had a poor memory as a student. One of his teachers told him bluntly, "You'll never amount to anything."

He was awarded the Nobel Prize in Physics in 1921 for his contribution to theoretical physics, especially for the discovery of photoelectric-effect law.

Early in 1939, the world was startled to learn that German scientists had converted atomic mass into energy in the laboratory, opening up the stunning possibility that such an explosive reaction could be converted into a weapon. After American physicists failed to convince the military leaders of the need for an atomic project, Einstein wrote a letter to President Franklin D. Roosevelt, calling attention to the possibility of an atomic bomb and urging that the United States commence research on this matter. This led to the now famous Manhattan Project.

Years later, Einstein served as chairman of the Emergency Committee of Atomic Scientists and urged outlawing the atomic and hydrogen bombs.

The year of his Nobel award, Einstein toured the United States with Chaim Weizmann and helped raise millions for the Jewish National Fund. When Weizmann, who had become the first President of Israel, died in 1952, Einstein was asked to stand for election of this office. He declined, saying, "I know a little about nature, but hardly anything of men."

When he died in 1955 at the age of 76, he was director of the School of Mathematics of the Institute for Advanced Study at Princeton, New Jersey.

His theories, which had once been said to be understood by only a dozen persons in the world, affected profoundly the ways scientists think and governments act.

E. JOSEPH ERLANGER
1874—1965

Born in 1874, Erlanger was graduated from Johns Hopkins University in 1899, and was a professor of physics at the University of Wisconsin Medical School. From 1910, he held the chair in physiology at Washington University School of Medicine in St. Louis.

In 1944, he was the co-recipient with Herbert Spencer Gasser of the Nobel Prize in Physiology and Medicine for his work on functional differentiation of nerves and on influence of pulse pressure on kidney secretion. Erlanger made fundamental contributions to the knowledge of the cardiovascular and nervous systems and to methods of physiology investigation. He was the inventor of a graphic method for measuring blood pressure.

RICHARD PHILLIPS FEYNMAN
1918—

Feynman was born in New York in 1918 and served on the staff of the first atomic bomb project at Princeton University and Los Alamos. In 1950, he became a member of the faculty of the California Institute of Technology, where he taught theoretical physics.

In 1965, Feynman was the co-recipient of the Nobel Prize in Physics with Sin-itiro Tomonaga of Japan and Julian S. Schwinger of the United States. This award was conferred in recognition of their research in quantum electrodynamics that contributed to the understanding of elementary particles in high-energy physics.

JAMES FRANCK
1882—1964

Born in 1882 in Germany, Dr. Franck moved to the United States in 1933 after the Nazis came to power. He became a member of the faculties of Johns Hopkins University and the University of Chicago, where he continued his research into the structure of matter, especially the kinetics of electrons.

In 1925, Franck was the co-recipient with Gustav Hertz of the Nobel Prize in Physics for their discovery of the laws governing the impact of an electron on an atom.

Franck was the developer of optical methods for determining dissociation temperatures of chemical combinations from molecular spectra, and confirmed the assumptions on which modern atomic theory rests.

MILTON FRIEDMAN
1912—

Born in 1912 in Rahway, New Jersey, Dr. Friedman

achieved international fame in economics for his association with the renaissance of the role of money in inflation and the consequent renewed understanding of the instrument of monetary policy.

A professor at the University of Chicago, he carried out a number of studies in the theory of economics in support of his analysis of the role of money.

At the beginning of the fifties, Friedman was a pioneer among those recommending the reorganization of the international monetary system based on free rates of exchange.

His major work, *A Monetary History of the United States 1867–1960*, is regarded as one of his most profound and distinguished achievements.

He was awarded the Nobel Prize in the field of Economics in 1976.

HERBERT SPENCER GASSER
1888—1963

Born in 1888 in Plattsville, Wisconsin, Gasser, whose field was neurophysiology, collaborated with Joseph Erlanger in investigating the electrical properties of nerve fibers, recording the electrical impulses passing over isolated nerve fibers. These studies were of great importance toward an understanding of the complexities of nerve impulse transmission.

Gasser was the co-recipient with Joseph Erlanger of the Nobel Prize in 1944 in the field of Physiology and Medicine.

Gasser was a director of the Rockefeller Institute from 1935 to 1953.

MURRAY GELL-MANN
1929—

Born in New York City in 1929, Dr. Gell-Mann is especially noted for his work in the theory of elementary particles of matter. He joined the Institute for Advanced Study at Princeton, New Jersey, in 1951, and in 1952 was a member of the faculty of the Institute of Nuclear Studies at the University of Chicago. He later became a member of the faculty of the California Institute of Technology.

In 1961, he announced his "Eightfold Way" system of classifying subatomic (elementary) particles. In 1964, Gell-Mann and Yuval Ne'eman of Israel published their book *The Eightfold Way*.

Gell-Mann was awarded the Nobel Prize in 1969 in the field of Physics for his research on the behavior of the subatomic particles, which he called "quarks."

DONALD ARTHUR GLASER
1926—

Born in 1926 in Cleveland, Ohio, Donald Glaser received his degree from the California Institute of Technology and was on the faculty of the University of Michigan.

In 1952, Glaser designed a "bubble chamber," which became an indispensable tool in observing tracks of moving subatomic particles in nuclear physics research.

He was awarded the Nobel Prize in Physics in 1960.

ROBERT HOFSTADTER
1915—

Born in 1915 in New York, Hofstadter attended City College of New York, originally intending to pursue the study of literature and philosophy. He switched his course study because he felt that the laws of physics could be tested and those of philosophy could not. After obtaining his doctorate at Princeton University in 1938, he worked during World War II at the National Bureau of Standards on the proximity fuse, which omitted radar signals and, when detecting an echo, detonated a shell. The proximity fuse thus became one of the most important antiaircraft weapons.

Dr. Hofstadter became a member of the faculty of Stanford University, and it was here that he began his work with the university's linear accelerator that brought him fame.

He was the co-recipient with Dr. Rudolf L. Mossbauer, of the Nobel Prize in Physics in 1961 for his investigations of atomic nuclei and discoveries relating to the structure of nucleons.

HENRY ALFRED KISSINGER
1923—

Heinz Alfred Kissinger, son of a high school teacher, was born in the Bavarian town of Fürth, Germany, in 1923. He was to become Secretary of State in January, 1973—the highest position ever attained by a Jew in any American administration.

The family fled Nazi Germany in 1938 and settled in New York City. Heinz became "Henry," and after excelling in high school, he commenced study at City College of New York. Drafted into the army in 1943, he soon became an interpreter, and when the American troops marched into Germany, Kissinger was with them. Kissinger became an army expert in civilian government and was soon setting up functional governments in areas of Germany captured by American troops. He left the army with the rank of captain and entered Harvard University. He completed his doctorate in 1954 in political science. Kissinger became associated with the Council on Foreign Relations, the Rockefeller Brothers Fund, and the Defense Studies Program at Harvard University.

It was during the administration of President John F. Kennedy that he became a part-time consultant to several policy-planning agencies, and in 1965 was a consultant to Ambassador Henry Cabot Lodge, Jr., who was posted in Vietnam. President Richard M. Nixon appointed Kissinger head of the powerful National Security Council, and he became the President's chief foreign policy advisor.

During the years 1968 to 1972, Kissinger, as Secretary of State, was involved in the Strategic Arms Limitation Talks (SALT), the initiation of the détente policy with Russia, and the opening of direct negotiations with China. He worked tirelessly in the pursuit of the right strategy for ending the Vietnam War, the longest in American history. After extended negotiations in Paris, final peace terms were signed on January 27, 1973.

For his efforts in negotiating an end to the war, Henry Kissinger was the co-recipient with Le Duc Tho, the North Vietnamese negotiator, of the Nobel Peace Prize.

Kissinger gave his share of the $122,000 prize money to establish a scholarship fund for the children of American servicemen killed or missing in action in Vietnam.

He was awarded the Medal of Freedom in 1976 by President Gerald R. Ford.

ARTHUR KORNBERG
1918—

Born in 1918 in Brooklyn, New York, Dr. Kornberg entered the United States Public Health Service in 1942. He was chief of the enzymes and metabolism section of the National Institute of Health. His advanced research was carried out at New York University, Washington University, and Stanford University School of Medicine. He was the co-recipient of the Nobel Prize with Severo Ochoa in the field of Physiology and Medicine, for discoveries in the biological synthesis in ribonucleic acids and deoxyribonuclei acids (DNA)—the carriers of hereditary characteristics in genetics.

KARL LANDSTEINER
1868—1943

Born in Vienna in 1868, Dr. Landsteiner came to New York in 1922 to become a member of the Rockefeller Institute for Medical Research. His research in hematology led to the successful typing of blood groups, which became the basis for matching donor and recipient in blood transfusions. He was awarded the Nobel Prize in 1930 in the field of Physiology and Medicine.

JOSHUA LEDERBERG
1925—

Born in 1925 in Montclair, New Jersey, Dr. Lederberg carried out research in microbial genetics at the University of Wisconsin and Stanford University, and was appointed director of Kennedy Laboratories for Molecular Biology and Medicine in 1961. For his studies on the organization of the genetic material in bacteria, Lederberg, with Edward L. Tatum, received the Nobel Prize for Medicine and Physiology in 1958. Lederberg's other fields of interest are the chemical origin and evolution of life, space biology, and the social and evolutionary consequences of genetic alterations in man.

In 1978, Lederberg was appointed president of Rockefeller University.

FRITZ ALBERT LIPMANN
1899—

Born in Koenigsberg, Germany in 1899, Dr. Lipmann came to the United States in 1939. As a biochemist, he carried out research at Cornell University, Massachusetts General Hospital, and Harvard University. In 1953 he was awarded the Nobel Prize in the field of Physiology and Medicine together with Hans Krebs for their biochemical studies on cell metabolism, including the discovery of coenzyme A, one of the most important substances in body metabolism. In 1966, President Lyndon B. Johnson presented him with the National Medal of Science, the nation's highest award for scientific achievement.

OTTO LOEWI
1873—1961

Born in 1873 in Germany, Loewi came to the United States in 1938 after being imprisoned by the Nazis. He taught pharmacology at New York University College of Medicine. He was awarded the Nobel Prize in 1936, together with Henry H. Dale, in the field of Physiology and Medicine, for discoveries relating to the chemical transmission of nerve impulses.

SALVADOR EDWARD LURIA
1912—

Born in 1912 in Turin, Italy, Luria was a member of the Institute of Radium in Paris. After the fall of France in 1940, he came to the United States, where he taught at Columbia University, Indiana University, the University of Illinois, and the Massachusetts Institute of Technology.

One of the pioneers in the field of microbial genetics, Luria was a co-recipient with Max Delbrueck and Alfred Hershey of the Nobel Prize in the field of Physiology and Medicine in 1969. The award was conferred on the three for their discoveries concerning the replication mechanism and the genetic structure of viruses.

OTTO MEYERHOF
1884—1951

Born in Germany in 1884, Meyerhof was a professor of physiological chemistry at the University of Kiel. In 1923, he was awarded the Nobel Prize in Physiology and Medicine together with A.V. Hill for their discovery of the fixed relationship between the consumption of oxygen and the metabolism of lactic acid in the muscle.

Forced to leave Germany in 1938, he became director of research at the Institut de Biologie Physicochimique in Paris. When the French surrendered to Germany in 1940, Dr. Meyerhof fled to southern France and then to the United

States, where he continued his research and taught at the University of Pennsylvania Medical School.

ALBERT ABRAHAM MICHELSON
1852—1931

Albert Abraham Michelson, born in Prussia in 1852, was the first American to receive the Nobel Prize.

Michelson came to the United States at the age of two and spent his youth in Virginia City, Nevada, when it was a boom town, and where his father owned a dry goods store.

Michelson wanted a career in the United States Navy and sought a Naval Academy appointment, but President Ulysses S. Grant had already used up his alloted ten appointments-at-large. However, Grant received such a strong endorsement for Michelson, he created an additional opening and gave Michelson the eleventh appointment. Michelson would later humorously state that his career was launched by an illegal act.

Michelson was graduated from the Naval Academy in 1873, and after two years at sea, resigned to become an instructor in physics at the Academy. When he left the Academy faculty after four years, he taught at Case School of Applied Science, Clark University, and for 37 years at the University of Chicago.

His breakthrough in methods of measuring the velocity of light catapulted him into the international scientific limelight at the age of 26. His further scientific experiments had a profound impact on the great theoretical developments in twentieth-century physics.

For his achievements in measuring the velocity of light, he was awarded the Nobel Prize in Physics in 1907, the first American to be so honored.

Just before Michelson's death in 1931, Albert Einstein stated that through Michelson's "marvelous experimental work, he paved the way for the development of the theory of relativity."

Michelson Hall, a science building at the Naval Academy, is named for this eminent Jewish scientist.

HERMANN JOSEPH MULLER
1890—1967

Born in New York City in 1890, Muller, a geneticist,

taught at Columbia University and the University of Texas, studied in Berlin on a Guggenheim Foundation Fellowship, and served as a senior geneticist at the Academy of Sciences in Russia. The central theme of his work was the nature and significance of changes in the stable gene material of the chromosome.

He received the Nobel Prize in Physiology and Medicine in 1946 for discovering the influence of X-rays in genetics. He was among the first to recognize that gene mutations constitute the basis for evolutionary change, and the extreme danger to genetic material in atomic activity.

MARSHALL W. NIRENBERG
1927—

Born in New York City in 1927, Nirenberg received his doctorate in biochemistry from the University of Michigan, Ann Arbor. He joined the National Institute of Health in 1960 and became chief of their biochemical genetics section in 1962.

Nirenberg and his co-workers laid the groundwork for the solution of the genetic code. He received the Nobel Prize in Physiology and Medicine in 1968 with Robert W. Holley and F. Gobind Khorana for the discovery of the process by which enzymes, consisting of a sequence of amino acids, determine a cell's function in genetic development.

ISIDOR ISAAC RABI
1898—

Born in 1898 in Austria, Rabi was brought to the United States when he was a year old. He became a tutor in physics at City College of New York and won fellowships to various European universities. In 1929 he returned to lecture at Columbia University and was appointed professor in 1937.

Continuing his research in nuclear physics, quantum mechanics, and magnetism, he was awarded the Nobel Prize in 1944 in the field of Physics for the discovery of resonance method of recording the magnetic properties of atomic nuclei.

During World War II, he served as a civilian researcher for the Office of Scientific Research and Development. In 1953, he was elected chairman of the advisory committee of the Atomic Energy Commission.

PAUL ANTHONY SAMUELSON
1915—

Born in 1915 in Gary, Indiana, Dr. Samuelson taught economics at Harvard University, the Massachusetts Institute of Technology, and served as a consultant to the National Resources Board and the War Production Board during World War II. He was chairman of the President's Task Force for Maintaining American Prosperity during the administration of President Harry S. Truman. An economic specialist in business cycles, econometrics, statistics, and mathematical programming, he was awarded the Nobel Prize in Economics in 1970 for his efforts to "raise the level of scientific analysis in economic theory."

JULIAN SEYMOUR SCHWINGER
1918—

Born in New York City in 1918, Dr. Schwinger received his doctorate at Columbia University in 1939. He became a physics research associate at the University of California. He later taught at Purdue University, the University of Chicago, and Harvard University.

He was the co-recipient of the Nobel Prize in Physics in 1965, together with Richard Feynman and Sin-itiro Tomonaga, for their research (conducted independently of one another) in the field of quantum electrodynamics, which contributed to the understanding of elementary particles in high-energy physics.

EMILIO GINO SEGRÉ
1905—

Born in Tivoli, Italy, in 1905, Dr. Segré came to the United States following the enactment of racial legislation in his native land.

A physicist, his research work at the University of California led to the synthesis of astatine. Following World War II, he participated in research on an elementary particle known as the "antiproton." In 1955, with his colleague, Dr. Owen Chamberlain, Dr. Segré reported on the discovery of the antiproton—a particle of mass identical to the proton but of opposite charge.

In 1959, Drs. Segré and Chamberlain shared the Nobel Prize in Physics for this achievement.

OTTO STERN
1888—1969

Born in Sorau, Germany in 1888, Otto Stern studied physics and worked with Albert Einstein in Prague and Zurich. In 1923, he was appointed professor of physical chemistry at Hamburg University. His research work was in developing a molecular beam method sufficiently sensitive to measure nuclear magnetic moments. His work confirmed the Planck quantum theory and the dual nature of matter.

In 1933, Stern left Germany when the Nazis came to power. The Buhl Foundation built a laboratory for him at the Carnegie Institute of Technology in Pittsburgh, and there, with I. Estermann, he continued his research in molecular physics. Dr. Stern was awarded the Nobel Prize in Physics in 1943 for his studies related to the magnetic properties of atoms and for his discovery of the magnetic moment of the proton.

SELMAN ABRAHAM WAKSMAN
1888—1973

Called the "wonder druggist," Selman Waksman is the scientist who gave the word antibiotics its modern meaning.

Born in Russia in 1888, Waksman came to the United States at the age of 22. He attended Rutgers University, and received his Ph.D. from the University of California.

At the New Jersey State Agricultural Experiment Station, where he became a microbiologist, he began his studies in the decomposition of organic matter by microorganisms and the production of antibiotic substances. These studies were to lead to the discovery of streptomycin and its value in the treatment and cure of tuberculosis.

He was awarded the Nobel Prize in Physiology and Medicine in 1952. Dr. Waksman donated 92 percent of all royalties from his discoveries to Rutgers State University's Research and Endowment Foundation.

He once recalled humorously that a Rutgers official had recommended his dismissal in 1941 because "all he seemed to be doing was playing with dirt and nothing would come of it."

THE PRESIDENCY
AND JEWRY

The Jew has always been the unconscious critic of his time. His treatment has been a barometer which indicated the level of the culture of the people in whose midst he lived. So, too, are the various expressions of sentiment made by American Presidents towards the Jews. They are a glimpse of the state of political morality of the time.

Of the thirty-nine presidencies, from George Washington to Jimmy Carter, it may be asserted that though the Jews have had widely differing political affiliations, every President has been sincerely concerned with safeguarding the rights of the nation's Jewish citizens. They have always enjoyed not only their constitutional rights, but also the genuine sympathetic interest of the President.

Many of the records of the presidencies in regard to their attitude towards the Jews are not readily available or have been lost to history. However, most archival material indicates that they have been not only friendly but, in many instances, actively militant on behalf of the Jews of America and in areas of oppression throughout the world.

GEORGE WASHINGTON
1732—1799
Federalist Party
Term of Office: 1789—1797

Washington's attitude toward the Jews was not one of condescension, but of deep respect and appreciation for their patriotism, as is evidenced by the three letters he wrote to separate Jewish congregations. Detesting the word "toleration," his letters were an eloquent expression and hope for religious harmony and are classic statements of the American ideal. His views on religious freedom were and remain authoritative expositions of fundamental American principles.

A strong believer in the ritual practices of the Jews, Washington, in a broadside issued by him to the Continental Army in 1777, called on his soldiers to live up to the standards maintained by "a great army of the children of Israel . . . that continued forty years in their different camps under the guidance and regulations of the wisest general that ever lived."

JOHN ADAMS
1735—1826
Federalist Party
Term of Office: 1797—1801

John Adams was the first President to express sympathy with the hope of a Jewish revival in Palestine—a view he voiced in a letter written in 1825, after his term of office, to Mordecai Manuel Noah: "I really wish the Jews again in Judea, an independent nation, for as I believe, the most enlightened men of it have participated in the amelioration of the philosophy of the age."

Adams had made a special study of the history of comparative religions, paying particular attention to Jewish tradition, and was known to have been a philo-Semite. In his correspondence with Thomas Jefferson, he wrote, "I will insist that the Hebrews have done more to civilize men than any other nation. If I were an atheist, and believed in blind eternal fate, I should still believe that fate had ordained the Jews to be the most essential instrument for civilizing nations."

When Adams, Thomas Jefferson, and Benjamin Franklin were members of a Congressional committee in 1777 to recommend a great seal for the new nation, the two future Presidents originally approved a design depicting the exodus of the Israelites from Egypt under the leadership of Moses.

THOMAS JEFFERSON
1743—1826
Democratic-Republican Party
Term of Office: 1801—1809

The impetus for religious freedom in the United States was given by Thomas Jefferson. In 1779, he introduced a statute, which later became the basis of the First Amendment, which called for the complete separation of church and state. This met with strong opposition by those who considered it a radical philosophy, and it was not adopted until 1785. He fought the inclusion of religious instruction in schools, and when he founded the University of Virginia, he barred religion from the curriculum. Jefferson regarded his role in the achievement of religious liberty, which he considered a human right, as his foremost contribution to the Republic.

In reply to an address by Mordecai M. Noah at the consecration of the Mill Street Synagogue in New York City, Jefferson wrote, "Your sect, by its suffering, has furnished a remarkable proof of the universal spirit of religious intolerance inherent in every sect, disclaimed by all while feeble, and practiced by all when in power . . . although we are free by law, we are not so in practice."

Jefferson was the first President to appoint a Jew to public office. In 1801, he named Reuben Etting of Maryland as United States Marshal for the state. Upon leaving office, he engaged in a notable correspondence with a number of eminent Jews of his time—Jacob de la Motta, Isaac Harby, and Mordecai M. Noah.

Following his death, the family of his close personal friend, Commodore Uriah P. Levy, purchased Monticello, Jefferson's estate, to keep it from falling into the hands of commercial realtors. The Levy family presented this landmark to the Government as a lasting memorial to Thomas Jefferson.

JAMES MADISON
1751—1836
Democratic-Republican Party
Term of Office: 1809—1817

Madison had a cordial relationship as a young man with Haym Salomon, who would often come to his aid when he was in financial difficulties. In a letter still extant, Madison wrote to Edmond Randolph, a fellow delegate to the Continental Congress, "The kindness of our friend in Front Street, near the coffee-house, is a fund which will preserve me from extremities, but I never resort to it without great mortification, as he obstinately rejects all recompense."

President Madison was the first chief executive to appoint a Jew to a diplomatic post. He named Mordecai M. Noah Consul-General to Tunis, a post he held from 1813 to 1816.

Madison was said to have been the only President able to read Hebrew, having studied the language at Princeton, where he attended classes to prepare for the ministry.

In a correspondence with Jacob de la Motta, a prominent doctor in Charleston, South Carolina, on the dedication of a synagogue in Savannah in 1820, Madison wrote, "Among the features peculiar to the political system of the United States is the perfect equality of rights which it secures to every religious sect. And it is particularly pleasing to observe in the citizenship of such as have been distrusted and oppressed elsewhere, a happy illustration of the safety and success of this experiment of a just and benign policy."

JAMES MONROE
1758—1831
Democratic-Republican Party
Term of Office: 1817—1825

President James Monroe was known to have had several personal and friendly relationships with a number of prominent Jews during his term of office. However, when President James Madison named Mordecai Manuel Noah Consul to Tunis for the purpose of ransoming a group of Americans held captive by the Barbary pirates, the then Secretary of State, James Monroe, dismissed Noah from the post on the ground that at the time of his appointment "it was not known that the religion which you profess would form any obstacle to the exercise of your consular functions." Ultimately, Noah was vindicated and the President conceded that his Judaism was no secret at the time of his appointment.

JOHN QUINCY ADAMS
1767—1848
Democratic-Republican Party
Term of Office: 1825—1829

John Quincy Adams was the first of several succeeding Presidents to concede that the use of the phrase "a Christian people" in official documents was irrelevant, although he continued its usage in spite of protests from the Jewish community.

Before becoming President, the most important of the many conversion societies of the nineteenth century had the support of Adams, who was an officer of the Society for Evangelizing Jews. Its main purpose was to convert European Jews and settle them in the United States.

In 1809, when Adams was appointed a minister to Russia by President James Madison, he strongly condemned the Czar's savage treatment of Jews in a number of his reports.

Following the end of his Presidency, he returned to the Capital as a member of Congress, where he gained a reputation as a tactless, brusque, but conscientious representative. In bitter partisan debates with David Levy Yulee of Florida—the first Jew to be elected to Congress—he sharply attacked him on many occasions as "that alien Jew delegate."

ANDREW JACKSON
1767—1845
Democratic Party
Term of Office: 1829—1837

While commanding the American forces at the Battle of New Orleans during the War of 1812, General Andrew Jackson immortalized the patriotic zeal and heroism of Judah Touro in his book *Narrative of the Defense of New Orleans.* Touro was later to become one of New Orleans' greatest benefactors, and a backer of Jackson in his political campaigns.

One of Jackson's close supporters and friend, Mordecai M.

Noah, head of the politically powerful Tammany Hall in New York, lined up strong support during the election of 1828 in which Jackson was elected President. Following his inauguration, the President appointed Noah Surveyor of the Port of New York.

Although President Jackson never joined a church during his administration because he felt it might be construed as a political gesture, he was firmly dedicated to the principles of religious freedom and the separation of church and state.

MARTIN VAN BUREN
1782—1862
Democratic Party
Term of Office: 1837—1841

President Martin Van Buren was the first Chief Executive to use the power of his office to intervene on behalf of Jews abroad. In 1840, he instructed the United States Consul in Alexandria, Egypt, to protest the conviction of several Jews in Damascus on false murder charges. It was the moral influence of this protest which was a determining factor in obtaining justice for the accused.

WILLIAM HENRY HARRISON
1773—1841
Whig Party
Term of Office: 1841

There is little on record of President William H. Harrison's attitudes towards the country's Jewish citizens, having died in office one month after his inauguration. He did, however, have a friendly correspondence with Simon and Hyman Gratz, Philadelphia merchants, when he served as Governor of the Indian Territory in 1810, in which he purchased supplies needed to equip and provision his troops who were protecting settlements against Indian attacks.

JOHN TYLER
1790—1862
Whig Party
Term of Office: 1841—1845

In the proclamation of a day of mourning for President William H. Harrison, Tyler spoke of the Americans as a "Christian people." This elicited a respectful, but vigorous protest from Jacob Ezekiel of Richmond, Virginia. Such a designation of the American people, Ezekiel contended, was contrary to one of the cardinal tenets of American political faith, namely the separation of church and state. In the President's reply to Ezekiel, he conceded that the use of the phrase was incorrect and, "For the people of whom you are one, I can feel none other than profound respect."

Two years later, the President received another letter of protest from one Joseph Simpson of Baltimore, who took exception to the announcement that General Winfield Scott, then General-in-Chief of the United States Army, would preside at a Christian missionary conference composed of army and navy officials. Tyler's reply is an historic document of great importance, in which he reaffirms in emphatic language his belief in the doctrine of separation of church and state and the absolute equality of all religious denominations and sects before the law "as a matter of right, not as a matter of favor."

President Tyler paid tribute in 1843 to Judah Touro, philanthropist from New Orleans, whose gift made possible the completion of the Bunker Hill monument.

JAMES KNOX POLK
1795—1849
Democratic Party
Term of Office: 1845—1849

President Polk appointed David Naar, one of New Jersey's most prominent Jews, to the post of United States Consul at St. Thomas, where he served from 1845 to 1848. Naar had been a political friend of Polk's and supported his candidacy for President by stumping the state for him during the 1844 election.

The First Hebrew Guards regiment of Baltimore,

Maryland, was organized in 1846 as a result of President Polk's call for volunteers to fight in the Mexican War.

ZACHARY TAYLOR
1784—1850
Whig Party
Term of Office: 1849—1850

As a general during the Mexican War, Taylor, the hero of the Battle of Buena Vista, was known to have had cordial relations with a number of Jews under his command. One, Henry Seeligson, a Texan volunteer who fought with Taylor, was complimented by him for his heroism and offered a second lieutenancy in the Second Dragoons.

Shortly after his inauguration, the President appointed Abraham Jonas, one of the early leaders of the Whig Party in Kentucky and Illinois, Postmaster of Quincy, Illinois. Jonas, a close personal friend of Abraham Lincoln, was one of the organizers of B'nai B'rith in Springfield.

Taylor is believed to be the first President to welcome a rabbi to the White House—Dr. Isaac Mayer Wise.

MILLARD FILLMORE
1800—1874
Whig Party
Term of Office: 1850—1853

It was during the Presidency of Millard Fillmore that B'nai B'rith set the precedent for its later historic diplomatic efforts on behalf of persecuted Jews abroad. The organization initiated a strong protest against a new treaty between the United States and Switzerland, which confirmed the right of Swiss cantons to deny residence to all Jews, including those who were American citizens.

In letters written by Dr. Sigmund Waterman, an early leader of B'nai B'rith, to President Fillmore; Daniel Webster, the Secretary of State; and Henry Clay, chairman of the Senate Foreign Relations Committee, he urged the United States not to ratify the treaty. In his message to the Senate, President Fillmore expressed "decisive objection" to the treaty on the ground that "neither by law, nor by treaty, nor by any other official proceeding is it competent for the government of the United States to establish any distinction between its citizens founded on differences in religious beliefs." It was this Presidential objection and the opposition of Webster and Clay which prompted the Senate to reject the treaty.

FRANKLIN PIERCE
1804—1869
Democratic Party
Term of Office: 1853—1857

President Pierce had the unique distinction of being the only President whose name appears on the charter of a synagogue. Until 1857, the laws of the District of Columbia discriminated against Jewish houses of worship. To put an end to this bias, Congress adopted legislation proclaiming that "all the rights, privileges, and immunities heretofore granted by law to the Christian churches in the city of Washington, be, and the same hereby are, extended to the Hebrew congregation of said city." When President Pierce put his name to this act, he made possible the establishment of the first synagogue, Washington Hebrew Congregation, in the nation's capital.

Pierce was the first President to offer a seat on the Supreme Court to a Jew—Judah P. Benjamin, Senator from Louisiana—which he declined. He appointed August Belmont to the post of Minister to The Hague, the first Jew to hold this rank in the American diplomatic service.

It was during his administration that the career of Julius Bien, one of the world's greatest cartographers and lithographers, was launched. After a meeting with President Pierce he suggested Bien apply for work with the then Secretary of War, Jefferson P. Davis. From that time until his retirement, there was scarcely a geographical or scientific publication issued by the government for which the maps and illustrations were not engraved by Bien.

JAMES BUCHANAN
1791—1868
Democratic Party
Term of Office: 1857—1861

In 1857, shortly after taking office, President Buchanan arranged an appointment with a delegation of prominent American rabbis—Isaac Mayer Wise, David Einhorn, and Isaac

Leeser—for the purpose of reviewing their objections to another proposed commercial treaty with Switzerland which discriminated against American Jews. While the President did make several changes in the treaty, complete emancipation was not accorded Jews in Switzerland until 1874.

During his Presidency, Buchanan was a strong supporter of the Southern cause, and many of the policies developed during his administration on the slavery issue and states' rights were initiated for him by Judah P. Benjamin, the Jewish Senator from Louisiana.

ABRAHAM LINCOLN
1809—1865
Republican Party
Term of Office: 1861—1865

Abraham Lincoln's friendship with Jews has been the subject of voluminous literature. Most prominent of these was Abraham Jonas who served with Lincoln in the Illinois legislature in 1842. It was Jonas who presided at the Lincoln-Douglas debates and first suggested his name for the Presidency. Although Jonas was one of Lincoln's most steadfast supporters before and during his Presidency, three of his sons served in the Confederate Army. When Jonas lay dying in 1863, his family interceded with Lincoln on behalf of one of his sons. Lincoln immediately issued orders for a three-week furlough for Charles Jonas who had been taken prisoner.

Soon after the outbreak of the Civil War, Lincoln played a key role in the satisfactory conclusion of the long and sometimes bitter struggle waged by Jewish leaders for the right of rabbis to serve as military chaplains. The legal status of Jewish chaplains had never been raised prior to the Civil War, and until the Mexican War, all chaplains were Protestants. When thousands of Jews from the North enlisted, the synagogues pressed for this right. The question became a national *cause célèbre* and was heatedly debated in Congress. It was not until Lincoln intervened that the discrimination against rabbis in uniform was resolved. Lincoln wrote to Rabbi Arnold Fishel that, "I shall try to have a new law broad enough to cover what is desired by you in behalf of the Israelites." In 1862, Congress passed, and Lincoln signed, the act which created a chaplaincy for Jews serving in the army.

Lincoln was the first President called upon to revoke an official act of anti-Semitism by a branch of the government. He canceled General Ulysses S. Grant's infamous Order No. 11, which expelled all Jews from the Army's Department of Tennessee during the Civil War.

It was to Isidor Bush of Missouri that Lincoln turned for help in developing a plan for a government loan of $100 million to finance the war. Joseph Seligman, the New York banker, was frequently called to the White House to discuss fiscal matters with the President, and was later able to float many of the government's war bond issues. Lincoln had offered Seligman the post of Secretary of the Treasury, but he declined.

Lincoln's close friend, Simon Wolf, known as the "Jewish ambassador to Washington" interceded with the President on behalf of a young Jewish soldier from New England who had been condemned to death for desertion after he had left his post in order to visit his mother on her deathbed. Wolf pleaded so eloquently that Lincoln pardoned the soldier at the risk of incurring the further displeasure of the War Department, which was critical of his leniency.

Philip J. Joachimson, a well-known Jewish leader in New Orleans, voiced the sentiment of Southern Jews following Lincoln's asassination: "And we, as Jews, had a distinct ground to love, respect and esteem him. I know that he, in his high position, appreciated those of our creed who had come forward to sustain him. His mind was not subject to the vulgar clamor against Jews."

ANDREW JOHNSON
1808—1875
Union Party
Term of Office: 1865—1869

In 1861, as a senator from Tennessee, Andrew Johnson made a number of scurrilous attacks against two prominent Jews in government. He berated Senator David Levy Yulee of Florida as "the contemptible little Jew" and referred to Senator Judah P. Benjamin of Louisiana, as "there's another Jew—that miserable Benjamin."

In spite of these attacks, Johnson had many Jewish friends in Nashville, and upon leaving office, was the keynote speaker at the dedication exercises of the Vine Street Temple in that city in 1874. He rode in a carriage with Rabbi Isaac Mayer Wise to the ceremony, and when he mounted the pulpit he said, "No one felt a deeper interest in the success and prosperity of them and their temple than he did," and he expressed the hope that "it would ever remain a monument to the industry, prosperity, and welfare of the Jewish citizens of Nashville."

ULYSSES S. GRANT
1822—1885
Republican Party
Term of Office: 1869—1877

In 1862, General Ulysses S. Grant signed Order No. 11— the most extensive anti-Semitic decree in American history. Grant always denied personal responsibility for this act, attributing it to a subordinate. Though the Order was in effect for less than a month and was personally revoked by President Lincoln, it caused great suffering and continued to haunt Grant all his life.

That Grant was probably misguided in this act and far from being an anti-Semite, is indicated by another act in which he set a unique precedent. In 1870, when the pogroms in Rumania shocked the world, President Grant appointed Benjamin Peixotto, who was head of B'nai B'rith, Consul to that country and gave him the specific assignment of investigating and reporting directly to him. In his charge to Peixotto, Grant said,

The humbler, poorer, more abject and more miserable a people be, be they black, white, Jew or Christian, the greater should be the concern of those in authority to extend protection, to rescue and redeem them and raise them up to equality with the most enlightened. The story of the sufferings of the Hebrews of Rumania profoundly touches every sensibility of our nature. It is one long series of outrages and wrongs . . . the United States, knowing no distinction between her own citizens on account of religion or nativity, naturally believes in a civilization the world over, which will secure the same universal views.

In 1868, during the Presidential election, when Democratic

party politicians sought to exploit Order No. 11 to antagonize Jews to vote against Grant, Simon Wolf, a well-known Washingtonian, defended Grant's record in an article in the *Boston Transcript,* establishing that he had no personal responsibility for the order. Up until that time, Grant chose to suffer the accusation in silence rather than be criticized for seeking the Jewish vote.

Wolf was later to write, "I distinctly state that during his eight years as President, Grant did more on and in behalf of American citizens of Jewish faith than all the Presidents prior thereto or since."

RUTHERFORD B. HAYES
1822—1893
Republican Party
Term of Office: 1877—1881

Rutherford Hayes was the first President to guarantee the right of civil servants to observe the Sabbath. Hayes personally intervened in a job appointment to the Department of the Interior by an applicant who refused to work on Saturday. The President was quoted as saying that anyone who would rather forgo an office than violate the Sabbath was a good citizen and worthy of the appointment.

In 1877, President Hayes named Benjamin Peixotto Consul to the court of St. Petersburg after he had completed his diplomatic mission to Rumania during the Grant administration. On instructions from the President, he was to report back on the Russian imposition of severe anti-Jewish policies against American citizens, thus initiating a long series of representations which ended in 1911 with the abrogation of the Russo-American commercial treaty. Before Peixotto could assume his new post, however, the Czar's government rejected him as an American diplomatic representative.

JAMES ABRAM GARFIELD
1831—1881
Republican Party
Term of Office: 1881—

During his short-lived administration, President James Garfield named Simon Wolf Consul-General to Egypt. In making the appointment, he said, "I am happy to name a descendant of a people who had been enslaved by the Egyptians as a representative to that country from a great free land."

In another review of the rights of Jewish-Americans living in Russia, which was made at the urgent request of B'nai B'rith, the Secretary of State, James G. Blaine, reported to President Garfield that "it would be, in the judgment of this government, absolutely inadmissible that a domestic law restraining native Hebrews residing in certain parts of the Empire might operate to hinder an American citizen."

When President Garfield was shot in a railroad station on July 2, 1881, he had to be removed to a hospital in Elberon, New Jersey, because there was no hospital in the capital to which he could be taken. At a special prayer service for Garfield, Adolphus Solomons, one of the founders of the American Red Cross, proposed that the city establish a hospital to be named for Garfield. The city adopted the idea and the first contributions toward the opening of Garfield Memorial Hospital came from the two Washington Jewish congregations.

CHESTER ALAN ARTHUR
1830—1886
Republican Party
Term of Office: 1881—1885

When Chester Arthur became President following the assassination of James Garfield, he had the distinction of recommending that the United States adhere to the Treaty of Geneva, by which the country became affiliated with the International Red Cross. When the Senate ratified the Treaty in 1882, the President named Adolphus Solomons, head of B'nai B'rith, and Clara Barton as the American representatives to the first International Red Cross Congress in Geneva.

In the Red Cross Museum in Washington, D. C., a number of historic objects connected with the first Geneva meeting are on exhibit. Among the mementos are Solomons' calling card, the State Department commission of appointment, and a dinner invitation from the President of Switzerland.

STEPHEN GROVER CLEVELAND
1837—1908
Democratic Party
Terms of Office: 1885—1889; 1893—1897

Grover Cleveland was the first President to pay tribute to a national Jewish organization. In a letter to B'nai B'rith on its golden jubilee in 1893, he stated,

> A society formed for the furtherance of such noble purposes as that of the B'nai B'rith should not only excite the enthusiasm of its members, but should also inspire the good wishes of all who desire to see humanity bettered and the higher instincts of our nature cultivated. Accept for your Order my sincere wish that the gratifying results which have followed its effort for good in the half century that has passed may be multiplied in the years to come.

During his first term, Cleveland appointed Oscar Straus of New York as United States Minister to Turkey, and had planned to name Isidor Straus, Oscar's brother, Secretary of the Treasury, but political obligations made that impossible.

When the Austrian government refused to accept John Kieley of Virginia as Minister-designate because Mrs. Kieley was Jewish, President Cleveland denounced the refusal and stated that the United States would not tolerate any religious distinction. Cleveland preferred to leave the post vacant throughout his administration rather than agree to an act of anti-Semitism.

During his second term, the issue of Russia's continuation of discriminatory practices against American Jews was again raised by B'nai B'rith. They protested this treatment and the fact that Russian consular officials in the United States were compelling Americans seeking visas to state their religion, and denied Jews the right to travel or visit relatives in Russia. On the basis of this protest, Cleveland instructed the Secretary of State to send a note to the Czar's government protesting this "religious inquisitorial function."

In the latter part of Cleveland's second term, during the height of the mass immigration to the United States from Russia and Poland, Congress passed a law providing for a

compulsory educational test for immigrants. Cleveland
promptly vetoed the bill on the grounds that it was discriminatory and was a radical departure from previous national
policy on immigration.

BENJAMIN HARRISON
1833—1901
Republican Party
Term of Office: 1889—1893

Benjamin Harrison, occupant of the White House in the interim between the two Cleveland administrations, was the
first President to accept a national petition from leaders of
American Jewry, urging an international conference "to
consider the Israelite claim to Palestine as their ancient
home." The Reverend William E. Blackstone, a prominent
Protestant clergyman, initiated the petition in 1891, six years
before Theodor Herzl convened the first Zionist Congress.
The petition was signed by many of the eminent figures in
American life, including J. Pierpont Morgan; Chief Justice
Melville Fuller; William McKinley, the future President; and
John D. and William Rockefeller.

When the stringent anti-Jewish edicts were being enforced
in Czarist Russia, Congress adopted a resolution calling upon
the State Department to protest these persecutions. President
Harrison, in a message to Congress, stated:

This government has found occasion to express in a
friendly spirit, but with much earnestness, to the government of the Czar its serious concern because of the harsh
measures now being enforced against the Hebrews in
Russia. By the revival of anti-Semitic laws, long in abey-
ance, great numbers of these unfortunate people have
been constrained to abandon their homes and leave the
empire by reason of the impossibility of finding subsist-
ence within the pale to which it is sought to confine
them . . .

The Hebrew is never a beggar; he always kept the
law—lives by toil—often under severe and oppressive
civil restrictions. It is also true that no race, sect, or
class has more fully cared for its own than the Hebrew
race.

WILLIAM MCKINLEY
1843—1901
Republican Party
Term of Office: 1897—1901

President McKinley on many occasions voiced his outrage at the persecution of Russian Jews which continued, in spite of the protests by the State Department and several former Presidents.

In 1898, at a meeting of the B'nai B'rith leaders at the White House regarding the plight of the Jews in Eastern Europe and the lack of recognition of the American passport in Russia, the President stated, "Nothing would give me greater pleasure than to comply with your request, and I have instructed the Secretary of State to bring this matter to the attention of the Russian government."

In 1897, the President and his entire cabinet attended exercises marking the laying of the cornerstone of the Washington Hebrew Congregation.

THEODORE ROOSEVELT
1858—1919
Republican Party
Term of Office: 1901—1909

Oscar S. Straus was the first Jew to serve in a Presidential cabinet. He was appointed Secretary of Commerce and Labor by President Theodore Roosevelt in 1906.

In 1918, when the President received the Nobel Peace Prize for his efforts while in office to settle the Russo-Japanese War, Roosevelt contributed part of the prize to the National Jewish Welfare Board.

In his annual message to Congress in December, 1904, Roosevelt commented on the notorious Kishnev pogroms of 1903. He stated:

I have felt a degree of personal sympathy and personal horror of this dreadful tragedy (Kishnev pogrom) as great as can exist in the minds of any of you gentlemen yourselves. Exactly as I should claim sympathy from any of you for any tragedy that happened to any Christian people, so I should hold myself unworthy of my present

286   POSTAL AND KOPPMAN

position if I failed to feel just as deep horror over an
outrage like this done to the Jewish people in any part of
the earth.

WILLIAM HOWARD TAFT
1857—1930
Republican Party
Term of Office: 1909—1913

William Taft's close association with the Jews of America
started as a young boy in Cincinnati, when he frequently accompanied his father to a synagogue to hear the sermons of
Rabbi Isaac Mayer Wise, who was a personal friend of the
elder Taft. During his Presidency, he spoke on two occasions
from synagogue pulpits and attended a Passover dinner at the
home of Colonel Harry Cutler in Providence, Rhode Island.

When the Russian "Black Hundreds" perpetrated massacres
in the Ukraine and the Crimea, the President leaned toward
abrogating a commercial treaty with Russia on the grounds
that "no humane government could look with favor on a
member of the family of nations which permitted such acts
within its borders." He was advised, however, that there was
no legal basis for the abrogation, and that it might invite
further atrocities against Jews.

When reports arrived of new Russian excesses, B'nai B'rith
launched a nationwide campaign to mobilize public sentiment
in favor of abrogation with mass meetings and, with the help
of Andrew D. White, former ambassador to Russia, organized the National Citizens Committee.

The long struggle for abrogation was finally approved by
Congress in 1911. President Taft later said that the efforts of
B'nai B'rith had been a decisive factor in changing public
opinion, and that it was the first time in American history
that a treaty was rescinded because of religious persecution.

THOMAS WOODROW WILSON
1856—1924
Democratic Party
Term of Office: 1913—1921

In the face of bitter opposition, Woodrow Wilson was the
first President to appoint a Jew to the Supreme Court. The
appointment of Louis D. Brandeis touched off one of the bit-

terest political arguments of the time. Amid anti-Semitic overtones, Wilson stood steadfast and succeeded in having Brandeis confirmed after the Senate debated the nomination for five months.

When he appointed Henry Morgenthau, Sr. as Ambassador to Turkey, he instructed him to "remember that anything you can do to improve the lot of your co-religionists is an act that will reflect credit upon America, and you can count on the full power of the administration to back you up."

Wilson genuinely believed in the Zionist cause and in his support of the Balfour Declaration, stated:

> I have before this expressed my personal approval of the Declaration of the British Government regarding Palestine. I am moreover persuaded that the Allied nations with the fullest concurrence of our own government and people are agreed that in Palestine there shall be laid the foundation of a Jewish Commonwealth.

Several days before sailing for Europe to attend the Peace Conference at Versailles, Wilson accepted the Gold Medal Award for 1918 from B'nai B'rith. He assured the leaders of B'nai B'rith that when terms of peace are agreed upon by the belligerents, he would do whatever he could for the displaced Jews of Europe. "I realize that, for one thing, one of the most difficult problems will be to secure the proper guarantees for the just treatment of the Jewish people in countries where they have not been justly dealt with, and unhappily there are several of which that may be said."

During an upsurge of anti-Semitism in the immediate post-World War I period, an appeal to leaders of public opinion was issued and signed by hundreds of the nation's leading citizens, with Wilson's name at the head of the list.

WARREN GAMALIEL HARDING
1865—1923
Republican Party
Term of Office: 1921—1923

When Harding served in the Senate during the long debate over the naming of Louis D. Brandeis to the Supreme Court, he voted against confirmation. It was charged that his opposition stemmed from the fact that Brandeis was Jewish. A friend, Alfred Cohen, defended Harding's vote in a number of newspaper articles on the ground that his sole objection to the appointment had been based on Brandeis' liberal economic and political views.

During his short term in office, Harding showed his friendship and sympathy for the Zionist cause in signing a Joint Congressional Resolution endorsing the Balfour Declaration in 1922. He wrote a personal letter to the Palestine Foundation Fund in which he stated hopes for a Jewish homeland in Palestine.

At the laying of the cornerstone of the Washington Jewish Center, he delivered a masterly address in which he stated, that "Hebraic mortar cemented the foundations of American democracy."

JOHN CALVIN COOLIDGE
1872—1933
Republican Party
Term of Office: 1923—1929

It was during the administration of Calvin Coolidge in 1924, when immigration to the United States was restricted to limited quotas, that a period of Jewish history in America came to an end. Immigration to America from the great centers of Jewish life in Europe, which had gone on for over 250 years in a migration that paralleled the Exodus in its reputed numbers, was to be severely limited.

Three weeks after becoming President, Coolidge, in a letter of greeting to the Jewish Welfare Board, said:

Every movement to maintain a close relationship between the community of today and the best achievements of the past is particularly worthy of encouragement. I recognize your organization as among those peculiarly devoted to this purpose and because of that, I have a particular pleasure in extending my best wishes to you.

When he appeared as the principal speaker at the dedication of the Jewish Community Center in Washington, D. C., in 1925, he stated:

About this institution will be organized, and from it will be radiated the influences of these civic works in which the genius of the Jewish people has always found such eloquent expression. Such an establishment, so noble in its physical proportions, so generous in its social purposes, is truly a part of the civic endowment of the nation's capital.

HERBERT CLARK HOOVER
1874—1964
Republican Party
Term of Office: 1929—1933

In 1932, Herbert Hoover became the second President to appoint the second Jew to the Supreme Court—Benjamin Cardozo. This appointment was an outstanding instance of Hoover's appreciation of the judicial qualities of Cardozo, who had been an outspoken member of the Democratic party.

As a food and relief administrator following the end of World War I, Hoover was visibly shocked at the shooting of 37 Jews in a pogrom in Poland. His secretary, Lewis Strauss, wrote, "It was then that we needed a champion and we needed one badly. If a strong man who was a non-Jew had not taken up the protest, the results of this propaganda would have had no repercussions in the United States." Hoover wrote several letters to Polish Premier Ignace Paderewski, protesting the massacre.

During his administration and after, Hoover strongly supported Zionist goals in Palestine. As a guest speaker at a Zionist function, he stated:

I have watched with genuine admiration the steady and unmistakable progress made in the rehabilitation of Palestine which, desolate for centuries, is now renewing its youth and vitality through the enthusiasm, hard work, and self-sacrifice of the Jewish pioneers who toil there in a spirit of peace and social justice.

When the persecution of Jews began in Germany in the thirties, Hoover added his name to a public protest:

I am glad to again evidence my own indignation and to join in an expression of public protest at the treatment of Jews in Germany. It is the duty of men everywhere to express our indignation not alone at the suffering these men are imposing on an innocent people, but at the blow they are striking at civilization.

In 1938, when the Federal Council of Churches in the United States condemned the Nazi treatment of the Jews as "the day of the inquisition in Germany," Hoover joined in the protest. He also was an outspoken advocate of a plan in 1939 to permit the entry of 20,000 German refugee children outside the prevailing quota.

FRANKLIN DELANO ROOSEVELT
1882—1945
Democratic Party
Term of Office: 1933—1945

Roosevelt's association with outstanding members of American Jewry dates back to the time following World War I when he served as Assistant Secretary of the Navy. At the Peace Conference, Roosevelt developed a close personal relationship with Felix Frankfurter, Louis Brandeis, and Stephen Wise, who were representatives to the assembly of nations on behalf of the rights of the Eastern European Jews and to further the implementation of the Balfour Declaration on Palestine.

Although many of his closest advisors were Jewish—among them Samuel Rosenman, Felix Frankfurter, Henry Morgenthau, Jr., Bernard Baruch, and David Lilenthal—there was an apparent apathy on his part toward the Nazi atrocities which began in 1933. It has been said that at a time when Roosevelt was the most influential public figure in the world, he seemed to content himself with a few pious words, intended more to calm his constituencies than to rebuke the German government.

In the famous incident of May, 1939, when the *SS St. Louis*, with its boatload of 907 German refugees bound for Cuba, was refused a permit to land, Roosevelt would not intervene on their behalf.

In the years following his death, there have been numerous examinations of Roosevelt's policies towards the Holocaust and the relationship of his administration with the German government during the pre-World War II period. Many of these studies indicate that his response to the Jewish plight was an ambivalent one from the beginning of his administration in 1933, a year both Roosevelt and Hitler came to power, through 1941.

During his first administration, he remained indifferent to

the American policy of six ex-presidents in their support of a Jewish homeland in Palestine. In his second administration, however, he did support Zionist aspirations, and in a statement to B'nai B'rith he said:

I know how long and ardently the Jewish people have worked and prayed for the establishment of Palestine as a free and democratic Jewish commonwealth. I am convinced that the American people give their support to this aim and I shall help to bring about its realization.

HARRY S. TRUMAN
1884—1972
Democratic Party
Term of Office: 1945—1953

In an informal conference before leaving the White House in January, 1953, President Truman said:

One of the proudest moments of my life occurred at 6:12 p.m. on Friday, May 14th, 1948, when I was able to announce recognition of the new State of Israel by the government of the United States. In view of the long friendship of the American people for the Zionist ideal, it was particularly appropriate that our government should be the first to recognize the new State.

The President had been under severe pressure in 1948 from such powerful groups as the State Department, the solid block of Arab countries in the United Nations, the British Foreign Office, and the Department of Defense, to oppose the recognition of Israel. Jewish history will gratefully record that in those critical, fateful days of Israel's rebirth, President Truman was a steadfast friend.

Subsequently, he continued on many occasions to demonstrate his warm friendship for Israel with generous loans to bolster the economy of the fledgling Jewish state. At a dinner tendered on the occasion of the establishment of the colony "K'far Truman," the Israeli ambassador, Abba Eban, said in addressing the President:

It is a good test of friendship for men and nations to recall their greatest loneliness and ask themselves who then stood at their side when all appeared lost. By this crucial

test President Truman must be surely accounted Israel's
most authentic and decisive friend.

DWIGHT DAVID EISENHOWER
1890—1969

Republican Party
Term of Office: 1953—1961

As Commander-in-Chief of the Allied forces in Europe
during World War II, General Dwight D. Eisenhower played
a significant role in contemporary Jewish history. As the
liberator of the pitiful handful of Jews who survived the Nazi
Holocaust, he was particularly concerned about their rehabilitation in the displaced persons camps in the American Zone
of Germany during the difficult months after their liberation.

While policies were being developed by the Allies regarding displaced persons, the surviving Jews of Europe were
regarded as semi-wards. Unable to return to their country of
origin, and barred by the British from entering Palestine,
their resettlement posed insurmountable problems.

At the end of the war, President Truman sent Earl Harrison, dean of the University of Pennsylvania Law School, to
Europe to survey the situation and report directly to him on
what priorities were needed to ease the suffering of these survivors. Upon receipt of a scathing report from Dean Harrison, President Truman immediately contacted Eisenhower,
demanding his personal attention to the plight of the Jewish
DP's. Eisenhower, in an unprecedented move, created a new
staff position, "Advisor on Jewish Affairs," and appointed
Chaplain Judah Nadich to this post.

Nadich's reports to Eisenhower made wide-ranging sugges-
tions for improving conditions in the camps. Cutting through
endless discussion and red tape, he issued directives which
created separate camps for Jewish DP's and educational and
work programs to prepare them for ultimate emigration to
Palestine.

Dwight Eisenhower was always steadfast in his opposition
to bigotry. Speaking at a United Jewish Appeal dinner in
1947, he said:

Only one who has seen, as I have, the mental and
physical effects of savagery, repression, and bigotry upon
the persecuted of Europe, can realize the full need for

material help and encouragement. The UJA is a demonstration of men united in mercy toward the stricken and an example that invites the world to renew with increased zeal the struggle against injustice, persecution and slavery.

In 1954, he was the guest speaker at the American Jewish Tercentenary dinner, marking the 300th anniversary of the founding of the first synagogue in North America, and the beginning of the American Jewish community. On this occasion, Eisenhower said that it was one of the enduring satisfactions of his life that he was privileged to lead the forces of the free world which finally crushed the brutal regime in Germany, freeing the remnant of Jews for a new life and hope in Israel.

JOHN FITZGERALD KENNEDY
1917—1963
Democratic Party
Term of Office: 1961—1963

Although Joseph Kennedy, father of the future President, had been accused of anti-Semitism and Nazi sympathies during his diplomatic appointment to Great Britain, subsequent studies indicate that in 1938, he sought permission of the State Department on a number of occasions to speak out against the persecution of the Jews in Germany. The senior Kennedy also protested the proposed abandonment of the Balfour Declaration and the British restriction of Jewish immigration to Palestine.

During John Fitzgerald Kennedy's campaigns for the Senate and the Presidency, the rumors about his father's anti-Jewish attitudes persisted. His right as a Roman Catholic to serve in the Presidency was strongly backed by the American Jewish community, who looked upon Kennedy as a victim of the same religious bigotry they had been subjected to.

In an address during the Presidential campaign before the American Society of Newspaper Editors, he asked:

Are we going to admit that a Jew can be elected mayor of Dublin, a Protestant can be chosen foreign minister of France, a Moslem can serve in the Israeli Parliament, but a Catholic cannot be President of the United States?

On Jewish matters, he was best known for the position he held and the measures he took on international questions of concern affecting Israel and Soviet Jewry. He favored American ratification of the United Nations Genocide Pact, and when he addressed the United Nations, he condemned the forced closing of synagogues in the Soviet Union.

On the day before his death, Kennedy announced that he would personally present the Enrico Fermi Award to Dr. J. Robert Oppenheimer at a White House ceremony scheduled for December 2nd, 1963. It was an atonement for the grave injustice done to Dr. Oppenheimer when he was suspended and denied security clearance as a consultant to the Atomic Energy Commission. His decision to personally present the award signified his determination to close the door on the McCarthy period.

President Kennedy appointed two Jews to his Cabinet— Abraham Ribicoff as Secretary of Health, Education, and Welfare, and Arthur Goldberg as Secretary of Labor.

LYNDON BAINES JOHNSON
1908—1973
Democratic Party
Term of Office: 1963—1969

With his wide knowledge and influence in Congress, President Johnson exerted his power in behalf of Israel in a number of crisis situations. His actions, he said, "were because I sincerely felt that Israel was in the right."

During his administration, the President maintained friendly relations with American Jewry and he was host on numerous occasions to Israel's top leadership. His views toward Israel always reflected a sympathy with their struggle for survival against formidable opposition, and he risked the grave displeasure of Arab countries when he appointed Arthur J. Goldberg ambassador to the United Nations in 1965.

Among his closest advisors were such notable Jews as Abe Fortas, Arthur Goldberg, Wilbur Cohen, Sheldon Kaplan, Emanuel Cohen, and Eugene Rostow. Abe Fortas was the first Jew to be nominated by a President for the office of Chief Justice of the Supreme Court.

On December 9, 1963, shortly after becoming President, Lyndon Johnson attended the funeral services at Temple Emanu-El for his close personal friend, Herbert H. Lehman.

During the same month, he took time out to deliver a speech at the dedication of Agudas Achim Synagogue's new building at Austin, Texas.

In 1967, the Jewish National Fund of America presented President Johnson with a silver Jerusalem Bible and several rare volumes of biblical and Jewish themes. The Bible was inscribed: "Presented to the Honorable Lyndon Baines Johnson, President of the United States, in recognition of his extraordinary qualities of humanity and leadership and in appreciation of his steadfast pursuit of peace and his championship of American-Israel friendship."

RICHARD MILHOUS NIXON
1913—
Republican Party
Term of Office: 1969—1974

Whatever history may say about President Nixon, Israel will recall with gratitude that it was his personal intervention, against major opposition, which brought about a major airlift of weapons during the Yom Kippur War and staved off the threat to Israel of near annihilation.

The President had a warm relationship with Israel's Prime Minister Golda Meir, and during his campaign for reelection in 1972, the Democrats alleged that as far as American Jewry was concerned the Nixon campaign operated out of the Israeli embassy in Washington, D.C. Though it was the Jewish vote which helped in Richard Nixon's reelection, their attitudes toward him were tempered with caution as he embarked on his policy of détente with the Soviet Union. However, in meetings with the Soviet leader, Leonid Brezhnev, the President, on several separate occasions, discussed an easement in the rigid Soviet policy towards Jewish emigration.

In 1974, on a trip to Israel, he visited Yad Vashem (Martyrs and Heroes Rememberence), one of the most venerated Jewish memorials to the victims of the Holocaust. After signing the guest book, he said it was the most awesome and impressive sight he had ever seen.

When the contents of several taped conversations Nixon had with aides were revealed in news media reports, there were charges that a number of them contained anti-Semitic remarks and ethnic epithets. Nixon issued a public denial over these allegations, citing his vigorous political and military backing of Israel and his appointment of Jews to key posts in his administration (Henry Kissinger, Leonard Garment, Herbert Stein, and Arthur Burns) as proof to the contrary.

GERALD RUDOLPH FORD
1913—
Republican Party
Term of Office: 1974—1976

As a Congressman, Gerald Ford was concerned about the plight of Soviet Jewry and was one of the signers of a declaration condemning the suppression of Jewish spiritual and cultural life in Russia. In 1970, he co-sponsored a resolution in the House calling upon the Soviets to commute the death penalties imposed on two Soviet Jews. Pleased when the sentences were commuted, he said, "Our elation should be tempered by the circumstances which gave rise to the incident . . . the fact that the Soviet Union is holding Jews in that country against their will is unconscionable."

When former Vice-President Spiro Agnew's novel was published, it was criticized as openly anti-Semitic and anti-Zionist. President Ford remarked that the Agnew book was "wrong, both substantively and morally," and that, "it is an unsavory footnote to a chapter in our history that best remain closed."

On an official visit to Poland in 1975, the President visited Brezezinka, where Auschwitz, one of the most notorious Nazi concentration camps, was located. After placing a wreath at the stone memorial to the four million victims who perished there, Ford was visibly moved when he said, "This monument and the memory of these it honors should be an inspiration to the dedicated pursuit of peace and the security of all people."

When General George S. Brown, chairman of the Joint Chiefs of Staff, complained in a lecture at Duke University about the extent of Israeli influence in the United States, he was rebuked by President Ford. In a statement issued by his press secretary, the President said, "I consider General Brown's remark ill-advised and poorly handled and in no way represents my view or the views of any senior officer of my administration—military or civilian."

President Ford made numerous Jewish appointments to important offices in his administration, among them Edward H. Levi as United States Attorney General—the first time a Jew had held this cabinet post. He reappointed Dr. Arthur Burns as chairman of the Federal Reserve Board and Henry Kissinger as Secretary of State. He named Alan Greenspan as chairman of the Council of Economic Advisors and Ron Nessen, a former television news reporter, as his press secretary.

JAMES EARL CARTER
1924—
Democratic Party
Term of Office: 1976—

Prior to his nomination for the Presidency, Jimmy Carter, in a letter to the Anti-Defamation League of B'nai B'rith, commented on a number of anti-Semitic remarks made by Spiro Agnew on a television show. He wrote, "The comments are false, malicious, and anti-Semitic. The preservation of a strong and viable State of Israel is not only in Israel's interest and in the interest of world Jewry, it is in the national interest of the United States as well."

Shortly after becoming President, Jimmy Carter, in a number of impassioned speeches, started his crusade for human rights. In seeking to promote this fundamental liberty, he reaffirmed the commitment of the United States to the principles contained in the United Nations Declaration on Human Rights, and stressed the right of Soviet Jewry to emigrate.

DOCUMENTS OF HONOR

Dating back to the American Revolution, a special niche in Jewish American history is reserved for the treasured documents which were written or received by various individuals and congregations. The documents have forged a link in the ongoing chronicle between an ancient people in a new world and the present American Jewish community—the largest in the world.

A number of these documents were received from American Presidents during and after their terms of office. Several represent published protests against anti-Semitism from well-remembered or forgotten figures of yesterday.

After becoming President, George Washington wrote three letters to Jewish congregations. The sentiments expressed in these letters are strong personal statements on political and religious freedom.

The first letter was sent to Mickve Israel Congregation of Savannah, Georgia. Levi Sheftall, president of the congregation, had sent a congratulatory message to George Washing to which he replied.

I thank you with great sincerity for your congratulation on my appointment to the office which I have the honor to hold by the unanimous choice of my fellow-citizens, and especially the expressions you are pleased to use in testifying the confidence that is reposed in me by your congregation.

As the delay which has naturally intervened between my election and your address has afforded me an opportunity for appreciating the merits of the Federal Government and for communicating your sentiments of its administration, I have rather to express my satisfaction rather than regret at a circumstance which demonstrates (upon experiment) your attachment to the former as well as approbation of the latter.

I rejoice that a spirit of liberality and philanthropy is much more prevalent than it formerly was among the enlightened nations of the earth, and that your brethren will benefit thereby in proportion as it shall become still more extensive; happily the people of the United States have in many instances exhibited examples of worthy of imitation, the salutary influence of which will doubtless extend much further if gratefully enjoying those blessings of peace which (under the favor of heaven) have been attained by fortitude in war, they shall conduct themselves with reverence to the Deity and charity towards their fellow-creatures.

May the same wonder-working Deity, who long since delivered the Hebrews from their Egyptian oppressors, planted them in the promised land, whose providential agency has lately been conspicuous in establishing these

302

United States as an independent nation, still continue to water them with the dews of heaven and to make the inhabitants of every denomination participate in the temporal and spiritual blessings of that people whose God is Jehovah.

G. Washington

+

The second letter received from George Washington was sent to the congregations of Savannah, Philadelphia, New York, and Richmond.

To the Hebrew Congregations in the Cities of Philadelphia, New York, Charleston, and Richmond:

Gentlemen:

The liberality of sentiment toward each other, which marks every political and religious denomination of men in this country, stands unparalleled in the history of nations.

The affection of such a people is a treasure beyond the reach of calculation, and the repeated proofs which my fellow-citizens have given of their attachment to me and approbation of my doings, form the purest source of my temporal felicity. The affectionate expressions of your address again excite my gratitude and receive my warmest acknowledgements.

The power and goodness of the Almighty, so strongly manifested in the events of our late glorious revolution, and His kind interposition in our behalf, have been no less visible in the establishment of our present equal government. In war He directed the sword, and in peace He has ruled in our councils. My agency in both has been guided by the best intentions and a sense of duty I owe to my country.

And as my exertions have hitherto been amply rewarded by the approbation of my fellow-citizens, I shall endeavor to deserve a continuance of it by future conduct.

May the same temporal and eternal blessings which you implore for me rest upon your congregation.

G. Washington

+

The third letter from George Washington was received by Congregation Jeshuat Israel of Newport, Rhode Island.

To the Hebrew Congregation in
Newport, Rhode Island
Gentlemen:

While I receive, with much satisfaction, your address replete with expressions of affection and esteem; I rejoice in the opportunity of assuring you that I shall always retain a grateful remembrance of the cordial welcome I experienced in my visit to Newport, from all classes of Citizens.

The reflection on the days of difficulty and danger which are past is rendered the more sweet, from a consciousness that they are succeeded by days of uncommon prosperity and security. If we have wisdom to make the best use of the advantages with which we are now favored, we cannot fail, under the just administration of a good Government, to become a great and happy people.

The Citizens of the United States of America have a right to applaud themselves for having given to mankind examples of an enlarged and liberal policy; a policy worthy of imitation. All possess alike liberty of conscience and immunities of citizenship. It is now no more than toleration is spoken of, as if it was by the indulgence of one class of people, that another enjoyed the exercise of their inherent natural rights. For happily the Government of the United States, which gives to bigotry no sanction, to persecution no assistance, requires only that they who live under its protection should demean themselves as good citizens, in giving it on all occasions their effectual support.

It would be inconsistent with the frankness of my character not to avow that I am pleased with your favorable opinion of my administration, and fervent wishes for my felicity. May the Children of the Stock of Abraham, who dwell in this land, continue to merit and enjoy the good will of the other inhabitants; while everyone shall sit in safety under his own vine and fig tree, and there shall be none to make him afraid. May the father of all mercies scatter light and not darkness in our paths, and make us all in our several vocations useful here, and in his own due time and way everlastingly happy.

G. Washington

✦

In correspondence with eminent Jews of his time after he left the White House, Thomas Jefferson continued to champion religious liberty and to oppose discrimination. The following letters indicate his deep commitment to this cause:

To Joseph Marx of Richmond, Virginia
. . . and with the regret I have ever felt at seeing a sect, the parent and basis of all those of Christendom, singled out by all of them for a persecution and oppression which prove they have profited nothing from the benevolent doctrines of Him whom they profess to make the model of their principles and practice.

To Mordecai M. Noah of New York
Your sect, by its suffereing, has furnished a remarkable proof of the universal spirit of religious intolerance inherent in every sect, disclaimed by all while feeble, and practiced by all in power. Our laws have applied the only antidote to this vice, protecting our religious, as they do our civil rights, by putting all men on an equal footing. But more remains to be done, for although we are free by the law we are not so in practice; public opinion erects itself into an inquisition, and exercises its office with as much fanaticism as fans the fires of an auto-da-fe. The prejudice still scowling on your section of our religion, although the elder one, cannot be unfelt by yourselves. It is to be hoped that individual dispositions will at length mould themselves to the model of the law.

To Isaac Harby of Charleston, South Carolina
I have thought it a cruel addition to the wrongs which that injured sect have suffered that their youth should be excluded from the instructions in science afforded to all others in our public seminaries by imposing upon them a course of theological reading which their consciences do not permit them to pursue; and in the university lately established here [*the University of Virginia which Jefferson founded*] we have set the example of ceasing to vio-

late the rights of conscience of the different sects
respecting their religion.

To Thomas Cooper, Monticello, Virginia
In our annual report to the legislature, after stating the
constitutional reasons against a public establishment of
any religious instruction, we suggest the expedience of
encouraging the different religious sects to establish, each
for itself, a professorship of their own tenets on the con-
fines of the university, so near as that their students may
attend the lectures there, and have the free use of our library and every other accommodation we can give
them; preserving however, their independence of us and
of each other . . . and by bringing the sects together
and mixing them with the mass of other students we
shall soften their asperities, liberalize and neutralize their
prejudices, and make the general religion a religion of
peace, reason and morality.

✦

In 1808, Jacob Henry was elected to the North Carolina
Legislature from Carteret County. The following year another
representative demanded that Henry be expelled from office
on the grounds that he had not taken his oath of office on the
New Testament, and the legislative body was compelled to
try him on the charges. When finally cleared, Henry rose to
speak:

Who among us feels himself so exalted above his fellows
as to have a right to dictate to them their mode of belief? Shall this free country set an example of
persecution which even the returning reason of enslaved
Europe would not submit to? Will you bind the
conscience in chains and fasten conviction upon the
mind in spite of the conclusions of reason? . . . Are you
prepared to plunge at once from the sublime heights of
moral legislation into the dark and gloomy caverns of
superstitious ignorance? Will you drive from your shores
and from the shelter of your constitutions all who do not
lay their oblations on the same altar, observe the same
ritual, and subscribe to the same dogmas? If so, which
among the various sects into which we are divided shall
be the favored one?

✦

During the Civil War, the Reverend M. J. Michelbacher, spiritual leader of Congregation Beth Ahabah of Richmond, Virginia, visited President Jefferson Davis and a number of Confederate generals to try to secure furloughs for the many Jewish soldiers to attend services on the High Holy Days and Passover. Answering the Rabbi's request, General Robert E. Lee wrote:

> I cannot . . . grant the general furlough you desire, but must leave it to individuals to make their own applications to their several commanders, in the hope that many will be able to enjoy the privilege you seek for them. Should any be deprived of the opportunity of offering up their prayers according to the rites of their Church, I trust their penitence may nevertheless be accepted by the Most High, and their petitions answered.

✝

During the Civil War General Ulysses S. Grant issued his infamous Order No. 11, December 17, 1862, which provided for the expulsion of all Jews "as a class" from the Department of Tennesssee within 24 hours. Three Jews from Paducah, Cesar Kaskel, J. W. Kaskel, his brother, and D. Wolff, took the lead in organizing a nationwide protest against the order. First they telegraphed the following protest to President Abraham Lincoln:

> This inhuman order, the carrying out of which would be the grossest violation of the Constitution and our rights as citizens under it, and would place us, besides a large number of other Jewish families of this town, as outlaws before the entire world.

They then hurried to Washington to see the President. En route, they wrote accounts of this expulsion for the press, arousing the whole country. Lincoln's reaction to their pleas has been preserved:

LINCOLN: And so the children of Israel were driven from the happy land af Canaan?

KASKEL: Yes, and that is why we have come unto Father Abraham's bosom, asking protection.

LINCOLN: And this protection they shall have at once.

Lincoln quickly had orders rescinding the decree telegraphed to Grant and told his three visitors that they may return to their home.

✛

When August Bondi, fervent abolitionist who fought with John Brown and later with the 5th Kansas Volunteer Cavalry during the Civil War, was offered the Republican nomination for Lieutenant-Governor of Kansas, he replied:

> I do not regret a single step or instance in my long life, to further and to assist the realization of my devout wishes that tyranny and despotism may perish, and bigotry and fanaticism may be wiped from the face of the earth. Never Orthodox, but a consistent Jew nevertheless, I believed in the continuance and upholding of all the ceremonial laws . . .

Following the end of the Civil War in which he served on the staff of Confederate General James Longstreet, Raphael J. Moses of Columbus, Georgia, was elected to the Georgia legislature. It was in the course of his political career that an opponent, a Mr. Tuggle, referred to Moses sneeringly as "a Jew." Moses' reply, printed in the *Columbus Daily Times* on August 29, 1876, is one of the most stinging indictments of religious prejudice in America:

> At West Point and in my absence, during your congressional campaign, you sought for me a term of reproach, and from your well-defined vocabulary selected the epithet of JEW.
>
> Had I served you to the extent of my ability in your recent political aspirations and your over-burdened heart had sought relief in some exhibition of unmeasured gratitude; had you a wealth of gifts and selected from your abundance your richest offering to lay at my feet, you could not have honored me more gratefully than by proclaiming me a Jew. I am proud of my lineage and my race; in your severest censure you can not name an act of my life which dishonors either, or which would mar the character of a Christian gentleman. I feel it an honor to be one of a race whom persecution can not crush; whom prejudice has in vain endeavored to subdue; who, despite the powers of man and the combined

governors of the world, protected by the hand of Deity
have burst the temporal bonds with which prejudice
would have bound them and after nineteen centuries of
persecution still survive as a nation, and assert their
manhood and intelligence, and give proof of "the Divin-
ity that stirs within them" by having become a great factor in the government of mankind.

Would you honor me? Call me a Jew. Would you
place in unenviable prominence your own un-Christian
prejudice and bigotry? Call me a Jew . . . Your narrow
and benighted mind, pandering to the prejudices of your
auditory, has attempted to taunt me by calling me a
Jew—one of that peculiar people at whose altars, according to the teachings of your theological masters,
God chose that His Son should worship.

Strike out the nationality of Judea, and you would
seek in vain for Christ and his apostles. Strike out of
sacred history the teachings of the Jews, and you would
be as ignorant of God and the soul's immortal mission
as you are of the duties and amenities of social life.

. . . while I thank you for the opportunity which you
have given me to rebuke your prejudice, confined to a
limited number distinguished for their bigotry and
sectarian feelings—of which you are a fit exemplar—I
pity you for having been cast in a mould impervious to
the manly and liberal sentiments which distinguish the
nineteenth century.

+

In Colonel George A. Forsyth's account, *Frontier Fights
and Thrilling Days of Army Life,* he paid the following
tribute to a 20-year-old Jewish clerk, Sigmund Shlesinger,
who became one of the heroes of a dramatic battle in
Colorado between his scouts and the Cheyenne Indians on
September 17, 1868:

> When the foe charged on the breastworks
> With the madness of despair,
> And the bravest of souls were tested,
> The little Jew was there.
>
> When the weary dozed on duty,
> Or the wounded needed care,

When another shot was called for,
The little Jew was there.

With the festering dead around them
Shedding poison in the air,
When the crippled chieftain ordered,
The little Jew was there.

In Newport, Rhode Island, the Old Cemetery, dating back
to 1677, is one of the oldest Jewish burial grounds in the
United States. When Henry Wadsworth Longfellow visited
Newport, the burial ground so inspired him that he composed
his famous poem "The Jewish Cemetery at Newport." The
following are a few stanzas which reflect his deep feeling and
interest:

How strange it seems! These Hebrews
   in their graves
Close by the street of this fair
   seaport town,
Silent beside the never-silent
   waves,
At rest in all this moving up and
   down!

And these sepulchral stones, so old
   and brown,
That pave with level flags their
   burial-place,
Seem like the tablets of the Law,
   thrown down
And broken by Moses at the
   mountain's base.

The very names recorded here are
   strange,
Of foreign accent, and of different
   climes;
Alvares and Rivera interchange
With Abraham and Jacob of old
   times.

How came they here? What burst
of Christian hate,
What persecution, merciless and
blind,
Drove o'er the sea—that desert
desolate—
These Ishmaels and Hagars of
mankind?

Pride and humiliation hand in
hand

Walked with them through the
world where'er they went,
Trampled and beaten were they
as the sand,
And yet unshaken as the continent.

✦

Touro Synagogue at Newport, Rhode Island, is the oldest existing synagogue building in North America, and the only Jewish house of worship to become a national shrine. On August 31, 1947, on the occasion of the designation as a National Historic Site, President Harry S. Truman sent Congregation Jeshuat Israel (Touro Synagogue) the following message:

The setting apart of this historic shrine as a national monument is symbolic of our tradition of freedom, which has inspired men and women of every creed, race, and ancestry to contribute their highest gifts to the development of our national culture.

I trust that through long centuries to come the spirit of good will and tolerance will ever dominate the hearts and minds of the American people.

✦

In 1940, on the 200th anniversary of Mikveh Israel Congregation in Philadelphia, the second oldest congregation in the United States, President Franklin D. Roosevelt sent the following message of congratulations to Rabbi Abraham A. Neuman:

Dear Rabbi Neuman:

My hearty congratulations to you and through you to the members of the historic Congregation Mikveh Israel on the happy occasion of the celebration of the 200th anniversary of its establishment.

That far away year 1740—which marked the beginning of this Synagogue—carries our minds back into our colonial past. The Declaration of Independence was not to be adopted until thirty-six years later but the thriving young city of Brotherly Love already gave promise of rich achievements in the arts and sciences, in statecraft and in all that through subsequent generations has gone into the enlargement and enrichment of our national culture.

In all the decades of two centuries, the Congregation Mikveh Israel has borne a notable part, as the roster of its rabbis and members reveals. It is therefore a genuine pleasure to send heartfelt greetings to this venerable body of which Haym Salomon was a devoted member and which was signally honored in the long ago through recognition by George Washington and Benjamin Franklin.

Distinguished alike in membership and leadership today, as through the two centuries which have elapsed since its foundation, the Congregation has my very best wishes that its beneficent influence in the future may be in keeping with the high traditions which are its priceless heritage.

Very sincerely yours,
Franklin D. Roosevelt.

DID YOU KNOW

DID YOU KNOW?

Who was the first Jewish military chaplain?

During the Civil War, a YMCA worker was shocked to discover that a Jew, Michael Allen of Philadelphia, was serving as the regimental chaplain of a Pennsylvania unit. The commanding officer of this unit, Colonel Max Friedman, and most of his officers and men were Jewish.

Allen, who had been selected, was unaware that the law required a chaplain to be "an ordained minister of a Christian denomination." Allen resigned his commission rather than face dismissal. Although qualified to lead services, he had not been ordained and was not a Christian. Col. Friedman commissioned Arnold Fischel of New York's Shearith Israel Congregation as his chaplain-designate but the application was turned down because he was a Jew

Rejecting this religious discrimination, Fischel organized a vigorous campaign to seek an amendment to the Chaplaincy Law. Both Jews and non-Jews spoke out on the issue and petitions were submitted to Congress.

Fischel met with President Lincoln who "believed that the exclusion of Jewish chaplains had been unintentional on the part of Congress, and agreed that something ought to be done to meet this case."

The President submitted an amendment to the Chaplaincy Law and on December 20, 1861, a bill amending the law was reported to the House. It substituted the word "religious" for the word "Christian," enabling ". . . a regularly ordained minister of some religious denomination" as the basic qualification for military chaplaincy.

When the bill became law on July 17, 1862, it ended the last Federal law sanctioning religious discrimination.

Rabbi Jacob Frankel of Rodeph Shalom Congregation in Philadelphia, was selected by the Board of Ministers of Hebrew Congregations for a commission as Army chaplain. He became the first Jewish chaplain to the Armerican Armed Service on September 18, 1862.

DID YOU KNOW?

One of the oddest occurrences in the annals of Arlington National Cemetery?

The famous Sir Moses Ezekeil memorial, costing $75,000 was paid for by the Daughters of the Confederacy. Facing South, the 33-foot monument, cast in bronze in Rome, Italy, in 1912, depicts the figure of a woman at the top holding in the left hand a laurel wreath. Below the figure are the words from Isaiah:

> "And they shall beat their swords
> into plough shares and their spears
> into pruning hooks."

Since the dedication of the memorial by President Woodrow Wilson in 1914, a number of legends have developed—some odd, some heroic. However, in the official annals of Arlington National Cemetery there are eye-witness accounts of a strange occurence on the first Decoration Day, 1869.

At the end of the Civil War, there were strong and overwhelming political objections to allowing any burial of Southern soldiers at Arlington. Eventually, the ban was lifted and a small area known as the "Confederate Section" was set aside for the burial of the Confederate dead.

On this first Federal celebration of Decoration Day, a group of Southern women went to Arlington for the purpose of placing flowers on the graves of their dead. They were refused admittance since regional feelings were still very bitter. That night, there was a violent storm and the flowers which had been placed on the Northern graves had all blown over to the "Confederate Section" creating a floral blanket over this small area.

James Ryder Randall in his poem entitled "At Arlington," refers to the incident in these excerpted lines:

> "...Rebuking wrong, rewarding right,
> Plucking the wreaths from those who won,
> The tempest heaped them dewy bright on
> Rebel graves at Arlington...."

DID YOU KNOW?

What was one of the most shocking and saddest moments in American-Jewish history?

On April 26, 1913, Mary Phagon, a 14-year old employee at Leo Frank's factory in Atlanta, Georgia, was found murdered. Frank, who had come to Atlanta from New York was president of the Atlanta B'nai B'rith Lodge and an upstanding member of the city, was arrested, tried, and convicted of the crime on the flimsiest evidence. The trial became the forum for a violent anti-Semitic campaign which was led by a Populist demogogue. Before the jury brought in its verdict, the presiding judge requested that the prisoner and his counsel leave the courtroom when the verdict was announced to avoid violence and a possible lynching in the event of an acquittal. Outside the courtroom a hostile mob waited for the verdict. Frank was sentenced to be hanged.

A long fight in the courts followed and when the case reached the Supreme Court, seven of the judges held that the prisoner's constitutional rights had not been violated because he and his counsel had agreed to be absent when the verdict was read.

A nationwide campaign to win a new trial followed. Jews and non-Jews were aroused by the biased verdict. A huge meeting was held in Chicago, while members of Congress and governors led a campaign addressed to the Georgia State Board of Pardons on Frank's behalf. This intense activity outside the state angered many Georgians who saw it as a reflection on their courts and themselves. Governor John Slaton eventually commuted Frank's sentence to life imprisonment while outraged Georgians called for the governor's impeachment. In prison, Frank was attacked by another prisoner and nearly died of his wounds. On the night of August 16, 1915, a mob broke into the prison and brought Frank to Marietta, 125 miles away where Mary Phagan had been born and where she was buried; there they hanged Frank from a tree.

David Marx, officiating rabbi of The Temple of Atlanta, had visited Frank regularly in prison and had received threats against his life because of his defense of Frank, who had been a member of his congregation. After the lynching, Marx was smuggled aboard the train that carried Frank's body to New York for burial. At the peril of his own life, Marx accompanied Mrs. Frank to New York where he then officiated at the funeral.

(Continued)

After 70 years, the trauma of the Frank case still remains in Atlanta. In 1983, an aged eye-witness to the murder of Mary Phagan gave sworn testimony that Frank was innocent and named the true murderer. Jewish organizations around the country petitioned the current governor, Joe F. Harris, to clear the name of Frank. Although he has not acted as of 1985, this matter is still pending.

DID YOU KNOW?

Who was the quartermaster General of the Confederate Army and has a fort named after him?

Colonel Abraham Charles Myers, quartermaster for Florida troops at an Army fort built in 1839, is memorialized by the Gulf Coast town, Fort Myers.

A close relative of Moses Cohen, the first rabbi in Charleston, South Carolina, Myers was an 1830 graduate of the United States Military Academy at West Point. He served with Federal troops in Seminole Indian Wars from 1836-1842 and with Generals Zachary Taylor and Winfield Scott during the Mexican War.

When the Civil War broke out in 1861, he was commanding general of the Quartermaster Department at New Orleans. He resigned his commission and was appointed to the same post in the Confederate Army. Harassed by shortages and critical commanders, Myers was blamed for the severe losses suffered by the South, and was removed from his post by Jefferson Davis in 1863.

In later recognition of his enormous contributions to the Confederate cause, the town and fort were named in his honor.

DID YOU KNOW?

What Kennedy was known for "The Jew Bill" in the Maryland Assembly in 1822?

Thomas Kennedy, non-Jewish member of the State Assembly of Maryland started the struggle in 1804 for full civil equality for the Jews of the state. As chairman of a committee appointed by the Assembly "to consider the justice and expediency of placing the Jewish inhabitants on equal footing with the Christians," Kennedy recommended that "Jews and Christians be placed on equal footing in regard to their civil rights." A bill known as "Kennedy's Jew Baby" was introduced, but was defeated in 1819. In 1822, Kennedy sponsored a universial version of this bill which would have extenced to all citizens of Maryland the same civil rights and privileges enjoyed under the Constitution of the United States. The "Jew Bill" was finally passed on February 26, 1825. A Colonel W.G.D. Worthington who supported the bill

(Continued)

submitted documents noting that "there were 150 Jews in the state with an estimated wealth of $10,500,000." Kennedy, who had spearheaded the long fight for the bill had never met a Jew until he became involved in the bill's struggle for passage!

There is a plaque honoring Thomas Kennedy in the lobby of Sinai Hospital in Baltimore. The inscription reads "A Christian gentleman and an earnest advocate of civil and religious liberty..."

He is buried in Hagerstown, Maryland. This grave is inscribed "One who loved his fellow man." This monument was erected in 1918 by Brith Sholom in recognition of the great vision and courage Kenndy displayed in behalf of civil equality in the early 19th century.

DID YOU KNOW?

Who organized the entire medical department of the Confederate Army during the Civil War?

David Camden DeLeon, born to one of the well-known, wealthy Sephardic families of South Carolina graduated from the medical school of University of Pennsylvania in 1836 and enlisted in the army as a surgeon during the Seminole Indian and Mexican Wars.

During the Mexican War, he was the only surviving officer at the battle of Chapultepec. Without any military training, he took command and lead his men to victory. This bold act earned him the title of "Fighting Doctor."

In 1860, in a letter to his brother Edwin, United States Consul General in Egypt, he revealed his uneasiness at the growing war clouds in the United States in the event the South seceded. He wrote, "Treason and patriotism are next door neighbors and only accident makes you strike the right knocker. Revolution is treason even if right...A Southern Confederacy seems as near a fact as human foresight can divine in the future...I have loved my country, I have fought under its flag, and every star and stripe is dear to me...But I am still convinced that no man can be a patriot who is afraid of being thought a traitor."

But when war came, he opted for the Confederacy. When he sent his army resignation to General Winfield Scott, his friend and commander, the General refused to accept it. He eventually was threatened with arrest and had to flee across the border to Virginia.

(Continued)

In Richmond, President Jefferson Davis assigned DeLeon the important and difficult task of organizing a medical department for the growing Confederate Army. He served most of the war in the capacity of Surgeon General.

He fled the United States to Mexico following the defeat of the Confederate forces as did many other Southern officials and celebrities. It was difficult to accept the defeat of his beloved South. He returned to the United States at the invitation of General Ulysses Grant, a former colleague, now one of the most famous men in America. He practiced medicine in New Mexico and died at the age of 59.

DID YOU KNOW?

Who was the hero of the battle of Beecher Island, Colorado, in 1868 between Forsyth's Scouts and the Cheyenne Indians?

It was Sigmund Shlesinger, a little 20-year old Jewish clerk. Shlesinger's role is recorded in official documents, but it is best told in his own words in a diary he kept during the fighting which is in the American Jewish Archives and in *Harper's New Monthly Magazine* of June, 1895.

Shlesinger arrived in New York in 1865 at the age of 15 and traveled to Leavenworth, Kansas, to work as a clerk. After several years of clerking, "Slinger," as he was known, moved west with the railroad workers earning his keep as a cook, mule driver, laborer, and peddler among the soldiers guarding the track-layers. In 1868, he signed up with Forsyth's Scouts, a volunteer company recruited to help the thinly stretched-out regular army units on the frontier.

Although many of the recruits had frontier experience in Indian country, Shlesinger was characterized "in all respects unfit for service; a Jew, small, with narrow shoulders, sunken chest, a piping voice, little knowledge of firearms and horsemandship—he was indeed unpromising as a son of Mars.

At the beginning of the fierce battle of Beecher Island, Forsyth lost his most experienced aide, however, he was to write that the loss was fully made up by the bravery, skill, and untiring activity of "the little Jew," and that "there was no sphere of gallantry or usefulness in which he was not conspicuous." Facing 600 Cheyenne

warriors, the Scouts lost every horse and mule. Awaiting reinforce-
ments, those who survived suffered from hunger, thirst, and cold.

Shlesinger's exploits are memorialized in a poetic tribute to him
published in *Forsyth's Frontier Fights and Thrilling Days in Army
Life*. The poem reads:

When the foe charged on the breastworks
With the madness of despair,
And the bravest of souls were tested,
The little Jew was there.

When the weary dozed on duty,
Or the wounded needed care,
When another shot was called for,
The little Jew was there.

With the festering dead around them,
Shedding poison in the air,
When the crippled chieftan ordered,
The little Jew was there.

DID YOU KNOW?

Who was one of the greatest bullfighters in the history of the sport?

Sidney Franklin (born Sidney Frumkin), a boy from Brooklyn,
New York, was the first non-Latin to win fame in the bull ring.

Born in 1903, one of nine children, he attended classes at Columbia University, but left home at 18 following a disagreement
with his father. He traveled to Mexico City where after attending
his first bull-fight, he was caught up in the excitement of the
crowd and the beauty of the matador's movements.

Accepting a dare to try the sport himself, Franklin secured a
letter of introduction to Rudolfo Gaona, one of the great bull-
fighters of the time. After some instruction, he was sent to a
ranch to practice with live bulls. Upon his return to Mexico City,
a promoter announced Franklin's debut within two days.
Franklin appearing in the arena, went through with the fight and
treated the crowd to a rare display of courage.

(Continued)

After successes in Mexican bull rings, he made his debut in Spain in 1929. He became close friends with Ernest Hemingway, who, in *Death in the Afternoon*, referred to Franklin: "He is a better, more scientific, more intelligent, and more finished matador than all but about six of the full matadors in Spain today."

Franklin died in 1975.

DID YOU KNOW?

Who was Secretary of Labor, United States Supreme Court Justice, and Ambassador to the United Nations within five years?

Arthur Goldberg was born in 1908 in Chicago, the youngest of 11 children of Russian immigrants. After graduation from Northwestern Law School, he practiced law in Chicago and won a national reputation as a labor lawyer. During World War II, he was appointed head of the labor division of the Office of Strategic Services (O.S.S.). In this capacity, he helped to establish operations with anti-Fascist trade union leaders behind Nazi lines to sabotage Nazi production.

As general counsel to the CIO, Goldberg helped draft the agreement merging the AFL and CIO in 1955. President John F. Kennedy named him Secretary of Labor in 1961. In this post, he worked to raise the minimum wage and to increase federal unemployment benefits. He was named by President Kennedy to the U.S. Supreme Court in 1962. Three years later, President Lyndon B. Johnson appointed him U.S. Ambassador to the United Nations.

DID YOU KNOW?

Two Jewish American Air Force officers took part in the atomic bombings of Hiroshima and Nagasaki?

At 9:15 AM on the morning of August 6, 1945, a B-29 Superfortress, the *Enola Gay*, piloted by Col. Paul W. Tibbet, Jr., dropped the first atomic bomb on Hiroshima. The radar officer was Lt. Jacob Beser, a one-time rabbinical student from Baltimore, Md.

On the afternoon of August 9, 1945, another Superfortress, the *Great Artiste*, piloted by Charles W. Sweeney, dropped the second atomic bomb on Nagasaki. The bombardier on the *Great Artiste* was Lt. Charles Levy of Philadelphia.

DID YOU KNOW?

Who donated the world's largest art collection to the American people?

Joseph Hirschhorn. An immigrant from Russian, Hirschhorn made his fortune in uranium mines in Canada. He donated more than 8,000 sculptures and paintings to the people of the United States. The gift was accepted by President Lyndon B. Johnson on May 17, 1966, after which Congress set aside a site and appropriated more than $15 million for the construction of a building to house this collection. It is an integral part of the Smithsonian Institution. President Gerald Ford dedicated the huge, four-level structure housing the museum and sculpture garden in 1974. The collection is valued in excess of $100 million.

DID YOU KNOW?

Who donated a copy of the original Bill of Rights to the Library of Congress?

Barney Balaban, a film industry magnate. The Library of Congress never owned an original copy of this document. The originals were given to the first 13 states and the National archives. Because the copy owned by the Archives had deteriorated badly and only Virginia and Connecticut still owned their original copies, Balaban's gift (purchased at auction on February 21, 1945), was one of the priceless historical acquisitions of the Library. The Balaban copy is on permanent display in a special shrine near the exhibit of originals of the Declaration of Independence and the Constitution.

DID YOU KNOW?

Who was the librettist for Wolfgang Amadeus Mozart's greatest opera?

Tucked away in the foyer of the Casa Italiana at Columbia University is a portrait of Lorenzo Da Ponte. Da Ponte was appointed professor of the Italian language at the college—the first to teach Italian in the United States. If his fame rested on this one

(Continued)

fact, he would have been just a poor, immigrant Italian teacher and writer whose name would soon be forgotten, had he not written librettos for Mozart.

Da Ponte had a varied career. He was born Emmanuele Conegliano in 1749, the child of a large family, in a town near Venice. Although descended from a Jewish family that had lived in Italy for many generations, his mercurial father had him baptized. At the age of 24, he changed his name to Lorenzo Da Ponte. His father thought he ought to join the priesthood and he did study at a seminary for a short time. The church, however, did not hold him long and a life full of unrest and danger was to follow him for the rest of his days. He taught music and languages for a time in Trieste, became a librettist at a large German opera house, and later was to be appointed theater poet and writer at the Vienna Opera House with the Emperor Joseph his patron.

As a result of a chance invitation to the home of the Jewish banker, Baron Raimund Wetzlar, he met a house guest who would eventually endow him with lasting fame and renown. The house guest was the musician and composer Wolfgang Amadeus Mozart. This was the start of one of the most creative collaborations in the history of music. His first libretto and Mozart's first opera was the sparkling comedy, *The Marriage of Figaro*, which was followed by *Cosi Fan Tutti* and *Don Giovanni*. Even the composer Richard Wagner, an avowed anti-Semite, considered the libretto and music of *Don Giovanni* one of the great operas of the day. Conveying the entire scope of deep human emotions from revenge to love, this joint masterpiece is written with humor and has remained fresh and delightful to the present day.

Following the death of the Emperor Joseph, his successor Leopold cared little for opera and disliked Da Ponte. He was expelled from Austria and fled to London where he received the appointment of poet to the Drury Lane Theater. Underpaid at his new post, he was eventually forced into debt and fled to New York to avoid prison.

With a precarious style of life, he moved from New York to Philadelphia, Elizabethtown, Sunbury, and eventually back to New York. In 1805, he opened a bookshop at 342 Broadway and taught Italian to a few students.

Although the young republic had not yet developed a taste for

(Continued)

opera, Da Ponte's linguistic talent became widely-known and when Columbia College expanded into a university, he was offered a teaching position. He set up a small theatre in his home and there his young students acted in Italian classics which Da Ponte produced. In 1823, at the age of 74, he wrote his *Memoirs*—a frank book which shocked the public. In his 84th year, he interested prominent citizens in a grandiose project to build a theatre for opera performances. The Italian Opera House was built on Church and Leonard Streets and the opening was the social event of the season. He produced 28 performances before the opera house was destroyed by fire. Depressed and impoverished, Da Ponte died in his new homeland at the age of 90.

There is no place in the world where great operas are performed that Lorenzo Da Ponte's name is not coupled with the world's most spontaneous musical genius, Wolfgang Amadeus Mozart.

Da Ponte is said to be buried on 11th Street and Sixth Avenue in New York City. This is the second oldest burial ground of the Spanish and Portuguese Congregation, and was dedicated on February 27th, 1805.

About the Author

Bernard Postal, editor, journalist, and author, is associate editor of *The Jewish Week,* editor of *The Jewish Digest,* and co-author of ten other books on travel, Jewish history, and Israel. He was the director of public relations of JWB for 25 years. Prior to that he was national public relations director of B'nai B'rith for eight years. He is a member of the executive council of the American Jewish Historical Society and the Jewish Historical Committee of B'nai B'rith. In 1954 he received the National Jewish Book Award (together with Lionel Koppman) for his contributions to American Jewish history. He was similarly honored by the American Jewish Historical Society.

Lionel Koppman, editor, writer, and publicist, is director of public information and publications for JWB. He is a former newspaperman in Texas; medical editor for the United States government; and winner of the National Jewish Book Award in 1954 (together with Bernard Postal) for his contributions to American Jewish history. He was also the recipient of the Outstanding Filmstrip of the Year Award for his filmstrip on Sholom Aleichem in 1970. He is the author of a number of manuals and plays on various aspects of American Jewish life. He has received a grant for a textbook in American Jewish history.

INDEX

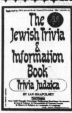